Practical .NET 2.0 Networking Projects

Wei-Meng Lee

Apress®

Practical .NET 2.0 Networking Projects

ISBN-13 (pbk): 978-1-59059-790-3

ISBN-10 (pbk): 1-59059-790-7

Printed and bound in the United States of America 9 8 7 6 5 4 3 2 1

Lead Editor: Ewan Buckingham
Technical Reviewer: Fabio Claudio Ferracchiati
Editorial Board: Steve Anglin, Ewan Buckingham, Gary Cornell, Jason Gilmore, Jonathan Gennick, Jonathan Hassell, James Huddleston, Chris Mills, Matthew Moodie, Dominic Shakeshaft, Jim Sumser, Keir Thomas, Matt Wade
Project Manager: Beth Christmas
Copy Edit Manager: Nicole Flores
Copy Editor: Kim Wimpsett
Assistant Production Director: Kari Brooks-Copony
Production Editor: Katie Stence
Compositor and Artist: Diana Van Winkle, Van Winkle Design
Proofreader: Linda Seifert
Indexer: Broccoli Information Management, Inc.
Cover Designer: Kurt Krames
Manufacturing Director: Tom Debolski

Distributed to the book trade worldwide by Springer-Verlag New York, Inc., 233 Spring Street, 6th Floor, New York, NY 10013. Phone 1-800-SPRINGER, fax 201-348-4505, e-mail orders-ny@springer-sbm.com, or visit http://www.springeronline.com.

For information on translations, please contact Apress directly at 2560 Ninth Street, Suite 219, Berkeley, CA 94710. Phone 510-549-5930, fax 510-549-5939, e-mail info@apress.com, or visit http://www.apress.com.

The source code for this book is available to readers at http://www.apress.com in the Source Code/ Download section.

Contents at a Glance

Contents

About the Author

 **WEI-MENG LEE** is a technologist and founder of Developer Learning Solutions (http://www.learn2develop.net), a technology company that specializes in hands-on training in the latest Microsoft technologies. Wei-Meng speaks regularly at international conferences and has authored and coauthored numerous books about .NET, XML, and wireless technologies, including *ASP.NET 2.0: A Developer's Notebook* and *Visual Basic 2005 Jumpstart* (both from O'Reilly Media). He is also the coauthor of *Programming Sudoku* (from Apress). Find out about the latest books and articles by Wei-Meng at his blog: http://weimenglee.blogspot.com/.

About the Technical Reviewer

FABIO CLAUDIO FERRACCHIATI is a senior consultant and a senior analyst/developer using Microsoft technologies. He works for Brain Force (http://www.brainforce.com) in its Italian branch (http://www.brainforce.it). He is a Microsoft Certified Solution Developer for .NET, a Microsoft Certified Application Developer for .NET, and a Microsoft Certified Professional, as well as a prolific author and technical reviewer. Over the past ten years he has written articles for Italian and international magazines and coauthored more than ten books about a variety of computer topics. Visit his blog at http://www.ferracchiati.com.

Acknowledgments

Although the "Acknowledgments" section of a book is always placed at the front, it is always the last thing an author writes; and after spending several months working on the book together with different groups of people, most names are not even mentioned (or at least mentioned in passing). Yet, without the collective efforts of these people, the book would never have been possible.

This book is no exception.

Now that this book is done, I can finally look forward to seeing it on the shelves of bookshops. I want to take this opportunity to thank my editor, Ewan Buckingham, for his guidance and valuable suggestions for making this book a better read. Fabio Claudio Ferracchiati, the technical reviewer for this book, also deserves special mention because he painstakingly tested every project in this book and made several good suggestions for improving the quality of the code. Thank you, Ewan and Fabio. And this book would never be possible without the great patience of its project manager, Beth Christmas. Beth was extremely patient with me while I was juggling writing this book and working on my daytime projects. For this, I am very grateful, Beth! To the production crew, Kim Wimpsett and Katie Stence—thanks for the great job of polishing my work!

I also want to thank Rod Paddock (editor-in-chief at *CoDeMagazine*) for publishing my RFID chapter as an article in the Nov/Dec 2006 issue of *CoDeMagazine*. And I want to express my gratitude to Ryan Clarke (from Parallax) and Matt Trossen and Jennie Jetter (from Phidgets USA) for their help in getting me started with RFID. They have been very patient in guiding an hardware-idiot (that's me) and for this I am very grateful to them! Last but not least, I want to thank Lori Piquet, my editor at DevX.com. Lori has always been very open to my new article ideas, and her support has provided me with the avenues to try new project ideas. For this, I am indebted and very grateful to you, Lori.

Finally, thank *you* for picking up this book, and I hope you have a great time with the various projects discussed in this book.

Introduction

Practical .NET 2.0 Networking Projects demonstrates some of the key networking technologies that are being made easily accessible through the .NET Framework 2.0. It discusses communication between wired machines and between networks and mobile devices. The book teaches you about the technologies by walking you through sample projects in a straightforward and direct way.

This book contains six chapters, each covering a specific aspect of network programming. You'll use the various APIs within the .NET Framework as well as third-party SDKs to build a variety of cutting-edge networking applications that cover everything from Bluetooth and RFID communication to sockets programming and chat servers. You'll build working examples for each project, which you can also customize and use for your own purposes. The featured projects cover the following.

Chapter 1:
Sockets Programming

Writing networked applications is one of the most interesting aspects of programming. This is especially intriguing when you see your applications successfully communicating over the network. In this chapter, you will build a chat application that works similarly to Windows Live Messenger (or ICQ) using TCP/IP. Using the chat application, you will learn how network programming happens in .NET and the various challenges you'll encounter when building a multiuser chat application.

Chapter 2:
Serial Communications

Serial communication is one of the oldest mechanisms for devices to communicate with each other. Starting with the IBM PC and compatible computers, almost all computers are equipped with one or more serial ports and one parallel port. As the name implies, a *serial* port sends and receives data serially, one bit at a time. In contrast, a *parallel* port sends and receives data eight bits at a time, using eight separate wires.

Despite the comparatively slower transfer speed of serial ports over parallel ports, serial communication remains a popular connectivity option for devices because of its simplicity and cost-effectiveness. Although consumer products today are using USB connections in place of serial connections, still a lot of devices use serial ports as their sole connections to the outside world.

In this chapter, you will learn how to communicate with other serial devices using the new SerialPort class available in the .NET Framework 2.0 and the .NET Compact Framework 2.0.

In particular, you will build three projects that illustrate how to use serial communications. The first project is a chat application that allows two computers (connected using either a serial cable or a Bluetooth connection) to communicate. And using the foundation of this application, you can extend it to communicate with other external serial devices such as cellular phones. You will learn how to use the AT commands to programmatically control your mobile phones through a serial Bluetooth connection. The second project is a Pocket PC chat application, which is similar to the first project. The third application shows how to communicate with a GPS receiver and then extract the useful data for displaying the current location on a map.

Chapter 3:
Incorporating Fingerprint Recognition into Your .NET Application

Biometric recognition is one of the most reliable ways to confirm the identity of an individual. And by now, most people should be familiar with the Microsoft Fingerprint Reader. Using the Microsoft Fingerprint Reader, you can now log in to your computer by placing your finger on the reader. You can also use the application provided by the Fingerprint Reader to save your user IDs and passwords for websites that require them for authentication. You can then use your fingerprint as a key to retrieve the user IDs and passwords for logging into these sites securely. The Microsoft Fingerprint Reader removes the hassle of remembering different passwords for different sites.

In this chapter, I will show you how you can use the GrFinger Fingerprint SDK to integrate the Microsoft Fingerprint Reader into your .NET 2.0 Windows applications. In particular, you will build a visitor identification system whereby users visiting your office can register at the reception desk. Once a user is registered, the next time the user visits the office, he can simply scan his fingerprint, and the system will register his visit. Schools can also adapt this application for attendance-taking purposes, such as in big lecture theaters where attendance must be taken rapidly and efficiently.

Chapter 4:
Infrared Programming

With all the buzz around WiFi, Bluetooth, and other wireless technologies, it's easy to overlook one of the simplest and most common forms of wireless communications—infrared. Anyone who has ever used a remote control has used it! Infrared uses the invisible spectrum of light just beyond red in the visible spectrum. You can use it in applications for short-range, point-to-point data transfer. Because it uses light, line-of-sight is a prerequisite for infrared. Despite this limitation, infrared is increasingly popular in devices such as digital cameras, PDAs, and notebook computers.

In this chapter, I will show you how to build an application that allows two devices (as well as computers) to communicate wirelessly using infrared. You can adapt the programming technique illustrated in this chapter for other programming tasks, such as writing wireless network games, and so on.

Chapter 5:
Fun with Radio Frequency Identifications (RFID)

Radio frequency identification (RFID) is one of the buzzwords receiving a lot of coverage in the IT world lately. An RFID system is an identification system that uses radio waves to retrieve data from a device called a *tag* or a *transponder*. RFID is all around us in our daily lives—in the supermarkets, libraries, bookstores, and so on. RFID provides a quick and efficient way to collect information, such as stocktaking in a warehouse or tracking the whereabouts of items.

In this chapter, you will learn how to build a Windows application that incorporates RFID technology for data collection. You will use two RFID readers and understand their pros and cons.

Chapter 6:
Interfacing with External Devices

Today, a webcam is a common peripheral that most people can easily afford; and it's used most often for video conferencing. But what can you do with your webcam besides video conferencing? For .NET developers, the answer is plenty; and you will be glad to know that integrating a webcam with a Windows application is not as difficult as you might imagine.

Besides integrating a webcam with your application, you can connect your Windows application to an external device such as a sensor to monitor the movements of the surroundings.

In this chapter, you will build a security system by interfacing a Windows application with an external sensor and a webcam so you can monitor for unwanted activities. You will be able detect the proximity of an intruder and use the webcam to record the intruder's movements.

CHAPTER 1

■■■

Sockets Programming

Writing networked applications is one of the most interesting aspects of programming. This is especially intriguing when you see your applications successfully communicating over the network. In this chapter, you will build a chat application that works similarly to Windows Live Messenger (or ICQ) using TCP/IP. Using the chat application, you will learn how network programming happens in .NET and the various challenges you'll encounter when building a multiuser chat application.

Introducing Sockets Programming

A *socket* is an abstract description of a means of sending and receiving data between computers/ applications on a network. It describes a connection between two communicating points (which may be on different computers or within the same computer).

In practice, socket programming is commonly associated with TCP/IP and UDP/IP communications (see the "Understanding IP, TCP, and UDP" sidebar for more information about TCP/IP and UDP/IP). When discussing sockets programming, three pieces of information are important:

- The protocol (such as TCP/IP or UDP/IP)

- The IP address (for example, 127.0.0.1)

- The port number (for example, port 80)

For example, you should be familiar with an address such as http://www.apress.com. This is an address that instructs your web browser to load the home page located at www.apress.com. The http part specifies the application protocol used (HTTP uses TCP/IP for data delivery), and www.apress.com specifies the address (the name www.apress.com will be resolved by the DNS service into an IP address). Because HTTP uses port 80 for communications, port 80 is implicitly implied and is not included in the address. As shown in Figure 1-1, for two parties to communicate, both must have an IP address.

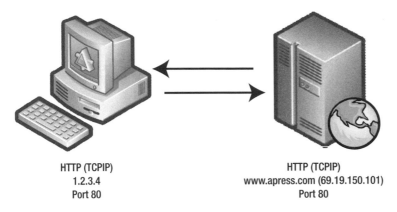

HTTP (TCPIP)   HTTP (TCPIP)
1.2.3.4   www.apress.com (69.19.150.101)
Port 80   Port 80

Figure 1-1. *Communication between a web browser and a web server*

Although a protocol such as TCP/IP takes care of delivering data from one point to another, it is the application protocol such as HTTP that specifies the *content* of the data to be transferred.

In the .NET Framework, socket communication is implemented by the Socket class (located in the System.Net.Sockets namespace).

UNDERSTANDING IP, TCP, AND UDP

For network programming, it is important that you have a good idea of some of the common protocols in use today. The first is Internet Protocol (IP). IP specifies the format as well as the addressing scheme of data packets (known as *datagrams*) that are to be sent from one point to another. Think of IP as the postal system where you can send a package from one location to another. You simply write the address of the recipient and drop the package in the postal box. The post office will then try to deliver the package to the recipient. However, you have no guarantee that the package will definitely arrive at the destination, and you won't know when the package does arrive.

To ensure that packages are delivered correctly, you have to use extra services such as registered mail. In a similar fashion, you use IP with other protocols to ensure guaranteed delivery of packets. One such protocol is Transmission Control Protocol (TCP). TCP is a connection-oriented network protocol that guarantees reliable and in-order delivery of packets (through acknowledgments). Coupled with IP, TCP has been adopted as a popular networking protocol by applications such as web browsers and email clients.

Although TCP ensures guaranteed delivery, it has its overhead. Just like registered mail, which costs more money to send, TCP adds overhead to the packets being sent and increases the packet size. Hence, sometimes developers use IP with User Datagram Protocol (UDP). UDP is a connectionless network protocol that sends packet from one point to another, with one exception—it does not provide reliable and guaranteed delivery. Since UPD does not guarantee delivery, the packets are more efficient and faster to deliver. Developers using UPD must devise their own logic to ensure packets are delivered correctly. This is analogous to the postal example, where you can manually call your recipient to see whether they have received the package you sent. If they have not received it, you may need to resend it. UDP is useful for applications that send small packets of data and require no elaborate assembling of data. These applications include Trivial File Transfer Protocol (TFTP), Domain Name System (DNS), and Voice over IP (VoIP).

Creating Your Own Multiuser Chat Application

In the first part of this chapter, you will first build a simple chat application that allows anyone who is connected to a central server to communicate. This will allow you to explore the basics of socket communications and learn how to broadcast messages to all connected users.

Figure 1-2 shows the application you will be building in the first part of the chapter.

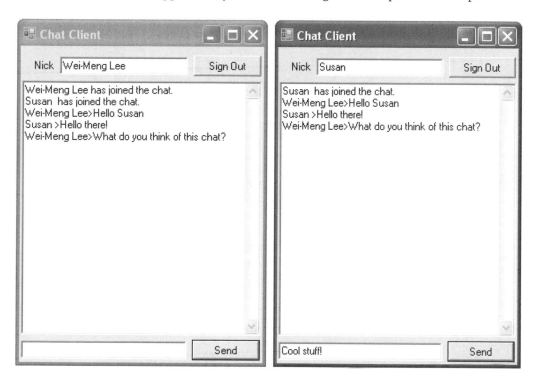

Figure 1-2. *The chat application you will create in the first part of the chapter*

Using the TcpClient and TcpListener Classes for Network Communications

Creating a chat application generally involves socket programming—creating a connection between a client and a server so that messages can be sent and received by both the client and the server. The System.Net.Sockets namespace provides the functionality required for socket programming. You will use two classes in the System.Net.Sockets namespace for this project: TcpClient and TcpListener.

The TcpClient class implements a socket for sending and receiving data using TCP. Because the connection to the remote device is represented as a stream, data can be read and written with .NET Framework stream-handling techniques.

The TcpListener class provides simple methods that listen for and accept incoming connection requests in blocking synchronous mode.

The following code example shows a simple implementation of a server (a console application) waiting for an incoming connection.

Visual Basic 2005

```vbnet
Imports System.Net.Sockets
Imports System.Text

Module Module1
    '---port number to use for listening---
    Const portNo As Integer = 500

    Sub Main()
        Dim localAdd As System.Net.IPAddress = _
            System.Net.IPAddress.Parse("127.0.0.1")

        '---listen at the local address---
        Dim listener As New TcpListener(localAdd, portNo)
        listener.Start()

        '---Accepts a pending connection request---
        Dim tcpClient As TcpClient = listener.AcceptTcpClient()

        '---use a NetworkStream object to send and receive data---
        Dim ns As NetworkStream = tcpClient.GetStream
        Dim data(tcpClient.ReceiveBufferSize) As Byte

        '---read incoming stream; Read() is a blocking call---
        Dim numBytesRead As Integer = ns.Read(data, 0, _
            CInt(tcpClient.ReceiveBufferSize))

        '---display data received---
        Console.WriteLine("Received :" & _
            Encoding.ASCII.GetString(data, 0, numBytesRead))

        '---prevent the console window from closing immediately---
        Console.ReadLine()
    End Sub

End Module
```

C# 2005

```csharp
using System;
using System.Collections.Generic;
using System.Text;
using System.Net.Sockets;

namespace Server_CS
{
```

```csharp
class Program
{
    //---port number to use for listening---
    const int portNo = 500;
    static void Main(string[] args)
    {
        System.Net.IPAddress localAdd =
            System.Net.IPAddress.Parse("127.0.0.1");

        //---listen at the local address---
        TcpListener listener = new TcpListener(localAdd, portNo);
        listener.Start();

        //---Accepts a pending connection request---
        TcpClient tcpClient = listener.AcceptTcpClient();

        //---use a NetworkStream object to send and receive
        // data---
        NetworkStream ns = tcpClient.GetStream();
        byte[] data = new byte[tcpClient.ReceiveBufferSize];

        //---read incoming stream; Read() is a blocking call---
        int numBytesRead = ns.Read(data, 0,
            System.Convert.ToInt32(tcpClient.ReceiveBufferSize));

        //---display data received---
        Console.WriteLine("Received :" +
            Encoding.ASCII.GetString(data, 0, numBytesRead));

        //---prevent the console window from closing
        // immediately---
        Console.ReadLine();
    }
}
}
```

To connect to the server and send it a string, the client code (a console application) will look like the following.

Visual Basic 2005

```vbnet
Imports System.Net.Sockets
Imports System.Text

Module Module1
    Const portNo As Integer = 500
    Sub Main()
        Dim tcpclient As New TcpClient
```

```
        '---connect to the server---
        tcpclient.Connect("127.0.0.1", portNo)

        '---use a NetworkStream object to send and receive data---
        Dim ns As NetworkStream = tcpclient.GetStream
        Dim data As Byte() = Encoding.ASCII.GetBytes("Hello")

        '---send the text---
        ns.Write(data, 0, data.Length)
    End Sub
End Module
```

C# 2005

```
using System;
using System.Collections.Generic;
using System.Text;
using System.Net.Sockets;

namespace Client_CS
{
    class Program
    {
        const int portNo = 500;
        static void Main(string[] args)
        {
            TcpClient tcpclient = new TcpClient();

            //---connect to the server---
            tcpclient.Connect("127.0.0.1", portNo);

            //---use a NetworkStream object to send and receive
            // data---
            NetworkStream ns = tcpclient.GetStream();
            byte[] data = Encoding.ASCII.GetBytes("Hello");

            //---send the text---
            ns.Write(data, 0, data.Length);
        }
    }
}
```

Note that the NetworkStream object works with byte arrays, and hence you need to use the Encoding.ASCII.GetString() and Encoding.ASCII.GetBytes() methods from the System.Text namespace to convert the byte array to a string, and vice versa.

The previous example is relatively simple—it contains the code for the server as well as the client. The service opens a socket at 127.0.0.1 using port 500 and listens for an incoming

TCP connection. When a connection is established, a NetworkStream object reads the data sent by the client. The data received is then displayed on the console. The client, on the other hand, opens a connection at 127.0.0.1 and then sends a string to the server using the NetworkStream object.

However, the problem becomes much more pronounced when the server needs to communicate with multiple clients and be able to both send and receive messages from clients, all at the same time. To do so, the following must be true:

- The server must be able to create connections with multiple clients.

- The server must be able to asynchronously read data from the client and be able to send messages to the client at any time.

- The client must be able to asynchronously read data from the server and be able to send messages to the server at any time.

The following sections will address these three problems.

Building the Server

The chat application has two components—server and client. Let's get started by first building the server. For the server, you will create a console application project using Visual Studio 2005. Name the project **Server**.

In the default Module1.vb/Program.cs file, first import the System.Net.Sockets namespace that will contain all the relevant classes you will use for this project.

Visual Basic 2005

```
Imports System.Net.Sockets
```

C# 2005

```
using System.Net.Sockets;
```

Next, declare a constant containing the port number to use for this application. For this application, I have used the port number 500.

Visual Basic 2005

```
Module Module1
    Const portNo As Integer = 500
```

C# 2005

```
class Program
{
    const int portNo = 500;
```

■**Tip** If you have a firewall installed on the server (or client), be sure to open port 500 for this application to work.

You also need to define the local address to listen to and then create an instance of the TcpListener class to use for listening for connections from TCP clients.

Visual Basic 2005

```
Sub Main()
    Dim localAdd As System.Net.IPAddress = _
        System.Net.IPAddress.Parse("127.0.0.1")
    Dim listener As New TcpListener(localAdd, portNo)
```

C# 2005

```
static void Main(string[] args)
{
    System.Net.IPAddress localAdd =
        System.Net.IPAddress.Parse("127.0.0.1");
    TcpListener listener = new TcpListener(localAdd, portNo);
```

In the Main() function, use the Start() method from the TcpListener class to start listening for incoming connection requests. The AcceptTcpClient() method is a blocking call, and execution will not continue until a connection is established. Because the server in this example needs to service multiple clients at the same time, you will create an instance of the ChatClient class (which you will define shortly) for each user. The server will loop indefinitely, accepting clients as they connect.

Visual Basic 2005

```
Sub Main()
    Dim localAdd As System.Net.IPAddress = _
        System.Net.IPAddress.Parse("127.0.0.1")
    Dim listener As New TcpListener(localAdd, portNo)
    listener.Start()
    While True
        Dim user As New ChatClient(listener.AcceptTcpClient)
    End While
End Sub
```

C# 2005

```
static void Main(string[] args)
{
    System.Net.IPAddress localAdd =
        System.Net.IPAddress.Parse("127.0.0.1");
```

```
TcpListener listener = new TcpListener(localAdd, portNo);
listener.Start();
while (true)
{
    ChatClient user = new
        ChatClient(listener.AcceptTcpClient());
}
}
}
```

The complete source for Module1.vb looks as follows.

Visual Basic 2005

```vb
Imports System.Net.Sockets

Module Module1
    Const portNo As Integer = 500
    Sub Main()
        Dim localAdd As System.Net.IPAddress = _
            System.Net.IPAddress.Parse("127.0.0.1")
        Dim listener As New TcpListener(localAdd, portNo)
        listener.Start()
        While True
            Dim user As New ChatClient(listener.AcceptTcpClient)
        End While
    End Sub
End Module
```

C# 2005

```csharp
using System;
using System.Collections.Generic;
using System.Text;
using System.Net.Sockets;

namespace server_CS
{
    class Program
    {
        const int portNo = 500;
        static void Main(string[] args)
        {
            System.Net.IPAddress localAdd =
                System.Net.IPAddress.Parse("127.0.0.1");
            TcpListener listener = new TcpListener(localAdd, portNo);
            listener.Start();
            while (true)
            {
```

```
            ChatClient user = new
                ChatClient(listener.AcceptTcpClient());
        }
    }
  }
}
```

The next step is to define the ChatClient class. You use the ChatClient class to represent information about each client connecting to the server.

Add a new Class item to your project in Visual Studio 2005, and name it **ChatClient.vb/ ChatClient.cs**. As usual, the first step is to import the System.Net.Sockets namespace (for the C# version of the code, you need to also import the System.Collections namespace).

Visual Basic 2005

```
Imports System.Net.Sockets
```

C# 2005

```
using System.Net.Sockets;
using System.Collections;
```

In the ChatClient class, first define the various private members (their uses are described in the comments in the code). You also declare a HashTable object (AllClients) to store a list of all clients connecting to the server. The reason for declaring it as a shared member is to ensure all instances of the ChatClient class are able to obtain a list of all the clients currently connected to the server.

Visual Basic 2005

```
Public Class ChatClient
    '---contains a list of all the clients---
    Public Shared AllClients As New HashTable

    '---information about the client---
    Private _client As TcpClient
    Private _clientIP As String
    Private _clientNick As String

    '---used for sending/receiving data---
    Private data() As Byte

    '---is the nickname being sent?---
    Private ReceiveNick As Boolean = True
```

C# 2005

```
class ChatClient
{
    //---contains a list of all the clients---
    public static Hashtable AllClients = new Hashtable();

    //---information about the client---
    private TcpClient _client;
    private string _clientIP;
    private string _clientNick;

    //---used for sending/receiving data---
    private byte[] data;

    //---is the nickname being sent?---
    private bool ReceiveNick = true;
```

When a client gets connected to the server, the server will create an instance of the ChatClient class and then pass the TcpClient variable (client) to the constructor of the class. You will also get the IP address of the client and use it as an index to identify the client in the HashTable object. The BeginRead() method will begin an asynchronous read from the NetworkStream object (client.GetStream) in a separate thread. This allows the server to remain responsive and continue accepting new connections from other clients. When the reading is complete, control will be transferred to the ReceiveMessage() function (which you will define shortly).

Visual Basic 2005

```
Public Sub New(ByVal client As TcpClient)
    _client = client

    '---get the client IP address---
    _clientIP = client.Client.RemoteEndPoint.ToString

    '---add the current client to the hash table---
    AllClients.Add(_clientIP, Me)

    '---start reading data from the client in a separate thread---
    ReDim data(_client.ReceiveBufferSize)
    _client.GetStream.BeginRead(data, 0, _
        CInt(_client.ReceiveBufferSize), _
        AddressOf ReceiveMessage, Nothing)
End Sub
```

C# 2005

```csharp
public ChatClient(TcpClient client)
{
    _client = client;

    //---get the client IP address---
    _clientIP = client.Client.RemoteEndPoint.ToString();

    //---add the current client to the hash table---
    AllClients.Add(_clientIP, this);

    //---start reading data from the client in a
    // separate thread---
    data = new byte[_client.ReceiveBufferSize];
    client.GetStream().BeginRead(data, 0,
        System.Convert.ToInt32(_client.ReceiveBufferSize),
        ReceiveMessage, null);
}
```

In the `ReceiveMessage()` function, you first call the `EndRead()` method to handle the end of an asynchronous read. Here, you check whether the number of bytes read is less than 1. If it is, it means that the client has disconnected, and you need to remove the client from the `HashTable` object (using the IP address of the client as an index into the hash table). You would also broadcast the message to all the clients that this particular client has left the chat using the `Broadcast()` function (which you will define shortly). For simplicity, assume that the client will send the nickname of the user the first time it connects to the server. Subsequently, you will just broadcast whatever was sent by the client to everyone. Once this is done, the server will proceed to perform the asynchronous read from the client again.

Visual Basic 2005

```vbnet
Public Sub ReceiveMessage(ByVal ar As IAsyncResult)
    '---read from client---
    Dim bytesRead As Integer
    Try
        SyncLock _client.GetStream
            bytesRead = _client.GetStream.EndRead(ar)
        End SyncLock

        '---client has disconnected---
        If bytesRead < 1 Then
            AllClients.Remove(_clientIP)
            Broadcast(_clientNick & _
                " has left the  chat.")
            Exit Sub
        Else
            '---get the message sent---
```

```vbnet
            Dim messageReceived As String = _
                System.Text.Encoding.ASCII. _
                GetString(data, 0, bytesRead)

            '---client is sending its nickname---
            If ReceiveNick Then
                _clientNick = messageReceived

                '---tell everyone client has entered the chat---
                Broadcast(_clientNick & _
                    " has joined the chat.")
                ReceiveNick = False
            Else
                '---broadcast the message to everyone---
                Broadcast(_clientNick & ">" & _
                    messageReceived)
            End If
        End If

        '---continue reading from client---
        SyncLock _client.GetStream
            _client.GetStream.BeginRead(data, 0, _
                CInt(_client.ReceiveBufferSize), _
                AddressOf ReceiveMessage, Nothing)
        End SyncLock

    Catch ex As Exception
        AllClients.Remove(_clientIP)
        Broadcast(_clientNick & _
            " has left the chat.")
    End Try
End Sub
```

C# 2005

```csharp
public void ReceiveMessage(IAsyncResult ar)
{
    //---read from client---
    int bytesRead;
    try
    {
        lock (_client.GetStream())
        {
            bytesRead = _client.GetStream().EndRead(ar);
        }

        //---client has disconnected---
```

```
        if (bytesRead < 1)
        {
            AllClients.Remove(_clientIP);
            Broadcast(_clientNick + " has left the chat.");
            return;
        }
        else
        {
            //---get the message sent---
            string messageReceived =
                System.Text.Encoding.ASCII.GetString(
                data, 0, bytesRead);

            //---client is sending its nickname---
            if (ReceiveNick)
            {
                _clientNick = messageReceived;

                //---tell everyone client has entered the
                // chat---
                Broadcast(_clientNick +
                    " has joined the chat.");
                ReceiveNick = false;
            }
            else
            {
                //---broadcast the message to everyone---
                Broadcast(_clientNick + ">" +
                    messageReceived);
            }
        }

        //---continue reading from client---
        lock (_client.GetStream())
        {
            _client.GetStream().BeginRead(data, 0,
                System.Convert.ToInt32(
                _client.ReceiveBufferSize),ReceiveMessage,
                null);
        }
    }
    catch (Exception ex)
    {
        AllClients.Remove(_clientIP);
        Broadcast(_clientNick + " has left the chat.");
    }
}
```

One issue to note in the previous code is that you need to use the SyncLock (lock in C#) statement to prevent multiple threads from using the NetworkStream object. This scenario is likely to occur when your server is connected to multiple clients and all of them are trying to access the NetworkStream object at the same time.

The SendMessage() function allows the server to send a message to the client.

Visual Basic 2005

```
Public Sub SendMessage(ByVal message As String)
    Try
        '---send the text---
        Dim ns As System.Net.Sockets.NetworkStream
        SyncLock _client.GetStream
            ns = _client.GetStream
        End SyncLock

        Dim bytesToSend As Byte() = _
         System.Text.Encoding.ASCII.GetBytes(message)
        ns.Write(bytesToSend, 0, bytesToSend.Length)
        ns.Flush()
    Catch ex As Exception
        Console.WriteLine(ex.ToString)
    End Try
End Sub
```

C# 2005

```
public void SendMessage(string message)
{
    try
    {
        //---send the text---
        System.Net.Sockets.NetworkStream ns;
        lock (_client.GetStream())
        {
            ns = _client.GetStream();
        }

        byte[] bytesToSend =
            System.Text.Encoding.ASCII.GetBytes(message);
        ns.Write(bytesToSend, 0, bytesToSend.Length);
        ns.Flush();
    }
    catch (Exception ex)
    {
        Console.WriteLine(ex.ToString());
    }
}
```

Finally, the Broadcast() function sends a message to all the clients stored in the AllClients HashTable object.

Visual Basic 2005

```vb
Public Sub Broadcast(ByVal message As String)
    '---log it locally---
    Console.WriteLine(message)
    Dim c As DictionaryEntry
    For Each c In AllClients
        '---broadcast message to all users---
        CType(c.Value, _
            ChatClient).SendMessage(message & vbLf)
    Next
End Sub
```

C# 2005

```csharp
public void Broadcast(string message)
{
    //---log it locally---
    Console.WriteLine(message);
    foreach (DictionaryEntry c in AllClients)
    {
        //---broadcast message to all users---
        ((ChatClient)(c.Value)).SendMessage(
            message + Environment.NewLine);
    }
}
```

Building the Client

Now that you've built the server, it is time to build the client. Using Visual Studio 2005, create a new Windows application (name it **WinClient**), and populate the default form with the controls shown in Figure 1-3. Set the MultiLine and ReadOnly properties of the txtMessageHistory control to True, and set its ScrollBars property to Vertical. Also, set the Enabled property of the btnSend control to False.

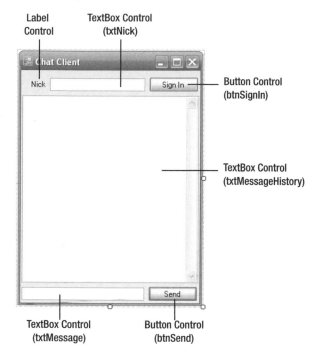

Figure 1-3. *Populating the Windows form with the various controls*

The client application logic is similar to the server, albeit more straightforward. Double-click the form to switch to the edit window. Import the following namespace.

Visual Basic 2005

```
Imports System.Net.Sockets
```

C# 2005

```
using System.Net.Sockets;
```

Define the following constant and variables within the form.

Visual Basic 2005

```
Public Class Form1
    Const portNo As Integer = 500
    Dim client As TcpClient
    Dim data() As Byte
```

C# 2005

```csharp
public partial class Form1 : Form
{
    const int portNo = 500;
    TcpClient client;
    byte[] data;
```

When the user signs in, you first connect to the server and send the nickname of the user using the SendMessage() subroutine. You then begin reading data from the server asynchronously and change the name of the button to **Sign Out**. When the user signs out from the chat application, you invoke the Disconnect() subroutine.

Visual Basic 2005

```vb
Private Sub btnSignIn_Click( _
    ByVal sender As System.Object, _
    ByVal e As System.EventArgs) _
    Handles btnSignIn.Click
    If btnSignIn.Text = "Sign In" Then
        Try
            '---connect to server---
            client = New TcpClient
            client.Connect("127.0.0.1", portNo)
            ReDim data(client.ReceiveBufferSize)
            SendMessage(txtNick.Text)

            '---read from server---
            client.GetStream.BeginRead( _
                data, 0, _
                CInt(client.ReceiveBufferSize), _
                AddressOf ReceiveMessage, Nothing)
            btnSignIn.Text = "Sign Out"
            btnSend.Enabled = True
        Catch ex As Exception
            MsgBox(ex.ToString)
        End Try
    Else
        '---disconnect from server---
        Disconnect()
        btnSignIn.Text = "Sign In"
        btnSend.Enabled = False
    End If
End Sub
```

C# 2005

```csharp
private void btnSignIn_Click(object sender, EventArgs e)
{
    if (btnSignIn.Text == "Sign In")
    {
        try
        {
            //---connect to server---
            client = new TcpClient();
            client.Connect("127.0.0.1", portNo);
            data = new byte[client.ReceiveBufferSize];

            //---read from server---
            SendMessage(txtNick.Text);
            client.GetStream().BeginRead(data, 0,
                System.Convert.ToInt32(
                client.ReceiveBufferSize),
                ReceiveMessage, null);
            btnSignIn.Text = "Sign Out";
            btnSend.Enabled = true;
        }
        catch (Exception ex)
        {
            MessageBox.Show(ex.ToString());
        }
    }
    else
    {
        //---disconnect from server---
        Disconnect();
        btnSignIn.Text = "Sign In";
        btnSend.Enabled = false;
    }
}
```

When the user clicks the Send button, you send a message to the server.

Visual Basic 2005

```vbnet
Private Sub btnSend_Click( _
    ByVal sender As System.Object, _
    ByVal e As System.EventArgs) _
    Handles btnSend.Click
    SendMessage(txtMessage.Text)
    txtMessage.Clear()
End Sub
```

C# 2005

```csharp
private void btnSend_Click(
    object sender,
    EventArgs e)
{
    SendMessage(txtMessage.Text);
    txtMessage.Clear();
}
```

Add the SendMessage() subroutine to allow the client to send a message to the server.

Visual Basic 2005

```vb
Public Sub SendMessage(ByVal message As String)
    Try
        '---send a message to the server---
        Dim ns As NetworkStream = client.GetStream
        Dim data As Byte() = _
         System.Text.Encoding.ASCII.GetBytes(message)
        '---send the text---
        ns.Write(data, 0, data.Length)
        ns.Flush()
    Catch ex As Exception
        MsgBox(ex.ToString)
    End Try
End Sub
```

C# 2005

```csharp
public void SendMessage(string message)
{
    try
    {
        //---send a message to the server---
        NetworkStream ns = client.GetStream();
        byte[] data =
            System.Text.Encoding.ASCII.GetBytes(message);

        //---send the text---
        ns.Write(data, 0, data.Length);
        ns.Flush();
    }
    catch (Exception ex)
    {
        MessageBox.Show(ex.ToString());
    }
}
```

The `ReceiveMessage()` subroutine asynchronously reads data sent from the server in a separate thread. When the data is received, it will display the data in the `txtMessageHistory` control. Because Windows controls are not thread-safe, you need to use a delegate (`delUpdateHistory()`) to update the controls.

THREAD SAFETY

By default, a Windows application uses a single thread of execution. And when you have multiple threads of execution (like what you did here with the `ReceiveMessage()` subroutine), things get a little complicated when you try to update the UI of the application from different threads.

It is important to note that you cannot directly access the properties of Windows controls on separate threads (other than on the main thread that it is running on), because Windows controls are not thread-safe. Trying to do so will also trigger a runtime error, a useful feature new in Visual Studio 2005. Instead, you should use a delegate and call it using the `Invoke()`/`BeginInvoke()` method of the controls/form you are trying to update.

Visual Basic 2005

```
Public Sub ReceiveMessage(ByVal ar As IAsyncResult)
    Try
        Dim bytesRead As Integer

        '---read the data from the server---
        bytesRead = client.GetStream.EndRead(ar)
        If bytesRead < 1 Then
            Exit Sub
        Else
            '---invoke the delegate to display the received
            ' data---
            Dim para() As Object = _
             {System.Text.Encoding.ASCII.GetString( _
              data, 0, bytesRead)}
            Me.Invoke(New delUpdateHistory( _
                AddressOf Me.UpdateHistory), para)
        End If

        '---continue reading...---
        client.GetStream.BeginRead( _
            data, 0, CInt(client.ReceiveBufferSize), _
            AddressOf ReceiveMessage, Nothing)
    Catch ex As Exception
        '---ignore the error; fired when a user signs off---
    End Try
End Sub
```

C# 2005

```csharp
public void ReceiveMessage(IAsyncResult ar)
{
    try
    {
        int bytesRead;

        //---read the data from the server---
        bytesRead = client.GetStream().EndRead(ar);
        if (bytesRead < 1)
        {
            return;
        }
        else
        {
            //---invoke the delegate to display the
            // received data---
            object[] para = {
                System.Text.Encoding.ASCII.GetString(
                data, 0, bytesRead) };
            this.Invoke(new delUpdateHistory(UpdateHistory),
                para);
        }
        //---continue reading...---
        client.GetStream().BeginRead(data, 0,
            System.Convert.ToInt32(client.ReceiveBufferSize),
            ReceiveMessage, null);
    }
    catch (Exception ex)
    {
        //---ignore the error; fired when a user signs off---
    }
}
```

You use the delUpdateHistory() delegate to invoke the UpdateHistory() function in the main thread.

Visual Basic 2005

```vb
'---delegate and subroutine to update the TextBox control---
Public Delegate Sub delUpdateHistory(ByVal str As String)
Public Sub UpdateHistory(ByVal str As String)
    txtMessageHistory.AppendText(str)
End Sub
```

C# 2005

```csharp
//---delegate and subroutine to update the TextBox control---
public delegate void delUpdateHistory(string str);
public void UpdateHistory(string str)
{
    txtMessageHistory.AppendText(str);
}
```

Finally, the `Disconnect()` subroutine disconnects the client from the server.

Visual Basic 2005

```vb
Public Sub Disconnect()
    Try
    '---Disconnect from server---
        client.GetStream.Close()
        client.Close()
    Catch ex As Exception
        MsgBox(ex.ToString)
    End Try
End Sub
```

C# 2005

```csharp
public void Disconnect()
{
    try
    {
        //---Disconnect from server---
        client.GetStream().Close();
        client.Close();
    }
    catch (Exception ex)
    {
        MessageBox.Show(ex.ToString());
    }
}
```

When the form is closed, call the `Disconnect()` subroutine to disconnect the client from the server.

Visual Basic 2005

```
Private Sub Form1_FormClosing( _
   ByVal sender As Object, _
   ByVal e As _
      System.Windows.Forms.FormClosingEventArgs) _
   Handles Me.FormClosing
     Disconnect()
End Sub
```

C# 2005

```
private void Form_Closing(
   object sender,
   FormClosingEventArgs e)
{
    Disconnect();
}
```

For the C# version of the code, you need to wire up the event handler for the FormClosing event of the form by adding the following code in bold in Form1.Designer.cs (in Solution Explorer, click the Show All Files button, and you will find this file located under Form1.cs):

```
private void InitializeComponent()
{
   ...
   this.FormClosing += new
      System.Windows.Forms.FormClosingEventHandler(this.Form_Closing);
}
```

Testing the Chat Applications

To test the applications, first run the server by pressing F5 in Visual Studio 2005. To launch multiple copies of the client to test the multiuser capabilities of the server, you can locate the .exe file of the client in the \bin folder of the WinClient project. Run multiple copies of WinClient.exe, and sign in and chat at the same time (see Figure 1-4).

■**Note** In the interest of simplicity, I have assumed that data sent over the TCP stream is sent and received in the same block. However, this is not always true. Data sent over the TCP stream is not guaranteed to arrive at once; you may receive a portion of the message in the current read cycle and receive the rest in the next read cycle, or several messages may be read at the same time. The project in the next section will show you how to take care of this.

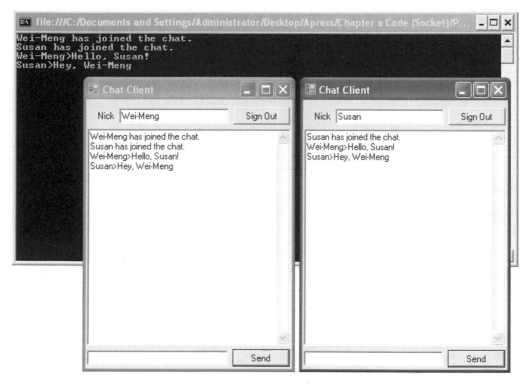

Figure 1-4. *Testing the multiuser chat application*

Building an Advanced Multiuser Chat Application

In the previous sections, you saw how to build a multiuser chat application that allows many users to chat simultaneously. Although the application is interesting, it is not very flexible because you cannot choose the users you want to privately chat with—all messages are broadcast to everyone in the chat.

In the following sections, based on the foundation covered in the earlier sections, you will enhance the application to allow private chats between selected users. You will also build FTP support into the application so you can transfer files between users.

Defining Your Own Communication Protocol

When you start to enhance the chat application, you'll realize that you have to define your own application protocol for the various functions. For example, when you want to chat with someone, you need to indicate the username to the server so that only messages destined for this particular user are sent to him. Similarly, when you need to perform a file transfer, there must be several handshaking processes to ensure that the recipient explicitly accepts the file transfer, and only then can you start sending the file.

The application will use the protocols defined and described in the next sections.

Protocol Description

The following sections describe the interaction between the users and the server.

Logging In

When a user (for example, User1) signs in to the server, the following happens:

- User1 sends [Join][User1] to the server indicating its presence.
- The server broadcasts [Join][User1] to all the users currently connected.

Requesting Usernames

When a user (for example, User1) logs in to the server, he needs to know who is currently online:

- User1 sends [Usrs] to the server asking for a list of users currently online.
- The server sends back to User1 [Usrs][User1,User2,UserN,] containing a list of all usernames.

Chatting

A user (for example, User1) wants to send a message ("Hello!") to other users (for example, User2 and User3):

- User1 sends [Talk][User2,User3,]User1>Hello! to the server.
- The server sends [Talk][User2,User3,]User1>Hello! to both User2 and User3.

Transferring Files

A user (for example, User1; IP address 1.2.3.4) wants to send a file named Filename.txt to another user (for example, User2; IP address 3.4.5.6):

- User1 sends [File][User1,User2,][Filename.txt] to the server.
- The server sends [File][User1][Filename.txt] to User2 to confirm he wants to receive the file.
- If User2 wants to receive the file, he will then send [Send_File][User1, User2] to the server indicating that he wants to receive the file.
- User2 starts to listen at port 501 for incoming data.
- The server looks up the IP address of User2 and sends [Send_File][3.4.5.6] to User1.
- User1 starts the FTP service by sending the file using the IP address (3.4.5.6) and port number 501.

■Note Note that for file transfers, the actual transferring of files takes place between the clients; the server is not involved.

Leaving a Chat

A user (for example, User1) signs out of the chat:

- User1 sends [Left][User1] to the server.

- The server broadcasts [Left][User1] to all users.

Walking Through the Features

Before you learn how to write the chat application, let's look at the application you are going to build in this part of the chapter.

When you log in to the server, a list of online users will appear on the ListBox control (see the left of Figure 1-5).

Figure 1-5. *Logging in to the server*

To chat with a user, simply select the user you want to chat with, and click the Send button to send the message (see Figure 1-6).

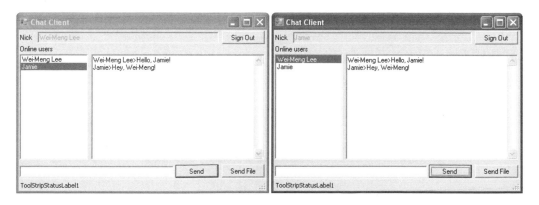

Figure 1-6. *Chatting with a user*

To chat with multiple users, Ctrl+click the users' names in the ListBox control (see Figure 1-7).

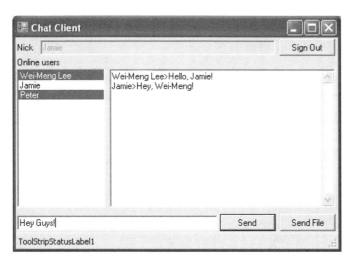

Figure 1-7. *Chatting with multiple users*

To send a file to another user, select the recipient's name, and click the Send File button. You will then select the file you want to send and click Open (see Figure 1-8).

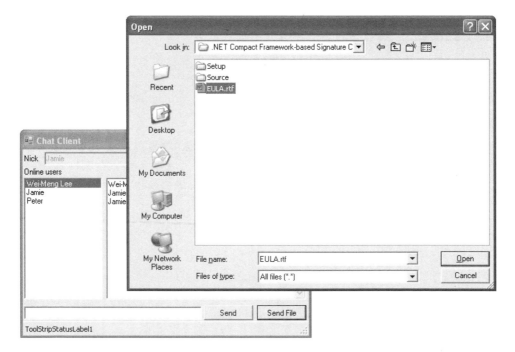

Figure 1-8. *Sending a file to another user*

On the recipient's end, he will get a prompt requesting to download the file. If he clicks Yes, the file is downloaded (see Figure 1-9).

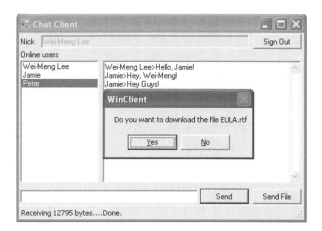

Figure 1-9. *Prompting the recipient to download the file*

As the file is downloaded, the status bar will display the number of bytes received so far (see Figure 1-10).

Figure 1-10. *Showing the progress of the download*

Building the Server

This chat application has two components: server and client. You will start by building the server. For the server, you will create a console application project using Visual Studio 2005. Name the project **Server**.

In the default Module1.vb file, populate it with the following.

Visual Basic 2005

```vb
Imports System.Net.Sockets
Module Module1
    Const portNo As Integer = 500
    Sub Main()
        Dim localAdd As System.Net.IPAddress = _
            System.Net.IPAddress.Parse("10.0.1.4")
        Dim listener As New System.Net.Sockets.TcpListener( _
            localAdd, portNo)
        listener.Start()
```

```
        While True
            Dim user As New ChatClient(listener.AcceptTcpClient)
        End While
    End Sub
End Module
```

C# 2005

```csharp
using System;
using System.Collections.Generic;
using System.Text;
using System.Net.Sockets;
namespace server_CS
{
    class Program
    {
        const int portNo = 500;
        static void Main(string[] args)
        {
            System.Net.IPAddress localAdd =
                System.Net.IPAddress.Parse("10.0.1.4");
            System.Net.Sockets.TcpListener listener = new
                System.Net.Sockets.TcpListener(localAdd, portNo);
            listener.Start();
            while (true)
            {
                ChatClient user = new
                    ChatClient(listener.AcceptTcpClient());
            }
        }
    }
}
```

USING A REAL IP ADDRESS

If you look closely at the code, you will realize that this time around I used a real IP address (and not the localhost address of 127.0.0.1). The IP address that I used here—10.0.1.4—is an address assigned by my router, and you will most likely have a different IP address for your own computer. The reason why I am using the real IP address is that in order to test the FTP feature of this project, you need to use at least two computers. One computer will host the server and the client, and the other one will host the client. Since the FTP feature will transfer files directly using each client's IP address, using the localhost address will result in an error. Also, if the server is on a different computer from the client's, you need to use the real IP address of the server.

For your own testing, be sure to use the IP address of the computer hosting the server.

The next step is to define the ChatClient class. You use the ChatClient class to represent information about each client connecting to the server. Add a new class to your project in Visual Studio 2005, and name it **ChatClient.vb**.

First, import the following namespace(s).

Visual Basic 2005

```vb
Imports System.Net.Sockets
```

C# 2005

```csharp
using System.Net.Sockets;
using System.Collections;
```

In the ChatClient class, first define the various private members (their uses are described in the comments in the code). You also declare a HashTable object (AllClients) to store a list of all clients connecting to the server. The reason for declaring it as a shared member is to ensure all instances of the ChatClient class are able to obtain a list of all the clients currently connected to the server.

Visual Basic 2005

```vb
'---class to contain information of each client---
Public Class ChatClient
    '---constant for linefeed character---
    Private Const LF As Integer = 10

    '---contains a list of all the clients---
    Public Shared AllClients As New Hashtable

    '---information about the client---
    Private _client As TcpClient
    Private _clientIP As String
    Private _clientNick As String

    '---used to store partial request---
    Private partialStr As String

    '---used for sending/receiving data---
    Private data() As Byte
```

C# 2005

```csharp
class ChatClient
{
    //---constant for linefeed character---
    const int LF = 10;
```

```
//---contains a list of all the clients---
public static Hashtable AllClients = new Hashtable();

//---information about the client---
private TcpClient _client;
private string _clientIP;
private string _clientNick;

//---used to store partial request---
private string partialStr;

//'---used for sending/receiving data---
private byte[] data;
```

When a client gets connected to the server, the server will create an instance of the ChatClient class and then pass the TcpClient variable (client) to the constructor of the class. You will also get the IP address of the client and use it as an index to identify the client in the HashTable object. The BeginRead() method will begin an asynchronous read from the NetworkStream object (client.GetStream) in a separate thread. This allows the server to remain responsive and continue accepting new connections from other clients. When the reading is complete, control will transfer to the ReceiveMessage() function (which you will define shortly).

Visual Basic 2005

```
'---when a client is connected---
Public Sub New(ByVal client As TcpClient)
    _client = client

    '---get the client IP address---
    _clientIP = client.Client.RemoteEndPoint.ToString

    '---add the current client to the hash table---
    AllClients.Add(_clientIP, Me)

    '---start reading data from the client in a separate thread---
    ReDim data(_client.ReceiveBufferSize - 1)
    _client.GetStream.BeginRead(data, 0, _
    CInt(_client.ReceiveBufferSize), _
    AddressOf ReceiveMessage, Nothing)
End Sub
```

C# 2005

```
//---when a client is connected---
public ChatClient(TcpClient client)
{
    _client = client;
```

```
//---get the client IP address---
_clientIP = client.Client.RemoteEndPoint.ToString();

//---add the current client to the hash table---
AllClients.Add(_clientIP, this);

//---start reading data from the client in a separate
// thread---
data = new byte[_client.ReceiveBufferSize];
_client.GetStream().BeginRead(data, 0,
    System.Convert.ToInt32(_client.ReceiveBufferSize),
    ReceiveMessage, null);
}
```

The SendMessage() function allows the server to send a message to the client.

Visual Basic 2005

```
'---send the message to the client---
Public Sub SendMessage(ByVal message As String)
    Try
        '---send the text---
        Dim ns As System.Net.Sockets.NetworkStream
        SyncLock _client.GetStream
            ns = _client.GetStream
            Dim bytesToSend As Byte() = _
            System.Text.Encoding. _
            ASCII.GetBytes(message) _
            ns.Write(bytesToSend, 0, _
            bytesToSend.Length)
            ns.Flush()
        End SyncLock
    Catch ex As Exception
        Console.WriteLine(ex.ToString)
    End Try
End Sub
```

C# 2005

```
//---send the message to the client---
public void SendMessage(string message)
{
    try
    {
        //---send the text---
        System.Net.Sockets.NetworkStream ns;
        lock (_client.GetStream())
        {
```

```
                ns = _client.GetStream();
                byte[] bytesToSend =
                    System.Text.Encoding.ASCII.GetBytes(message);
                ns.Write(bytesToSend, 0, bytesToSend.Length);
                ns.Flush();
            }
        }
        catch (Exception ex)
        {
            Console.WriteLine(ex.ToString());
        }
}
```

The Broadcast() function sends a message to all the clients stored in the AllClients HashTable object.

Visual Basic 2005

```
'---broadcast message to selected users---
Public Sub Broadcast(ByVal message As String, _
   ByVal users() As String)

    If users Is Nothing Then
        '---broadcasting to everyone---
        Dim c As DictionaryEntry
        For Each c In AllClients
            '---broadcast message to all users---
            CType(c.Value, _
                ChatClient).SendMessage(message & vbLf)
        Next
    Else
        '---broadcasting to selected ones---
        Dim c As DictionaryEntry
        For Each c In AllClients
            Dim user As String
            For Each user In users
                If CType(c.Value, ChatClient). _
                _clientNick = user Then
                    '---send message to user
                    CType(c.Value, ChatClient). _
                    SendMessage(message & vbLf)
                    '---log it locally
                    Console.WriteLine("sending -----> " _
                    & message)
                    Exit For
                End If
            Next
        Next
```

```
    End If
End Sub
```

C# 2005

```csharp
//---broadcast message to selected users---
public void Broadcast(string message, string[] users)
{
    if (users == null)
    {
        //---broadcasting to everyone---
        foreach (DictionaryEntry c in AllClients)
        {
            ((ChatClient)(c.Value)).SendMessage(
                message + "\n");
        }
    }
    else
    {
        //---broadcasting to selected ones---
        foreach (DictionaryEntry c in AllClients)
        {
            foreach (string user in users)
            {
                if (((ChatClient)(c.Value)).
                    _clientNick == user)
                {
                    ((ChatClient)(c.Value)).SendMessage(
                        message + "\n");
                    //---log it locally
                    Console.WriteLine("sending -----> "
                        + message);
                    break;
                }
            }
        }
    }
}
```

■**Note** All messages sent to the client end with the linefeed (vbLf in Visual Basic and \n in C#) character.

In the ReceiveMessage() function, you first call the EndRead() method to handle the end of an asynchronous read. Here, you check whether the number of bytes read is less than 1. If it is, the client has disconnected, and you need to remove the client from the HashTable object (using the IP address of the client as an index into the hash table). You also want to broadcast a message to all the clients telling them that this particular client has left the chat. You do this using the Broadcast() function. In this ReceiveMessage() function, you check the various message formats sent from the client and take the appropriate action. For example, if the client initiates a FTP request, you need to repackage the message (as described in the earlier section "Protocol Description") and send it to the recipient.

It is important to note that incoming data may not arrive all at once—a request may be broken up and received separately, or multiple requests may come in at the same time. The sidebar "Receiving Incoming Data" discusses the three possible scenarios.

RECEIVING INCOMING DATA

Here are the three possible scenarios.

Scenario 1

The first scenario is the ideal scenario. Here, the string sent by a client is received in its entirety. The following illustration shows a talk request sent by User1 to User2 and User3. The request ends with an LF character, and the rest of the byte array contains null characters (0).

Scenario 2

The second scenario happens when a request is broken up and received separately. In the following illustration, the request sent by User1 to User2 and User3 is broken up into two parts. Only the second portion of the request ends with the LF character.

Scenario 3

The third scenario occurs when two separate requests are received together, as shown in the following illustration. Here, the first request is separated from the second request by an LF character.

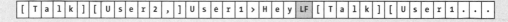

Visual Basic 2005

```
'---receiving a message from the client---
Public Sub ReceiveMessage(ByVal ar As IAsyncResult)

'---read from client---
    Dim bytesRead As Integer
```

```vb
Try
    SyncLock _client.GetStream
        bytesRead = _client.GetStream.EndRead(ar)
    End SyncLock

    '---client has disconnected---
    If bytesRead < 1 Then
        AllClients.Remove(_clientIP)
        Broadcast("[Left][" & _clientNick & _
            "] has left the chat.", Nothing)
        Exit Sub
    Else
        Dim messageReceived As String
        Dim i As Integer = 0
        Dim start As Integer = 0

        '---loop until no more chars---
        While data(i) <> 0

            '---do not scan more than what is read---
            If i + 1 > bytesRead Then Exit While

            '---if LF is detected---
            If data(i) = LF Then
                messageReceived = _
                    partialStr & _
                    System.Text.Encoding.ASCII.GetString( _
                    data, start, i - start)
                Console.WriteLine("received <----- " & _
                    messageReceived)

                If messageReceived.StartsWith("[Join]") Then

                    '====client is sending its nickname====
                    '---e.g. [Join][User1]---

                    '---extract user's name---
                    Dim nameLength As Integer = _
                        messageReceived.IndexOf("]", 6)
                    _clientNick = messageReceived.Substring( _
                        7, nameLength - 7)

                    '---tell everyone client has entered the
                    ' chat---
                    Broadcast(messageReceived, Nothing)
```

```vb
ElseIf messageReceived.StartsWith("[Usrs]") _
Then

    '===client is requesting for all users
    ' names===
    '--- e.g. [Usrs]---

    '---get all the users---
    Dim allUsers As String = "[Usrs]["
    Dim c As DictionaryEntry
    For Each c In AllClients

        '---get all the users' name---
        allUsers += _
            CType(c.Value, _
            ChatClient)._clientNick & ","
    Next
    allUsers += "]"

    '--- e.g. [Usrs][User1,User2,etc]---
    Broadcast(allUsers, Nothing)

ElseIf messageReceived.StartsWith("[Talk]") _
Then
    '===Chatting with someone===
    '---e.g. [Talk][User2,User3]User1>Hello
    ' everyone!---

    '---get all users---
    Dim users() As String = _
        messageReceived.Substring(7, _
        messageReceived.IndexOf("]", 7) - _
        8).Split(",")

    '---send to specified users---
    Broadcast(messageReceived, users)

ElseIf messageReceived.StartsWith("[File]") _
Then
    '===FTP request===
    '---e.g.
    ' [File][User1,User2][Filename.txt]---

    '---get all users---
    Dim users() As String = _
        messageReceived.Substring(7, _
        messageReceived.IndexOf("]", 7) - _
```

```vb
      8).Split(",")
    Dim index As Integer = _
      messageReceived.IndexOf("]", 7) + 2
    Dim filename As String = _
      messageReceived.Substring(index, _
      messageReceived.Length - index - 1)

    '---see who initiated the request---
    Dim from As String = users(0)

    '---remove the first user (initiator)---
    For j As Integer = 1 To users.Length - 1
        users(j - 1) = users(j)
    Next
    users(users.Length - 1) = String.Empty

    '---send to user---
    '---e.g. [File][User1][Filename.txt]---
    Broadcast("[File][" & from & "][" & _
    filename & "]", users)

ElseIf _
   messageReceived.StartsWith("[Send_File]") _
Then
    '===send file via FTP===
    '---e.g. [Send_File][User1,User2]---

    '---send file from User1 to User2---
    '---check send to who---
    Dim users() As String = _
       messageReceived.Substring(12, _
       messageReceived.IndexOf("]", 12) - _
       12).Split(",")

    Dim RecipientIP As String = String.Empty

    '---find out the recipient's IP address---
    Dim c As DictionaryEntry
    For Each c In AllClients
        If CType(c.Value, ChatClient)._
          _clientNick = users(1) Then

            '---send message to user---
            RecipientIP = _
               CType(c.Value, ChatClient). _
               _clientIP.Substring(0, _
                _clientIP.IndexOf(":"))
```

```
                        Exit For
                    End If
                Next
                users(1) = String.Empty

                '---e.g. [Send_File][1.2.3.4]---
                Broadcast("[Send_File][" & RecipientIP & _
                "]", users)
            End If
            start = i + 1
        End If
        i += 1
    End While

    '---partial string---
    If start <> i Then
        partialStr = _
            System.Text.Encoding.ASCII.GetString( _
            data, start, i - start)
    End If
End If

    '---continue reading from client
    SyncLock _client.GetStream
        _client.GetStream.BeginRead(data, 0, _
        CInt(_client.ReceiveBufferSize), _
        AddressOf ReceiveMessage, Nothing)
    End SyncLock
Catch ex As Exception
    AllClients.Remove(_clientIP)
    Broadcast("[Left][" & _clientNick & _
            "] has left the chat.", Nothing)
End Try
End Sub
```

C# 2005

```csharp
//---receiving a message from the client---
public void ReceiveMessage(IAsyncResult ar)
{
    //---read from client---
    int bytesRead;
    try
    {
        lock (_client.GetStream())
        {
            bytesRead = _client.GetStream().EndRead(ar);
        }
```

```
//---client has disconnected---
if (bytesRead < 1)
{
    AllClients.Remove(_clientIP);
    Broadcast("[Left][" + _clientNick +
        "] has left the chat.", null);
    return;
}
else
{
    string messageReceived;
    int i = 0;
    int start = 0;

    //---loop until no more chars---
    while (data[i] != 0)
    {

        //---do not scan more than what is read---
        if (i + 1 > bytesRead)
        {
            break;
        }

        //---if LF is detected---
        if (data[i] == LF)
        {
            messageReceived = partialStr +
                System.Text.Encoding.ASCII.GetString(
                data, start, i - start);
            Console.WriteLine("received <----- " +
                messageReceived);
            if (messageReceived.StartsWith("[Join]"))
            {
                //====client is sending its
                // nickname====
                //---e.g. [Join][User1]---

                //---extract user's name---
                int nameLength =
                    messageReceived.IndexOf("]", 6);
                clientNick =
                    messageReceived.Substring(
                    7, nameLength - 7);

                //---tell everyone client has entered
                // the chat---
                Broadcast(messageReceived, null);
```

```
          }
          else if
             (messageReceived.StartsWith("[Usrs]"))
          {
             //===client is requesting for all
             // users names===
             //---e.g. [Usrs]---

             //---get all the users---
             string allUsers = "[Usrs][";

             foreach (DictionaryEntry c in
                AllClients)
             {
                //---get all the users' name---
                allUsers +=
                ((ChatClient)(c.Value)).
                _clientNick + ",";
             }
             allUsers += "]";

             //---e.g. [Usrs][User1,User2,etc]---
             Broadcast(allUsers, null);
          }
          else if
             (messageReceived.StartsWith("[Talk]"))
          {
             //===Chatting with someone===
             //---e.g.
             // [Talk][User2,User3]User1>Hello
             // everyone!---

             //---get all users---
             string[] users =
                messageReceived.Substring(
                7, messageReceived.IndexOf("]", 7)
                - 8).Split(',');

              //---send to specified users---
             Broadcast(messageReceived, users);
          }
          else if
             (messageReceived.StartsWith("[File]"))
          {
             //===FTP request===
             //---e.g.
             // [File][User1,User2][Filename.txt]---
```

```csharp
//---get all users---
string[] users =
   messageReceived.Substring(
   7, messageReceived.IndexOf("]", 7)
   - 8).Split(',');
int index =
   messageReceived.IndexOf("]", 7)
   + 2;
string filename =
   messageReceived.Substring(
   index, messageReceived.Length -
   index - 1);

//---see who initiated the request---
string from = users[0];

//---remove the first user
// (initiator)---
for (int j = 1; j <= users.Length - 1;
   j++)
{
    users[j - 1] = users[j];
}
users[users.Length - 1] =
   string.Empty;

//---send to user---
//---e.g. [File][User1][Filename.txt]
// ---
Broadcast("[File][" + from + "][" +
   filename + "]", users);
}
else if
   (messageReceived.StartsWith(
   "[Send_File]"))
{
   //===send file via FTP===
   //---e.g. [Send_File][User1,User2]---

   //---send file from User1 to User2---
   //---check send to who---
   string[] users =
      messageReceived.Substring(
      12, messageReceived.IndexOf("]",
      12) - 12).Split(',');
   string RecipientIP = string.Empty;
```

```
                        //---find out the recipient's IP
                        // address---
                        foreach (DictionaryEntry c in
                          AllClients)
                        {
                            if (((ChatClient)(c.Value)).
                              _clientNick == users[1])
                            {
                                //---send message to user---
                                RecipientIP =
                                  ((ChatClient)(c.Value)).
                                  _clientIP.Substring(
                                  0, _clientIP.IndexOf(":"));
                                break;
                            }
                        }

                        users[1] = string.Empty;
                        //---e.g. [Send_File][1.2.3.4]---
                        Broadcast("[Send_File][" +
                            RecipientIP + "]", users);
                    }
                    start = i + 1;
                }
                i += 1;
            }

            //---partial string---
            if (start != i)
            {
                partialStr =
                    System.Text.Encoding.ASCII.GetString(data,
                    start, i - start);
            }
        }

        //---continue reading from client
        lock (_client.GetStream())
        {
            _client.GetStream().BeginRead(
                data, 0, System.Convert.ToInt32(
                _client.ReceiveBufferSize), ReceiveMessage,
                null);
        }
    }
    catch (Exception ex)
    {
```

```
        AllClients.Remove(_clientIP);
        Broadcast("[Left][" + _clientNick +
            "] has left the chat.", null);
    }
}
```

Building the Client

Now that you've built the server, it is time to build the client. Using Visual Studio 2005, create a new Windows application (name it **WinClient**), populate the default form with the controls shown in Figure 1-11, set the MultiLine and ReadOnly properties of txtMessageHistory to True, and set the ScrollBars property to Vertical. Also, set the SelectionMode property of lstUsers to MultiExtended.

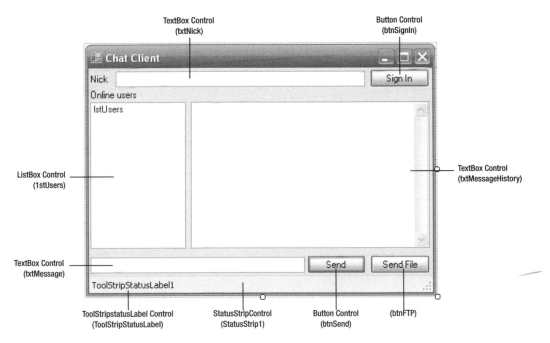

Figure 1-11. *Populating the Windows form with the various controls*

Double-click the form to switch to the code-behind. Import the following namespaces.

Visual Basic 2005

```
Imports System.Net.Sockets
Imports System.IO
```

C# 2005

```
using System.Net.Sockets;
using System.IO;
```

Within the Form1 class, define the following variables and constants.

Visual Basic 2005

```
Public Class Form1
    '---get own IP address---
    Private ips As Net.IPHostEntry = _
        Net.Dns.GetHostEntry(Net.Dns.GetHostName())

    '---port numbers and server IP address---
    Const PORTNO As Integer = 500
    Const FTPPORTNO As Integer = 501
    Const SERVERIP As String = "10.0.1.4"

    Private client As TcpClient

    '---used for sending and receiving data---
    Private data() As Byte

    '---for FTP use---
    Private fs As System.IO.FileStream
    Private filename As String
    Private fullfilename As String

    '---used to store partial request---
    Private partialStr As String
```

C# 2005

```
public partial class Form1 : Form
{
    //---get own IP address---
    private System.Net.IPHostEntry ips =
        System.Net.Dns.GetHostEntry(System.Net.Dns.GetHostName());

    //---port numbers and server IP address---
    const int PORTNO = 500;
    const int FTPPORTNO = 501;
    const string SERVERIP = "10.0.1.4";
    private TcpClient client;

    //---used for sending and receiving data---
    private byte[] data;

    //---for FTP use---
    private System.IO.FileStream fs;
    private string filename;
    private string fullfilename;
    //---used to store partial request---
    private string partialStr;
```

When the user signs in, the client first connects to the server and sends the nickname of the user using the SendMessage() subroutine (defined shortly). Then it begins reading data from the server asynchronously and changes the name of the Sign In button to Sign Out. It will also ask for a list of users currently logged in.

When the user signs out from the chat application, you invoke the Disconnect() subroutine (defined shortly).

Visual Basic 2005

```
'--Sign in to server---
Private Sub btnSignIn_Click( _
   ByVal sender As System.Object, _
   ByVal e As System.EventArgs) _
   Handles btnSignIn.Click

   If btnSignIn.Text = "Sign In" Then
       '---Sign in to the server---
       Try
           client = New TcpClient

           '---connect to the server---
           client.Connect(SERVERIP, PORTNO)
           ReDim data(client.ReceiveBufferSize - 1)

           '---inform the server of your nickname---
           ' e.g. [Join][User1]
           SendMessage("[Join][" & txtNick.Text & "]")

           '---begin reading data asynchronously from the server---
           client.GetStream.BeginRead( _
               data, 0, CInt(client.ReceiveBufferSize), _
               AddressOf ReceiveMessage, Nothing)

           '---change the button and textbox---
           btnSignIn.Text = "Sign Out"
           btnSend.Enabled = True
           txtNick.Enabled = False

           '---get all users connected---
           ' e.g. [Usrs]
           SendMessage("[Usrs]")

       Catch ex As Exception
           MsgBox(ex.ToString)
       End Try
   Else
       '---Sign off from the server---
       Disconnect()
       lstUsers.Items.Clear()
```

```
            '---change the button and textbox---
            btnSignIn.Text = "Sign In"
            btnSend.Enabled = False
            txtNick.Enabled = True
        End If
End Sub
```

C# 2005

```csharp
//---Sign in to server---
private void btnSignIn_Click(object sender, EventArgs e)
{
    if (btnSignIn.Text == "Sign In")
    {
        //---Sign in to the server---
        try
        {
            client = new TcpClient();

            //---connect to the server---
            client.Connect(SERVERIP, PORTNO);

            data = new byte[client.ReceiveBufferSize];

            //---inform the server of your nickname---
            SendMessage("[Join][" + txtNick.Text + "]");

            //---begin reading data asynchronously from the
            // server---
            client.GetStream().BeginRead(
                data, 0, System.Convert.ToInt32(
                client.ReceiveBufferSize), ReceiveMessage,
                null);

            //'---change the button and textbox---
            btnSignIn.Text = "Sign Out";
            btnSend.Enabled = true;
            txtNick.Enabled = false;

            //---get all users connected---
            SendMessage("[Usrs]");
        }
        catch (Exception ex)
        {
            MessageBox.Show(ex.ToString());
        }
    }
```

```
    else
    {
        //---Sign off from the server---
        Disconnect();
        lstUsers.Items.Clear();

        //---change the button and textbox---
        btnSignIn.Text = "Sign In";
        btnSend.Enabled = false;
        txtNick.Enabled = true;
    }
}
```

The Send button sends a message to the server. Note that you need to select a user in the
ListBox control before you can send a message.

Visual Basic 2005

```
'---Send Button---
Private Sub btnSend_Click( _
    ByVal sender As System.Object, _
    ByVal e As System.EventArgs) _
    Handles btnSend.Click
      ' e.g. [Talk][User2,User3,etc]User1>Hello world!

    '---select users to chat---
    If lstUsers.SelectedItems.Count < 1 Then
        MsgBox("You must select who to chat with.")
        Exit Sub
    End If

    '---formulate the message---
    Dim Message As String = "[Talk]["

    '---check who to chat with---
    Dim user As Object
    For Each user In lstUsers.SelectedItems
        Message += user & ","
    Next
    Message += "]" & txtNick.Text & ">" & txtMessage.Text

    '---update the message history---
    txtMessageHistory.Text += txtNick.Text & _
    ">" & txtMessage.Text & vbCrLf

    '---send message---
    SendMessage(Message)
    txtMessage.Clear()
End Sub
```

C# 2005

```csharp
//---Send Button---
private void btnSend_Click(object sender, EventArgs e)
{
    // e.g. [Talk][User2,User3,etc]User1>Hello world!

    //---select users to chat---
    if (lstUsers.SelectedItems.Count < 1)
    {
        MessageBox.Show("You must select who to chat with.");
        return;
    }

    //---formulate the message---
    string Message = "[Talk][";

    //---check who to chat with---
    foreach (object user in lstUsers.SelectedItems)
    {
        Message += user + ",";
    }
    Message += "]" + txtNick.Text + ">" + txtMessage.Text;

    //---update the message history---
    txtMessageHistory.Text += txtNick.Text + ">" +
        txtMessage.Text + Environment.NewLine;

    //---send message---
    SendMessage(Message);
    txtMessage.Clear();
}
```

The SendMessage() subroutine, used in the previous code, allows the client to send a message to the server.

Visual Basic 2005

```vb
'---Sends the message to the server---
Public Sub SendMessage(ByVal message As String)
    '---adds an LF char---
    message += vbLf
    Try
        '---send the text---
        Dim ns As System.Net.Sockets.NetworkStream
        SyncLock client.GetStream
            ns = client.GetStream
            Dim bytesToSend As Byte() = _
            System.Text.Encoding. _
```

```
                ASCII.GetBytes(message)

            '---sends the text---
            ns.Write(bytesToSend, 0, bytesToSend.Length)
            ns.Flush()
        End SyncLock
    Catch ex As Exception
        MsgBox(ex.ToString)
    End Try
End Sub
```

C# 2005

```
//---Sends the message to the server---
public void SendMessage(string message)
{
    //---adds a linefeed char---
    message += "\n";
    try
    {
        //---send the text---
        System.Net.Sockets.NetworkStream ns;
        lock (client.GetStream())
        {
            ns = client.GetStream();
            byte[] bytesToSend =
                System.Text.Encoding.ASCII.GetBytes(message);
            //---sends the text---
            ns.Write(bytesToSend, 0, bytesToSend.Length);
            ns.Flush();
        }
    }
    catch (Exception ex)
    {
        MessageBox.Show(ex.ToString());
    }
}
```

The ReceiveMessage() subroutine asynchronously reads data sent from the
server in a separate thread. When the data is received, it will display the data in the
txtMessageHistory control. Because Windows controls are not thread-safe, you need to use a
delegate, delUpdateHistory(),(), to update the controls. Like before, you need to take special
note that the request may not come in its entirety.

Visual Basic 2005

```
'---Receives a message from the server---
Public Sub ReceiveMessage(ByVal ar As IAsyncResult)
```

```vb
    Try
        Dim bytesRead As Integer
        bytesRead = client.GetStream.EndRead(ar)
        If bytesRead < 1 Then
            Exit Sub
        Else
            Dim messageReceived As String
            Dim i As Integer = 0
            Dim start As Integer = 0
            '---loop until no more chars---
            While data(i) <> 0
                '---do not scan more than what is read---
                If i + 1 > bytesRead Then Exit While

                '---if LF is detected---
                If data(i) = 10 Then
                    messageReceived = _
                        partialStr & _
                        System.Text.Encoding.ASCII.GetString( _
                            data, start, i - start) & _
                        vbCrLf

                    '---update the message history---
                    Dim para() As Object = {messageReceived}
                    Me.Invoke(New delUpdateHistory(AddressOf _
                        Me.UpdateHistory), para)
                    start = i + 1
                End If
                i += 1
            End While

            '---partial request---
            If start <> i Then
                partialStr = _
                    System.Text.Encoding.ASCII.GetString( _
                    data, start, i - start)
            End If
        End If

        '---continue reading for more data---
        client.GetStream.BeginRead(data, 0, _
            CInt(client.ReceiveBufferSize), _
            AddressOf ReceiveMessage, Nothing)
    Catch ex As Exception
        MsgBox(ex.ToString)
    End Try
End Sub
```

C# 2005

```
//---Receives a message from the server---
public void ReceiveMessage(IAsyncResult ar)
{
    try
    {
        int bytesRead;
        bytesRead = client.GetStream().EndRead(ar);
        if (bytesRead < 1)
        {
            return;
        }
        else
        {
            string messageReceived;
            int i = 0;
            int start = 0;
            //---loop until no more chars---
            while (data[i] != 0)
            {
                //---do not scan more than what is read---
                if (i + 1 > bytesRead)
                {
                    break;
                }

                //---if LF is detected---
                if (data[i] == 10)
                {
                    messageReceived = partialStr +
                        System.Text.Encoding.ASCII.
                        GetString(data, start, i - start) +
                        Environment.NewLine;

                    //---update the message history---
                    object[] para = { messageReceived };
                    this.Invoke(new
                        delUpdateHistory((this.UpdateHistory)),
                        para);
                    start = i + 1;
                }
                i += 1;
            }

            //---partial request---
            if (start != i)
            {
```

```
                partialStr = System.Text.Encoding.ASCII.
                    GetString(data, start, i - start);
            }
        }

        //---continue reading for more data---
        client.GetStream().BeginRead(
            data, 0, System.Convert.ToInt32(
            client.ReceiveBufferSize),
            ReceiveMessage, null);
    }
    catch (Exception ex)
    {
        MessageBox.Show(ex.ToString());
    }
}
```

You use the delUpdateHistory() delegate to invoke the UpdateHistory() function in the main thread.

Visual Basic 2005

```
'---delegate to update the textboxes in the main thread---
Public Delegate Sub delUpdateHistory(ByVal str As String)
```

C# 2005

```
//---delegate to update the textboxes in the main thread---
public delegate void delUpdateHistory(string str);
```

In the UpdateHistory() subroutine, you examine the message format and perform the appropriate action. For example, if the user has left a chat (through the [Left] message), you must remove the username from your ListBox.

Visual Basic 2005

```
Public Sub UpdateHistory(ByVal str As String)
    If str.StartsWith("[Join]") Then
        'e.g. [Join][User1]

        '---extract user's name---
        Dim nameLength As Integer = str.IndexOf("]", 6)

        '---display in the ListBox---
        lstUsers.Items.Add(str.Substring(7, _
        nameLength - 7))

        Exit Sub
```

```vb
ElseIf str.StartsWith("[Left]") Then
    'e.g. [Left][User1]

    '---extract user's name---
    Dim nameLength As Integer = str.IndexOf("]", 6)

    '---remove the user from the listbox---
    Try
        lstUsers.Items.RemoveAt( _
        lstUsers.Items.IndexOf( _
        str.Substring(7, nameLength - 7)))

    Catch ex As Exception
    End Try
    Exit Sub

ElseIf str.StartsWith("[Usrs]") Then
    'e.g. [Usrs][User1,User2,User3,etc]

    '---extract the usernames---
    Dim users() As String = _
        str.Substring(7, str.Length - 8).Split(",")

    Dim user As String
    lstUsers.Items.Clear()
    '---add the user to ListBox---
    For Each user In users
        lstUsers.Items.Add(user)
    Next
    '---remove the last empty user---
    lstUsers.Items.RemoveAt(lstUsers.Items.Count - 1)
    Exit Sub

ElseIf str.StartsWith("[File]") Then
    'e.g. [File][User1][Filename.ext]

    '---get username---
    Dim users() As String = _
    str.Substring(7, str.IndexOf("]", 7) _
    - 7).Split(",")

    '---extract filename---
    Dim index As Integer = str.IndexOf("]", 7) + 2
    Dim filename As String = str.Substring(index, _
    str.Length - index - 3)

    '---prompt the user---
```

```vb
            Dim response As MsgBoxResult
            response = MsgBox( _
            "Do you want to download the file " & _
            filename, MsgBoxStyle.YesNo)

            '---proceed with download---
            If response = MsgBoxResult.Yes Then
                '---tell the client that he can proceed to
                ' send the file---
                ' e.g. [Send_File][User1,User2]
                SendMessage("[Send_File][" & users(0) & "," _
                & txtNick.Text & "]")

                '---start the FTP process---
                FTP_Receive(filename)
            End If
            Exit Sub

        ElseIf str.StartsWith("[Send_File]") Then
            'e.g. [Send_File][1.2.3.4]

            '---extract the IP address of file recipient---
            Dim userIP As String = _
            str.Substring(12, str.Length - 15)

            '---start the FTP process---
            FTP_Send(fullfilename, userIP)
            Exit Sub

        ElseIf str.StartsWith("[Talk]") Then
            'e.g. [Talk][User1]Hello!

            '---display the message in the textbox---
            str = str.Substring(str.IndexOf("]", 7) + 1)
            txtMessageHistory.AppendText(str)
        End If
End Sub
```

C# 2005

```csharp
public void UpdateHistory(string str)
{
    if (str.StartsWith("[Join]"))
    {
        //---e.g. [Join][User1]---
        //---extract user's name---
        int nameLength = str.IndexOf("]", 6);
```

```
        //---display in the ListBox---
        lstUsers.Items.Add(str.Substring(7, nameLength - 7));
        return;
    }
    else if (str.StartsWith("[Left]"))
    {
        //---e.g. [Left][User1]---
        //---extract user's name---
        int nameLength = str.IndexOf("]", 6);
        try
        {
            //---remove the user from the listbox---
            lstUsers.Items.RemoveAt(
                lstUsers.Items.IndexOf(str.Substring(7,
                nameLength - 7)));
        }
        catch (Exception ex)
        {
        }
        return;
    }
    else if (str.StartsWith("[Usrs]"))
    {
        //---e.g. [Usrs][User1,User2,User3,etc]---
        //---extract the usernames---
        string[] users = str.Substring(
            7, str.Length - 8).Split(',');
        lstUsers.Items.Clear();

        //---add the user to ListBox---
        foreach (string user in users)
        {
            lstUsers.Items.Add(user);
        }

        //---remove the last empty user---
        lstUsers.Items.RemoveAt(lstUsers.Items.Count - 1);
        return;
    }
    else if (str.StartsWith("[File]"))
    {
        //---e.g. [File][User1][Filename.ext]---
        //---get username---
        string[] users = str.Substring(
            7, str.IndexOf("]", 7) - 7).Split(',');

        //---extract filename---
```

```
            int index = str.IndexOf("]", 7) + 2;
            string filename = str.Substring(
                index, str.Length - index - 3);

            //---prompt the user---
            DialogResult response;
            response = MessageBox.Show(
                "Do you want to download the file " + filename,
                "Download", MessageBoxButtons.YesNo);

            //---proceed with download---
            if (response == DialogResult.Yes)
            {
                //---tell the client that he can proceed to
                // send the file---
                //---e.g. [Send_File][User1,User2]---
                SendMessage("[Send_File][" + users[0] + "," +
                    txtNick.Text + "]");

                //---start the FTP process---
                FTP_Receive(filename);
            }
            return;
        }
        else if (str.StartsWith("[Send_File]"))
        {
            //---e.g. [Send_File][1.2.3.4]---
            //---extract the IP address of file recipient---
            string userIP = str.Substring(12, str.Length - 15);

            //---start the FTP process---
            FTP_Send(fullfilename, userIP);
            return;
        }
        else if (str.StartsWith("[Talk]"))
        {
            //---e.g. [Talk][User1]Hello!---
            //---display the message in the textbox---
            str = str.Substring(str.IndexOf("]", 7) + 1);
            txtMessageHistory.AppendText(str);
        }
    }
}
```

When a user clicks the Send File button, check to see that a recipient user is selected and then prompt the user to select a file to send.

Visual Basic 2005

```vb
'---Send File button---
Private Sub btnFTP_Click( _
    ByVal sender As System.Object, _
    ByVal e As System.EventArgs) Handles btnFTP.Click

    '---formulate the message---
    '---e.g. [FILE][User1,User2,User3,][Filename.ext]---
    Dim Message As String = "[File][" & _
    txtNick.Text & ","

    Dim user As Object
    If lstUsers.SelectedItems.Count < 1 Then
        MsgBox("You must select who to send to.")
        Exit Sub
    End If

    '---check who to send to---
    For Each user In lstUsers.SelectedItems
        Message += user & ","
    Next

    '---select the file to send---
    Dim openFileDialog1 As New OpenFileDialog()

    openFileDialog1.InitialDirectory = "c:\"
    openFileDialog1.Filter = _
    "txt files (*.txt)|*.txt|All files (*.*)|*.*"

    openFileDialog1.FilterIndex = 2
    openFileDialog1.RestoreDirectory = True

    If openFileDialog1.ShowDialog() = _
    DialogResult.OK Then
        fullfilename = openFileDialog1.FileName

        filename = _
        fullfilename.Substring( _
        fullfilename.LastIndexOf("\") + 1)

        Message += "][" & filename & "]"
        SendMessage(Message)
    End If
End Sub
```

C# 2005

```csharp
//---Send File button---
private void btnFTP_Click(object sender, EventArgs e)
{
    //---formulate the message---
    //---e.g. [FILE][User1,User2,User3,][Filename.ext]---
    string Message = "[File][" + txtNick.Text + ",";

    if (lstUsers.SelectedItems.Count < 1)
    {
        MessageBox.Show("You must select who to send to.");
        return;
    }

    //---check who to send to---
    foreach (object user in lstUsers.SelectedItems)
    {
        Message += user + ",";
    }

    //---select the file to send---
    OpenFileDialog openFileDialog1 = new OpenFileDialog();
    openFileDialog1.InitialDirectory = "c:\\";
    openFileDialog1.Filter =
        "txt files (*.txt)|*.txt|All files (*.*)|*.*";
    openFileDialog1.FilterIndex = 2;
    openFileDialog1.RestoreDirectory = true;
    if (openFileDialog1.ShowDialog() == DialogResult.OK)
    {
        fullfilename = openFileDialog1.FileName;
        filename =
            fullfilename.Substring(
            fullfilename.LastIndexOf("\\") + 1);
        Message += "][" + filename + "]";
        SendMessage(Message);
    }
}
```

The FTP_Send() subroutine sends a file to the recipient through the TCP port 501. It sends files in blocks of 8,192 bytes (the maximum buffer size).

Visual Basic 2005

```vb
'---FTP process - Send file---
Public Sub FTP_Send( _
    ByVal filename As String, _
    ByVal recipientIP As String)
```

```vb
    '---connect to the recipient---
    Dim tcpClient As New System.Net.Sockets.TcpClient
    tcpClient.Connect(recipientIP, FTPPORTNO)
    Dim BufferSize As Integer = _
    tcpClient.ReceiveBufferSize
    Dim nws As NetworkStream = tcpClient.GetStream

    '---open the file---
    Dim fs As FileStream
    fs = New FileStream(filename, FileMode.Open, _
    FileAccess.Read)

    Dim bytesToSend(fs.Length - 1) As Byte
    Dim numBytesRead As Integer = fs.Read(bytesToSend, _
    0, bytesToSend.Length)

    Dim totalBytes As Integer = 0
    For i As Integer = 0 To fs.Length \ BufferSize
        '---send the file---
        If fs.Length - (i * BufferSize) > BufferSize Then
            nws.Write(bytesToSend, i * BufferSize, _
            BufferSize)
            totalBytes += BufferSize
        Else
            nws.Write(bytesToSend, i * _
                BufferSize, fs.Length - (i * BufferSize))
            totalBytes += fs.Length - (i * BufferSize)
        End If
        '---update the status label---
        ToolStripStatusLabel1.Text = _
            "Sending " & totalBytes & " bytes...."
        Application.DoEvents()
    Next
    ToolStripStatusLabel1.Text = _
        "Sending " & totalBytes & " bytes....Done."
    fs.Close()
    tcpClient.Close()
End Sub
```

C# 2005

```csharp
//---FTP process - Send file---
public void FTP_Send(string filename, string recipientIP)
{
    //---connect to the recipient---
    System.Net.Sockets.TcpClient tcpClient = new
        System.Net.Sockets.TcpClient();
```

```
tcpClient.Connect(recipientIP, FTPPORTNO);
int BufferSize = tcpClient.ReceiveBufferSize;
NetworkStream nws = tcpClient.GetStream();

//---open the file---
FileStream fs;
fs = new FileStream(filename, FileMode.Open,
    FileAccess.Read);
byte[] bytesToSend = new byte[fs.Length];
int numBytesRead = fs.Read(bytesToSend, 0,
    bytesToSend.Length);
int totalBytes = 0;
for (int i = 0; i <= fs.Length / BufferSize; i++)
{
    //---send the file---
    if (fs.Length - (i * BufferSize) > BufferSize)
    {
        nws.Write(bytesToSend, i * BufferSize,
            BufferSize);
        totalBytes += BufferSize;
    }
    else
    {
        nws.Write(bytesToSend, i * BufferSize,
            (int)fs.Length - (i * BufferSize));
        totalBytes += (int)fs.Length - (i * BufferSize);
    }
     //---update the status label---
    ToolStripStatusLabel1.Text = "Sending " + totalBytes +
        " bytes....";
    Application.DoEvents();
}
ToolStripStatusLabel1.Text = "Sending " + totalBytes +
    " bytes....Done.";
fs.Close();
tcpClient.Close();
}
```

The FTP_Receive() subroutine receives an incoming file through TCP port 501. It saves the file to the C:\temp directory.

■**Note** For simplicity, be sure you have the C:\temp folder created on the computer running the client.

Visual Basic 2005

```vbnet
'---FTP Process = Receive Files---
Public Sub FTP_Receive(ByVal filename As String)
    Try
        '---get the local IP address---
        Dim localAdd As System.Net.IPAddress = _
        System.Net.IPAddress. _
        Parse(ips.AddressList(0).ToString)

        '---start listening for incoming connection---
        Dim listener As New _
           System.Net.Sockets.TcpListener( _
           localAdd, FTPPORTNO)
           listener.Start()

        '---read incoming stream---
        Dim tcpClient As TcpClient = _
        listener.AcceptTcpClient()
        Dim nws As NetworkStream = tcpClient.GetStream

        '---delete the file if it exists---
        If File.Exists("C:\temp\" & filename) Then
            File.Delete("C:\temp\" & filename)
        End If

        '---create the file---
        fs = New System.IO.FileStream("c:\temp\" & _
        filename, _
           FileMode.Append, FileAccess.Write)

        Dim counter As Integer = 0
        Dim totalBytes As Integer = 0
        Do
            '---read the incoming data---
            Dim bytesRead As Integer = _
               nws.Read(data, 0, _
               tcpClient.ReceiveBufferSize)
            totalBytes += bytesRead
            fs.Write(data, 0, bytesRead)

            '---update the status label---
            ToolStripStatusLabel1.Text = "Receiving " & _
            totalBytes & " bytes...."
            Application.DoEvents()
            counter += 1
```

```vbnet
                Loop Until Not nws.DataAvailable
                ToolStripStatusLabel1.Text = "Receiving " & _
                totalBytes & " bytes....Done."
                fs.Close()
                tcpClient.Close()
                listener.Stop()

        Catch ex As Exception
            MsgBox(ex.ToString)
        End Try
    End Sub
```

C# 2005

```csharp
//---FTP Process = Receive Files---
public void FTP_Receive(string filename)
{
    try
    {
        //---get the local IP address---
        System.Net.IPAddress localAdd =
            System.Net.IPAddress.Parse(
            ips.AddressList[0].ToString());

        //---start listening for incoming connection---
        System.Net.Sockets.TcpListener listener = new
            System.Net.Sockets.TcpListener(localAdd,
            FTPPORTNO);
        listener.Start();

        //---read incoming stream---
        TcpClient tcpClient = listener.AcceptTcpClient();
        NetworkStream nws = tcpClient.GetStream();

        //---delete the file if it exists---
        if (File.Exists("c:\\temp\\" + filename))
        {
            File.Delete("c:\\temp\\" + filename);
        }

        //---create the file---
        fs = new System.IO.FileStream("c:\\temp\\" + filename,
            FileMode.Append, FileAccess.Write);
        int counter = 0;
        int totalBytes = 0;
        do
        {
```

```
            //---read the incoming data---
            int bytesRead = nws.Read(data, 0,
               tcpClient.ReceiveBufferSize);
            totalBytes += bytesRead;
            fs.Write(data, 0, bytesRead);

             //---update the status label---
            ToolStripStatusLabel1.Text = "Receiving " +
                totalBytes + " bytes....";
            Application.DoEvents();
            counter += 1;
        } while (nws.DataAvailable);
        ToolStripStatusLabel1.Text = "Receiving " + totalBytes
            + " bytes....Done.";
        fs.Close();
        tcpClient.Close();
        listener.Stop();
    }
    catch (Exception ex)
    {
        MessageBox.Show(ex.ToString());
    }
}
```

When the user closes the form (by clicking the X button on the window), disconnect the client from the server.

Visual Basic 2005

```
Private Sub Form1_FormClosing( _
  ByVal sender As Object, _
  ByVal e As System.Windows.Forms.FormClosingEventArgs) _
  Handles Me.FormClosing
    Disconnect()
End Sub
```

C# 2005

```
private void Form_Closing(
    object sender,
    FormClosingEventArgs e)
{
    Disconnect();
}
```

Finally, the Disconnect() subroutine disconnects the client from the server.

Visual Basic 2005

```vbnet
'---disconnect from the server---
Public Sub Disconnect()
    Try
        client.GetStream.Close()
        client.Close()
    Catch ex As Exception
        MsgBox(ex.ToString)
    End Try
End Sub
```

C# 2005

```csharp
//---disconnect from the server---
public void Disconnect()
{
    try
    {
        client.GetStream().Close();
        client.Close();
    }
    catch (Exception ex)
    {
        MessageBox.Show(ex.ToString());
    }
}
```

Testing the Application

To test the application, first run the server by pressing F5 in Visual Studio 2005. You need to launch multiple copies of the client to test the multiuser capabilities of the server. To do this, compile the code files provided in the Source Code/Download section of the Apress website (http://www.apress.com) into an .exe file. Run multiple copies of the application, sign in, and chat at the same time! To test the FTP feature of the application, be sure to run the client on different computers.

Summary

In this chapter, you saw how the TcpClient class allows you to perform asynchronous communication between two computers. The two chat applications developed in this chapter illustrate how you can design your own communication protocols, and this lays the foundation for building more complicated chat applications. For now, have fun with the chat applications!

CHAPTER 2

Serial Communications

Serial communication is one of the oldest mechanisms for devices to communicate with each other. Starting with the IBM PC and compatible computers, almost all computers are equipped with one or more serial ports and one parallel port. As the name implies, a *serial* port sends and receives data serially, one bit at a time. In contrast, a *parallel* port sends and receives data eight bits at a time, using eight separate wires.

Tip For serial communication to work, you just need a minimum of three wires—one to send, one to receive, and one signal ground. For parallel communication, you need eight wires.

Despite the comparatively slower transfer speed of serial ports over parallel ports, serial communication remains a popular connectivity option for devices because of its simplicity and cost-effectiveness. Figure 2-1 shows some of the devices that use a serial port to connect to the computer. Using a serial port, you can connect to a modem, a mouse, or a device such as a bridge/router for configuration purposes.

Figure 2-1. *Some common serial devices—modem, mouse, and router*

Although consumer products today are using USB connections in place of serial connections, still a lot of devices use serial ports as their sole connections to the outside world.

In this chapter, you will learn how to communicate with other serial devices using the new SerialPort class available in the .NET Framework 2.0 and the .NET Compact Framework 2.0. In particular, you will build three projects that illustrate how to use serial communications. The first project is a chat application that allows two computers (connected using either a serial cable or a Bluetooth connection) to communicate. And using the foundation of this application, you can extend it to communicate with other external serial devices such as cellular phones. You will learn how to use the AT commands to programmatically control your mobile phones through a serial Bluetooth connection. The second project is a Pocket PC chat application, which is similar to the first project. The third application shows how to communicate with a GPS receiver and then extract the useful data for displaying the current location on a map.

Some Serial Communication Basics

As mentioned, a serial device sends and receives data one bit at a time. Some devices can send and receive data at the same time and are known as *full-duplex* devices. Others that can either send or receive at any one time are known as *single-duplex*.

To initiate transmission, a device first transmits a *start bit*, followed by the *data bits*. The data bits can be five, six, seven, or eight bits, depending on what has been agreed upon. Both the sender and the receiver must be set to the same data bits for communication to take place correctly. Once the data bits are sent, a *stop bit* is sent. A stop bit can be one, one and a half, and two bits. The *baud rate* is the speed of transmission of data from one device to another. Baud rate is usually measured in *bits per second* (bps).

■**Note** Most serial devices transmit in seven or eight bits.

To detect that the data has been sent correctly, an optional *parity bit* can be included together with the data bits. A parity bit can be one of the following: odd, even, mark, space, or none (mark and space parity are almost always used). Using a parity bit provides a basic mechanism to detect corruption of data that was sent and does not guarantee that the data received is free from error. Nevertheless, a parity bit is useful for improving the integrity of the data sent.

Most serial ports adhere to the RS232C standard, which specifies a connector either with 25 pins or with 9 pins (see Figure 2-2). Most serial devices use the nine-pin connector.

 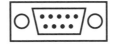

Figure 2-2. *The 25-pin and 9-pin serial connectors*

Chatting Using Serial Ports

The first application you will build in this chapter is a chat application. This chat application will allow two users whose computers are connected using a serial connection to communicate.

■**Tip** Notice that I mention serial *connection*, not a serial cable. This is because two users who are connected by Bluetooth can also use this application to communicate—you can establish a serial connection between two computers paired using Bluetooth.

The most common scenario is to connect two computers using a null modem cable (see Figure 2-3).

Figure 2-3. *A null modem cable*

Figure 2-4 shows the finished project. To start the chat, select the COM number corresponding to the serial port that is connected to the remote computer. Click Connect, and you are ready to talk!

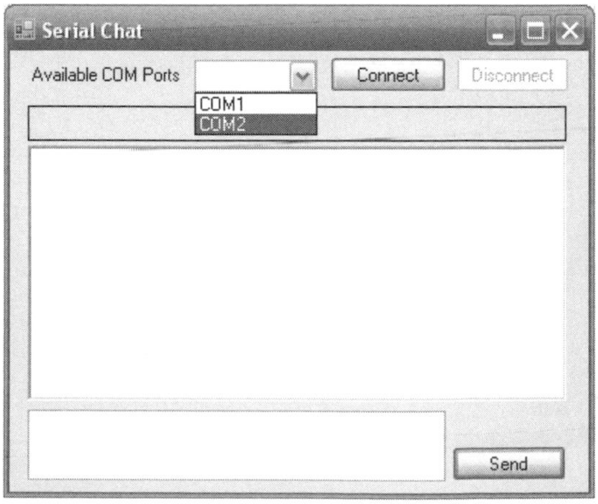

Figure 2-4. *Selecting a serial port to start chatting*

Hardware Needed

To test serial communications, you have a couple of options:

Computer to computer: As mentioned, you can connect two computers using a null modem cable.

Single computer: You can connect two serial ports on the same computer using a null modem cable. If your computer has only one serial port, you can convert a USB port to a serial port using a USB-to-serial-port converter (see the next section for more information about this).

Bluetooth connection: You can create a serial connection between two Bluetooth-paired computers.

USB-to-Serial-Port Converters

Unless you have two computers, you won't be able to test serial communications. However, you can use a null modem cable to connect two serial ports on the same computer to simulate two computers communicating over serial ports. But most computers today come with at most one serial port (and some notebooks do not even have one). One good solution is to use a USB-to-serial-port adapter to convert a USB port to a serial port. Hence, if your computer does not have any serial ports, you will need a pair of USB-to-serial-port adapters and a null modem cable (see Figure 2-5). Then, connect each USB-to-serial-port adapter to a USB connection.

Figure 2-5. *A USB-to-serial-port adapter and a null modem cable*

The USB-to-serial-port adapter comes with its own drivers. After installing the drivers, right-click My Computer on the desktop, and select Properties. In the System Properties dialog box, click the Hardware tab, and click the Device Manager button. Expand the Ports (COM & LPT) item, and locate the two newly added COM ports (see Figure 2-6).

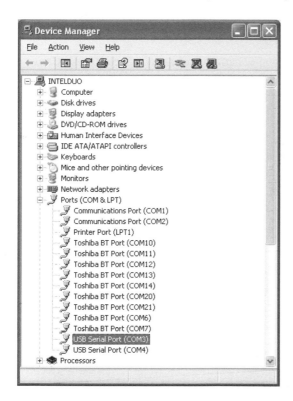

Figure 2-6. *Locating the newly created serial ports*

In this example, the two USB serial ports are COM3 and COM4.

Bluetooth Adapters

Besides using a null modem cable to connect two serial ports, you can also use Bluetooth to pair two computers. You can equip each computer with a Bluetooth adapter (see Figure 2-7).

Figure 2-7. *A USB Bluetooth adapter*

You can then pair the two computers and establish a serial connection between them.

■Note Refer to the documentation that comes with your Bluetooth adapter to learn how to establish a serial connection between two Bluetooth-paired computers.

Building the Chat Application

Using Visual Studio 2005, create a new Windows application, and name it **SerialCommChat**. Populate the default Form1 as shown in Figure 2-8.

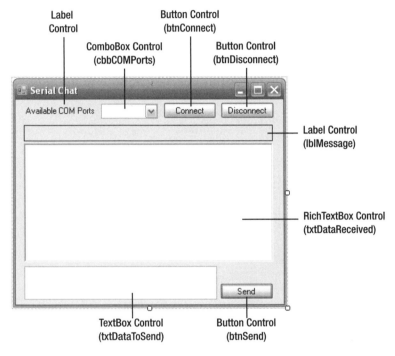

Figure 2-8. *Populating the default Form1 with the various controls*

Set the properties for the various controls as shown in Table 2-1.

Table 2-1. *Setting the Properties for the Various Controls*

Control	Property	Value
Form1	Text	"Serial Chat"
Form1	AcceptButton	btnSend
lblMessage	BorderStyle	FixedSingle
txtDataReceived	ScrollBars	Vertical
txtDataReceived	MultiLine	True
txtDataToSend	MultiLine	True

In .NET 2.0, there is now a new SerialPort Windows Forms control located on the Components tab in the Toolbox (see Figure 2-9). This SerialPort control encapsulates all the required functionality that you need to access in order to communicate using serial communications. You can either drag and drop a SerialPort control to your project or instantiate one from code (you will use this method for this project).

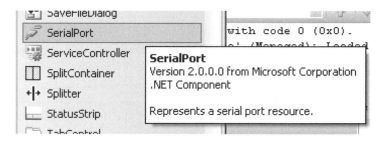

Figure 2-9. *The SerialPort control in the Toolbox*

Switch to Code View for Form1 to start coding the application.

Instantiating the SerialPort Class

First, declare the member variable serialPort to represent the serial port you want to use.

Visual Basic 2005

```
Public Class Form1
    Private WithEvents serialPort As New IO.Ports.SerialPort
```

C# 2005

```
public partial class Form1 : Form
{
    private System.IO.Ports.SerialPort serialPort =
        new System.IO.Ports.SerialPort();
```

■**Note** You can use the SerialPort control as mentioned earlier, or you can use the IO.Ports.SerialPort class; both are the same.

Notice that for Visual Basic 2005, you need to declare it with the WithEvents keyword. This is because the SerialPort class has the DataReceived event that is fired when data arrives at the serial port, and hence you need to service this event to receive the data. For C# 2005, the event handler for the DataReceived event will be added in the Form1_Load event.

Listing All the Available Serial Port Names

When the form is first loaded, you will retrieve all the available serial port names on your computer and then add these port names to the ComboBox control. Double-click the form to switch to the code-behind of the form, and the Form1_Load event handler will automatically be shown. Code the event as follows.

■**Note** Henceforth in this chapter, to make Visual Studio 2005 automatically create the event handler for a control (such as a form's Load event or a button's Click event), double-click the control to create the event handler.

Visual Basic 2005

```
Private Sub Form1_Load( _
    ByVal sender As System.Object, _
    ByVal e As System.EventArgs) _
    Handles MyBase.Load

    '---display all the serial port names on the local computer---
    For i As Integer = 0 To _
       My.Computer.Ports.SerialPortNames.Count - 1
          cbbCOMPorts.Items.Add( _
             My.Computer.Ports.SerialPortNames(i))
    Next
    btnDisconnect.Enabled = False
End Sub
```

C# 2005

```
private void Form1_Load(object sender, EventArgs e)
{
    //---set the event handler for the DataReceived event---
    serialPort.DataReceived += new
       System.IO.Ports.SerialDataReceivedEventHandler(
       DataReceived);

    //---display all the serial port names on the local
    // computer---
    string[] portNames =
       System.IO.Ports.SerialPort.GetPortNames();
    for (int i = 0; i <= portNames.Length - 1; i++)
    {
        cbbCOMPorts.Items.Add(portNames[i]);
    }
    btnDisconnect.Enabled = false;
}
```

HANDLING EVENTS IN C#

In the C# version of the `Form1_Load` event, I have also added an event handler for the `SerialPort` class's `DataReceived` event. This event will be fired when there is incoming data at the serial port. You don't need to wire this event handler in Visual Basic 2005 because you can use the `Handles` keyword to wire up event handlers.

   Also note that for the C# version of the code, before you press F5 to test the code, you need to comment out the following section of the code because the `DataReceived()` event handler has not been defined yet:

```
//---set the event handler for the DataReceived event---
// serialPort.DataReceived += new
// System.IO.Ports.SerialDataReceivedEventHandler(
// DataReceived);
```

Figure 2-10 shows how the ComboBox control will look when the form is first loaded.

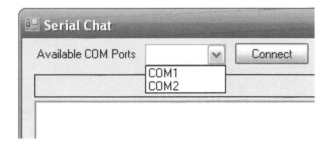

Figure 2-10. *The ComboBox control displaying all the serial port names*

Opening a Serial Port

Once a port name is selected, the user clicks the Connect button to open the selected port. You accomplish this with the following method.

Visual Basic 2005

```
'---Event handler for the Connect button---
Private Sub btnConnect_Click( _
   ByVal sender As System.Object, _
   ByVal e As System.EventArgs) _
   Handles btnConnect.Click
    '---close the serial port if it is open---
    If serialPort.IsOpen Then
        serialPort.Close()
    End If

    Try
        '---configure the various parameters of the serial port---
```

```
        With serialPort
            .PortName = cbbCOMPorts.Text
            .BaudRate = 9600
            .Parity = IO.Ports.Parity.None
            .DataBits = 8
            .StopBits = IO.Ports.StopBits.One
        End With

        '---open the serial port---
        serialPort.Open()

        '---update the status of the serial port and
        ' enable/disable the buttons---
        lblMessage.Text = cbbCOMPorts.Text & " connected."
        btnConnect.Enabled = False
        btnDisconnect.Enabled = True
    Catch ex As Exception
        MsgBox(ex.ToString)
    End Try
End Sub
```

C# 2005

```
//---Event handler for the Connect button---
private void btnConnect_Click(object sender, EventArgs e)
{
    //---close the serial port if it is open---
    if (serialPort.IsOpen)
    {
        serialPort.Close();
    }
    try
    {
        //---configure the various parameters of the serial
        // port---
        serialPort.PortName = cbbCOMPorts.Text;
        serialPort.BaudRate = 9600;
        serialPort.Parity = System.IO.Ports.Parity.None;
        serialPort.DataBits = 8;
        serialPort.StopBits = System.IO.Ports.StopBits.One;

        //---open the serial port---
        serialPort.Open();

        //---update the status of the serial port and
        // enable/disable the buttons---
        lblMessage.Text = cbbCOMPorts.Text + " connected.";
```

```
            btnConnect.Enabled = false;
            btnDisconnect.Enabled = true;
        }
        catch (Exception ex)
        {
            MessageBox.Show(ex.ToString());
        }
    }
}
```

In particular, you set the various properties of the SerialPort class, such as PortName, BaudRate, Parity, and so on.

Note The two communicating parties must have the same properties set. That is, they must have the same baud rate, parity, data bits, and stop bit.

Disconnecting a Serial Port

The Disconnect button closes the currently open serial port.

Visual Basic 2005

```
'---Event handler for the Disconnect button---
Private Sub btnDisconnect_Click( _
   ByVal sender As System.Object, _
   ByVal e As System.EventArgs) _
   Handles btnDisconnect.Click
    Try
        '---close the serial port---
        serialPort.Close()

        '---update the status of the serial port and
        ' enable/disable the buttons---
        lblMessage.Text = serialPort.PortName & " disconnected."
        btnConnect.Enabled = True
        btnDisconnect.Enabled = False
    Catch ex As Exception
        MsgBox(ex.ToString)
    End Try
End Sub
```

C# 2005

```
//---Event handler for the Disconnect button---
private void btnDisconnect_Click(object sender, EventArgs e)
{
```

```
    try
    {
        '---close the serial port---
        serialPort.Close();

        //---update the status of the serial port and
        // enable/disable the buttons---
        lblMessage.Text = serialPort.PortName +
            " disconnected.";
        btnConnect.Enabled = true;
        btnDisconnect.Enabled = false;
    }
    catch (Exception ex)
    {
        MessageBox.Show(ex.ToString());
    }
}
```

Sending Data Using the Serial Port

To send data to the recipient through the serial port, use the Write() method of the
SerialPort class.

Visual Basic 2005

```
'---Event handler for the Send button---
Private Sub btnSend_Click( _
    ByVal sender As System.Object, _
    ByVal e As System.EventArgs) _
    Handles btnSend.Click
    Try
        '---write the string to the serial port---
        serialPort.Write(txtDataToSend.Text & vbCrLf)

        '---append the sent string to the TextBox control---
        With txtDataReceived
            .AppendText(">" & txtDataToSend.Text & vbCrLf)
            .ScrollToCaret()
        End With

        '---clears the TextBox control---
        txtDataToSend.Text = String.Empty
    Catch ex As Exception
        MsgBox(ex.ToString)
    End Try
End Sub
```

C# 2005

```csharp
//---Event handler for the Send button---
private void btnSend_Click(object sender, EventArgs e)
{
    try
    {
        //---write the string to the serial port---
        serialPort.Write(txtDataToSend.Text +
            Environment.NewLine);

        //---append the sent string to the TextBox control---
        txtDataReceived.AppendText(">" + txtDataToSend.Text +
            Environment.NewLine);
        txtDataReceived.ScrollToCaret();

        //---clears the TextBox control---
        txtDataToSend.Text = string.Empty;
    }
    catch (Exception ex)
    {
        MessageBox.Show(ex.ToString());
    }
}
```

Receiving Data on the Serial Port

One nice feature of the SerialPort class is that you don't need to constantly poll for incoming data. Instead, you just need to service the DataReceived event, and it will automatically fire when incoming data is detected. However, because this event is running on a separate thread, any attempt to update the main form directly will result in an error. Hence, you need to use a delegate to update controls on the main thread (Form1).

Visual Basic 2005

```vbnet
'---Event handler for the DataReceived event---
Private Sub DataReceived( _
    ByVal sender As Object, _
    ByVal e As System.IO.Ports.SerialDataReceivedEventArgs) _
    Handles serialPort.DataReceived
        '---invoke the delegate to retrieve the received data---
        txtDataReceived.BeginInvoke(New _
            myDelegate(AddressOf updateTextBox), _
            New Object() {})
End Sub
```

C# 2005

```
//---Event handler for the DataReceived event---
private void DataReceived(object sender,
    System.IO.Ports.SerialDataReceivedEventArgs e)
{
    //---invoke the delegate to retrieve the received data---
    txtDataReceived.BeginInvoke(new
        myDelegate(updateTextBox));
}
```

Define the delegate and the updateTextBox() subroutine as follows.

Visual Basic 2005

```
'---Delegate and subroutine to update the TextBox control---
Public Delegate Sub myDelegate()
Public Sub updateTextBox()
    '---append the received data into the TextBox control---
    With txtDataReceived
        .AppendText(serialPort.ReadExisting)
        .ScrollToCaret()
    End With
End Sub
```

C# 2005

```
//---Delegate and subroutine to update the TextBox control---
public delegate void myDelegate();
public void updateTextBox()
{
    //---append the received data into the TextBox control---
    txtDataReceived.AppendText(serialPort.ReadExisting());
    txtDataReceived.ScrollToCaret();
}
```

Testing the Application

You are now ready to test the application. Press F5 in Visual Studio 2005 to debug the application. You need to run another instance of the application in order to test the chat functionality. To do so, find the SerialCommChat.exe application within the Debug folder contained in the directory where you have stored the solution.

In the first instance of the application, select port 3 (based on the port number on my computer; check the port number on your computer), and click Connect. On the other instance, select port 4, and click Connect. You can now start chatting (see Figure 2-11)!

Figure 2-11. *Chatting via two COM ports*

Transmitting Unicode Characters

By default, the SerialPort class transmits ASCII characters only. This is set in the Encoding property of the SerialPort class. If you want to converse in other languages (such as Chinese or Japanese), you need to set the Encoding property of the SerialPort class to Unicode so that the data can be sent and received correctly.

■Tip The current versions of the .NET Framework 2.0 and the .NET Compact Framework 2.0 do not work correctly when you use the ReadExisting() method to read Unicode characters. Hence, instead of using the ReadExisting() method to read incoming Unicode characters, you will use the Read() method.

First, you need to set the Encoding property in the SerialPort class to Unicode.

Visual Basic 2005

```
With serialPort
    .PortName = cbbCOMPorts.Text
    .BaudRate = 9600
    .Parity = IO.Ports.Parity.None
    .DataBits = 8
    .StopBits = IO.Ports.StopBits.One
    '---set the encoding the Unicode---
    .Encoding = System.Text.Encoding.Unicode
End With
```

C# 2005

```
serialPort.PortName = cbbCOMPorts.Text;
serialPort.BaudRate = 9600;
serialPort.Parity = System.IO.Ports.Parity.None;
serialPort.DataBits = 8;
serialPort.StopBits = System.IO.Ports.StopBits.One;
//---set the encoding the Unicode---
serialPort.Encoding = System.Text.Encoding.Unicode;
```

Then, modify the updateTextBox() subroutine to read the incoming Unicode characters correctly.

Visual Basic 2005

```
Public Sub updateTextBox()
    '---UNICODE work-around---
    With txtDataReceived
        '---find out the number of bytes to read---
        Dim bytesToRead As Integer = serialPort.BytesToRead

        '---declare a char array---
        Dim ch(bytesToRead) As Char

        '---read the bytes into the ch array---
        Dim bytesRead As Integer = 0
        bytesRead = serialPort.Read(ch, 0, bytesToRead)

        '---convert the ch array into a string---
        Dim str As String = New String(ch, 0, bytesRead)

        '---append the received string into the TextBox control---
        .AppendText(str)
        .ScrollToCaret()
    End With
End Sub
```

C# 2005

```
public void updateTextBox()
{
    //---UNICODE work-around---
    //---find out the number of bytes to read---
    int bytesToRead = serialPort.BytesToRead;

    //---declare a char array---
    char[] ch = new char[bytesToRead];
    int bytesRead = 0;

    //---read the bytes into the ch array---
    bytesRead = serialPort.Read(ch, 0, bytesToRead);

    //---convert the ch array into a string---
    string str = new string(ch, 0, bytesRead);

    //---append the received string into the TextBox
    // control---
    txtDataReceived.AppendText(str);
    txtDataReceived.ScrollToCaret();
}
```

Figure 2-12 shows sending and receiving Chinese characters.

Figure 2-12. *Sending and receiving Chinese characters*

Connecting to Other Serial Devices

One interesting use for the chat application is using it to communicate with serial devices. One good candidate to test on is your Bluetooth-enabled mobile phone (and modem). Most mobile phones support the AT command set, which means you can programmatically interact with the phone by issuing AT commands.

To see how the example application communicates with a Bluetooth handset, you first need the following hardware:

- A Bluetooth-enabled handset, such as the Sony Ericsson T68i or the Motorola E398

- A Bluetooth adapter for your computer

Before running the application, first pair the computer with the Bluetooth-enabled handset. Your Bluetooth driver (on your computer) will tell you which serial port is being used to connect to the handset. Suppose that COM1 is used to connect to a Sony Ericsson T68i. You will now connect COM1 in the application and then issue the AT command (see Figure 2-13).

■Note When communicating with external devices, remember to change the encoding from Unicode to the default ASCII.

Figure 2-13. *Issuing an AT command to a handset*

You should see "AT OK" returned by the phone. You can try the sample AT commands listed in Table 2-2.

Table 2-2. *Some AT Commands*

Command	Usage	Example Response
AT	Attention.	AT OK
AT*	List all supported AT commands.	*EACS, *EAID, *EALR, *EALS, *EAM, *EAMS, *EAPM, *EAPN, and so on
AT+CGMI	Request manufacturer identification.	ERICSSON
AT+CGMM	Request model identification.	1130202-BVT68
ATDT+Number	Dial a number.	
AT*EVA	Answer a call.	
AT+CBC?	Check battery charge.	+CBC: 0,44 (44 means the battery is 44 percent charged)
AT+CSQ	Signal quality.	+CSQ: 14,99 (signal strength is from 0 to 31; 14 is the signal strength)

■**Note** Not all phones support the same AT command set. Refer to the manual for your handset for the actual AT commands supported.

Two interesting AT commands are ATDT and AT*EVA. You can use them to make and receive calls, respectively.

■**Note** Not all phones support ATDT and AT*EVA. I tested the two commands using the Sony Ericsson T68i.

To allow users to control their mobile phones using their computers, I added the controls as shown in Figure 2-14.

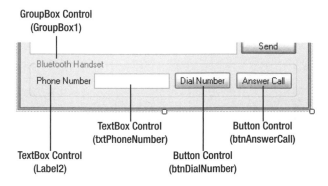

Figure 2-14. *Adding the controls to Form1*

The code for the Dial Number and Answer Call buttons is as follows.

Visual Basic 2005

```
'---Event handler for the Dial Number button---
Private Sub btnDialNumber_Click( _
   ByVal sender As System.Object, _
   ByVal e As System.EventArgs) _
   Handles btnDialNumber.Click
     '---write the AT command ATDT to the serial port---
     serialPort.Write("ATDT " & txtPhoneNumber.Text & vbCrLf)
End Sub

'---Event handler for the Answer Call button---
Private Sub btnAnswerCall_Click( _
   ByVal sender As System.Object, _
   ByVal e As System.EventArgs) _
   Handles btnAnswerCall.Click
     '---write the AT command AT*EVA to the serial port---
     serialPort.Write("AT*EVA" & vbCrLf)
End Sub
```

C# 2005

```
//---Event handler for the Dial Number button---
private void btnDialNumber_Click(object sender, EventArgs e)
{
    //---write the AT command ATDT to the serial port---
    serialPort.Write("ATDT " + txtPhoneNumber.Text +
        Environment.NewLine);
}

//---Event handler for the Answer Call button---
private void btnAnswerCall_Click(object sender, EventArgs e)
{
    //---write the AT command AT*EVA to the serial port---
    serialPort.Write("AT*EVA" + Environment.NewLine);
}
```

Press F5 to test the application. You can now enter a phone number and click the Dial Number button, and your mobile phone will automatically dial the number! When the phone rings, click the Answer Call button to answer the call.

Chatting Using Serial Ports on the Pocket PC

In the previous sections, you saw how to use the `SerialPort` class to send and receive data through the serial ports on your computer. In fact, the `SerialPort` class has greatly simplified the life of serial communication programmers by encapsulating all the important functionalities into a single class. Fortunately, the `SerialPort` class is also available in the .NET Compact Framework 2.0. This means it is now easy to write network applications on the Pocket PC.

To see how easily you can use the `SerialPort` class using the .NET Compact Framework, you will now port the chat application from the previous project to the Pocket PC platform.

Hardware Needed

For the application in this section, you need two Bluetooth-enabled Pocket PCs. Most new Pocket PCs on the market today come with built-in Bluetooth functionality, and hence you are not required to purchase additional hardware. For this example, I used the iMate JASJAR (see Figure 2-15), which runs on the latest Windows Mobile 5.0 platform and has built-in Bluetooth, WiFi, and 3G support.

Figure 2-15. *The iMate JASJAR*

■**Note** There are some known issues when using the `SerialPort` class on some older devices, such as those running on platforms prior to Windows Mobile 5.0. On some devices, the `SerialPort` class has problems receiving data and will drain the battery power of your device rapidly.

Building the Application

Launch Visual Studio 2005, and create a new smart-device application. Choose the Windows Mobile 5.0 Pocket PC project type, and then select the Device Application template (see Figure 2-16).

■**Note** Out of the box, Visual Studio 2005 does not ship with the Windows Mobile 5.0 for Pocket PC SDK. You can download it by going to http://www.microsoft.com/downloads/ and searching for *Windows Mobile 5.0 for Pocket PC SDK*.

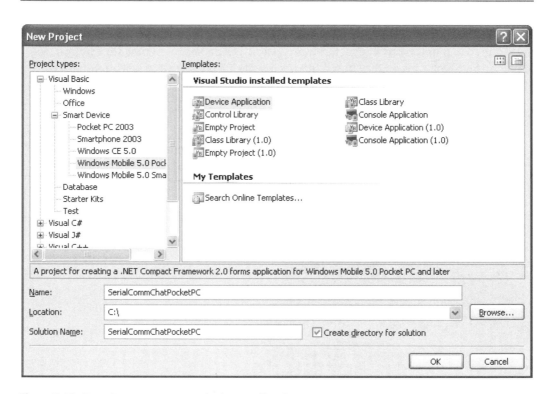

Figure 2-16. *Creating a new smart-device application*

Populate the default Form1 with the controls shown in Figure 2-17, and set the properties of the various controls as shown in Table 2-3.

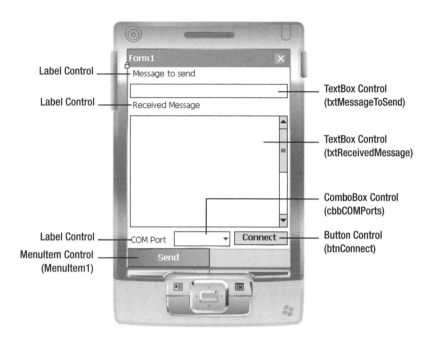

Figure 2-17. *Populating the default Form1*

Table 2-3. *Setting the Properties for the Various Controls*

Control	Property	Value
txtReceivedMessage	ScrollBars	Vertical
txtReceivedMessage	MultiLine	True
cbbCOMPorts	Items	COM0, COM1, COM2, COM3, COM4, COM5, COM6, COM7, COM8, COM9 (all separated by carriage returns)

Coding the Application

Switch to the code-behind of Form1, and instantiate a SerialPort object.

Visual Basic 2005

```
Private WithEvents serialPort As New IO.Ports.SerialPort
```

C# 2005

```
private System.IO.Ports.SerialPort serialPort =
    new System.IO.Ports.SerialPort();
```

Next, add the following subroutines.

■**Note** The code here is similar to the code listed in the previous sample application. Hence, I will not spend too much time explaining its usage.

Visual Basic 2005

```vb
'---Event handler for the DataReceived---
Private Sub DataReceived( _
       ByVal sender As Object, _
       ByVal e As System.IO.Ports.SerialDataReceivedEventArgs) _
       Handles serialPort.DataReceived
    txtReceivedMessage.BeginInvoke(New _
       myDelegate(AddressOf updateTextBox), _
       New Object() {})
End Sub

'---Delegate to update the TextBox control---
Public Delegate Sub myDelegate()
Public Sub updateTextBox()
    txtReceivedMessage.Text = _
       serialPort.ReadExisting & _
       txtReceivedMessage.Text
End Sub

'---Send menu item---
Private Sub MenuItem1_Click( _
    ByVal sender As System.Object, _
    ByVal e As System.EventArgs) _
    Handles MenuItem1.Click
    Try
        serialPort.WriteLine(txtMessageToSend.Text)
        txtReceivedMessage.Text = ">" & _
           txtMessageToSend.Text & vbCrLf & _
           txtReceivedMessage.Text
        txtMessageToSend.Text = String.Empty
    Catch ex As Exception
        MsgBox(ex.ToString)
    End Try
End Sub

'---Connect button---
Private Sub btnConnect_Click( _
    ByVal sender As System.Object, _
    ByVal e As System.EventArgs) _
    Handles btnConnect.Click
    Try
```

```
            If serialPort.IsOpen Then
                serialPort.Close()
            End If
            With serialPort
                .PortName = cbbCOMPorts.Text
                .BaudRate = 9600
                .Parity = IO.Ports.Parity.None
                .DataBits = 8
                .StopBits = IO.Ports.StopBits.One
            End With
            serialPort.Open()
            MsgBox("Port opened successfully!")
        Catch ex As Exception
            MsgBox(ex.ToString)
        End Try
End Sub
```

C# 2005

```
//---Form Load event---
private void Form1_Load(object sender, EventArgs e)
{
    serialPort.DataReceived += new
        System.IO.Ports.SerialDataReceivedEventHandler(
        DataReceived);
}


//---Event handler for the DataReceived---
private void DataReceived(object sender,
    System.IO.Ports.SerialDataReceivedEventArgs e)
{
    txtReceivedMessage.BeginInvoke(new
        myDelegate(updateTextBox));
}


//---Delegate to update the TextBox control---
public delegate void myDelegate();
public void updateTextBox()
{
    //---for receiving plain ASCII text---
    txtReceivedMessage.Text = (serialPort.ReadExisting()) +
        txtReceivedMessage.Text;
    txtReceivedMessage.ScrollToCaret();
}


//---Send menu item---
private void MenuItem1_Click(object sender, EventArgs e)
{
```

```
    try
    {
        serialPort.Write(txtMessageToSend.Text + "\r");
        txtReceivedMessage.Text = ">" + txtMessageToSend.Text
            + "\r" + txtReceivedMessage.Text;
        txtMessageToSend.Text = string.Empty;
    }
    catch (Exception ex)
    {
        MessageBox.Show(ex.ToString());
    }
}


//---Connect button---
private void btnConnect_Click(object sender, EventArgs e)
{
    if (serialPort.IsOpen)
    {
        serialPort.Close();
    }
    try
    {
        serialPort.PortName = cbbCOMPorts.Text;
        serialPort.BaudRate = 9600;
        serialPort.Parity = System.IO.Ports.Parity.None;
        serialPort.DataBits = 8;
        serialPort.StopBits = System.IO.Ports.StopBits.One;
        serialPort.Open();
        MessageBox.Show("Port opened successfully!");
    }
    catch (Exception ex)
    {
        MessageBox.Show(ex.ToString());
    }
}
```

To test the application, connect a Pocket PC device to your computer and ensure that it is connected via ActiveSync. In Visual Studio 2005, select Windows Mobile 5.0 Pocket PC Device (see Figure 2-18) in the Target Device drop-down list, and press F5. This will cause the application to be deployed on the Pocket PC. Repeat this process for the second Pocket PC.

Once the two Pocket PCs are loaded with the application, you need to pair them up using Bluetooth. In addition, ensure that you establish a serial connection between these two paired Pocket PCs, and take note of the respective serial port numbers. On each Pocket PC, you can then launch the application (by default it is installed in the \Program Files\ SerialCommChatPocketPC directory).

Finally, select the respective serial port number on the application, and click Connect. You are now ready to chat!

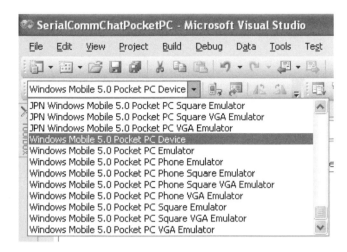

Figure 2-18. *Selecting a target device to deploy your application*

Creating a Mapping Application Using a GPS Receiver and Microsoft Virtual Earth

In the final project of this chapter, you will learn how to build a mapping application using Microsoft Virtual Earth and a GPS receiver. Microsoft Virtual Earth (VE) is a map and search system comprising maps, aerial images, business directories, and so on. Using VE, you can search for businesses and addresses, as well as ask for directions (see Figure 2-19).

■**Tip** You can access VE via MSN Virtual Earth at `http://local.live.com/`.

To developers, Microsoft exposes the VE Map control that allows you to embed VE maps into your own application. You can then build your own custom solution using the mapping services provided by VE. The VE Map control consists of a JavaScript page and a stylesheet. The VE Map control is hosted at `http://dev.virtualearth.net/mapcontrol/v3/mapcontrol.js`. The CSS is located at `http://local.live.com/css/MapControl.css`.

■**Note** Besides Microsoft Virtual Earth, another popular mapping solution is Google Maps. Google Maps also exposes APIs for developers to integrate mapping abilities into their custom applications. However, Google Maps will work only on Web browsers; it does not allow developers to embed Google Maps within a Windows application. Hence, if you want to include a mapping functionality in your Windows application, Microsoft VE is the way to go.

Figure 2-19. *Microsoft Virtual Earth*

In this project, you will build a Windows application that allows you to track your location in real time by getting positioning information from your GPS receiver and then feeding the data to VE. For this to work, I am assuming you have Internet connectivity, possibly through wireless hotspots or General Packet Radio Service (GPRS). In addition, this application is also able to plot traveled paths by extracting GPS data from a file. For example, you can track your traveled path by saving all the positioning information using a GPS receiver (and a Pocket PC or notebook). When you return to the office, you can upload the saved data to the application, and it will display the path you have traveled using VE.

This application will use a Bluetooth-enabled GPS receiver (such as the Holux GPSlim 236; see Figure 2-20) that connects to your computer (such as Pocket PC or computer) via Bluetooth (through a serial communication).

Figure 2-20. *The Holux GPSlim 236 GPS receiver*

Figure 2-21 shows how the completed project will look. You can view the maps of a particular location as well as pan and zoom into specific areas.

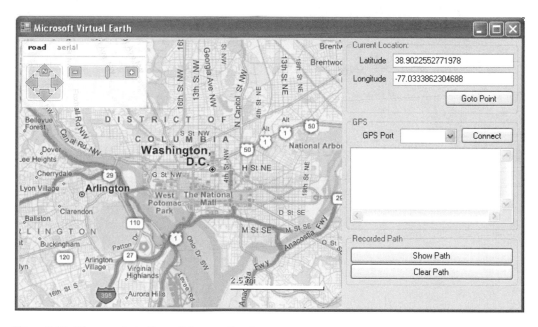

Figure 2-21. *The user interface of the application*

Besides viewing the roads of an area, you can also choose to view the aerial images (see Figure 2-22).

Figure 2-22. *Viewing aerial images*

Depending on the locations you have specified, you can also zoom into specific areas and view the highly detailed map (see Figure 2-23).

Figure 2-23. *Zooming and viewing the highly detailed map*

Building the Application

Let's now build the application. Launch Visual Studio 2005, and create a new Windows application project. Name the application **VirtualEarth**.

Populate the default Form1 with the controls shown in Figure 2-24.

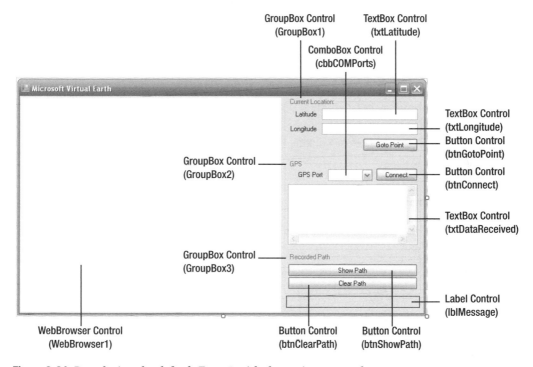

Figure 2-24. *Populating the default Form1 with the various controls*

In addition, add a Timer control to the form. Configure the controls on the form with the values shown in Table 2-4.

Table 2-4. *Configuring the Controls on Form1*

Control	Property	Value
Form1	BackColor	Khaki
WebBrowser1	Size	460,380
txtDataReceived	MultiLine	True
txtDataReceived	ScrollBars	Both
Timer1	Interval	1000

Creating the HTML File Containing the Virtual Earth Map

The next step is to create an HTML file containing all the necessary JavaScript functions to interact with the VE map.

Add an HTML page to the project (right-click the project name in Solution Explorer, select Add ➤ New Item, and then select HTML Page). Name the HTML page **Map.html**.

Populate the HTML page with the following:

```
<html xmlns="http://www.w3.org/1999/xhtml">
<head>
    <title>My Virtual Earth</title>
    <link href="http://local.live.com/css/MapControl.css"
        type="text/css" rel="stylesheet" />
    <script type="text/javascript"
        src="http://dev.virtualearth.net/mapcontrol/v3/mapcontrol.js">
    </script>
    <script type="text/javascript">

    var map = null;
    // Update the position of the map in the TextBox controls
    function updatePosition(e)
    {
        window.external.mapPositionChange(
            e.view.latlong.latitude,e.view.latlong.longitude);
    }
    // Go to a particular location on the map
    function goto_map_position(lat, lng)
    {
        map.PanToLatLong(lat, lng);
    }

    // Add a pushpin to the map
    function addPushpin(id, text, Lat, Long)
    {
        map.AddPushpin(id, Lat, Long, 15, 40, 'pin', '<b>' + text +
            '</b>', 1);
    }

    // Remove a particular pushpin
    function removePushpin(id)
    {
        map.RemovePushpin(id);
    }

    // Load the map
    function loadMap()
    {
        var params = new Object();
```

```
        params.latitude = 38.898748;
        params.longitude = -77.037684;
        params.zoomlevel = 12;
        params.mapstyle = Msn.VE.MapStyle.Road;
        params.showScaleBar = true;
        params.showDashboard = true;
        params.dashboardSize = Msn.VE.DashboardSize.Normal;
        params.dashboardX = 2;
        params.dashboardY = 2;

        container = document.getElementById("VirtualEarthMap");
        container.style.width = 460;
        container.style.height = 380;

        map = new Msn.VE.MapControl(container, params);
        map.Init();

        // Attach the event handlers for the various events
        map.AttachEvent("onendcontinuouspan", updatePosition);
        map.AttachEvent("onendzoom", updatePosition);
        map.AttachEvent("onclick", updatePosition);
    }
    </script>
</head>
<body onload="loadMap()" style="margin: 0px">
    <div id="VirtualEarthMap"></div>
</body>
</html>
```

The `Map.html` page contains a reference to the VE Map control (`.js`) as well as to the CSS file (`.css`). It also contains five JavaScript functions:

`updatePosition():():` Displays the currently selected position on the map by calling the `mapPositionChange()` method defined in the code-behind of Form1 (more about this later).

`goto_map_position():():` Goes to a particular location on the map based on the latitude and longitude specified.

`addPushpin():():` Adds a pushpin to the map using the caption specified in the parameter.

`removePushpin():():` Removes a particular pushpin on the map.

`loadMap():():` Loads the map with the various parameters such as size of the map, zoom level, latitude and longitude, and so on. It also attaches event handlers to the various events so that when certain events happen, the appropriate event handler will be fired.

You also need to set the `Copy to Output Directory` property of `Map.html` to `Copy if newer` (via the Properties window) so that the HTML page is deployed during runtime.

Coding the Application

Once the HTML page is populated, switch to the code-behind of Form1. For this application, you need to programmatically interact with the map displayed within the WebBrowser control, and hence you need to mark the Form1 class as "COM visible" using the ComVisibleAttribute class.

Visual Basic 2005

```
<System.Runtime.InteropServices.ComVisibleAttribute(True)> _
Public Class Form1
...
```

C# 2005

```
[System.Runtime.InteropServices.ComVisibleAttribute(true)]
public partial class Form1 : Form
...
```

Next, declare the following member variables.

Visual Basic 2005

```
'---index of the pushpin---
Private pushpin As Integer = 0

'---keeping track of the points---
Private pointCounter As Integer

'---used for remembering the lines read
' from a file containing coordinates---
Private lineIndex As Integer = 0
Dim line() As String

'---serial port for communicating with GPS receiver---
Private WithEvents serialPort As New IO.Ports.SerialPort
```

C# 2005

```
//---index of the pushpin---
private int pushpin = 0;

//---keeping track of the points---
private int pointCounter;

//---used for remembering the lines read
// from a file containing coordinates---
private int lineIndex = 0;
string[] line;
```

```
//---serial port for communicating with GPS receiver---
private System.IO.Ports.SerialPort serialPort = new
    System.IO.Ports.SerialPort();
```

In the Form1_Load event, you first display a list of available serial ports on the computer, then read the content of the Map.html file, and finally load it into the WebBrowser control.

Visual Basic 2005

```
Private Sub Form1_Load( _
    ByVal sender As System.Object, _
    ByVal e As System.EventArgs) _
    Handles MyBase.Load

    '---display the available COM port on the computer---
    For i As Integer = 0 To _
        My.Computer.Ports.SerialPortNames.Count - 1
        cbbCOMPorts.Items.Add( _
            My.Computer.Ports.SerialPortNames(i))
    Next

    '---Load the WebBrowser control with the Virtual Earth map---
    Dim fileContents As String

    '---remember to set the Copy to Output Directory
    ' property of Map.html to "Copy if newer"---
    fileContents = My.Computer.FileSystem.ReadAllText( _
        Application.StartupPath & "\Map.html")

    WebBrowser1.DocumentText = fileContents
    WebBrowser1.ObjectForScripting = Me
End Sub
```

C# 2005

```
private void Form1_Load(object sender, EventArgs e)
{
    //---set the event handler for the DataReceived event---
    serialPort.DataReceived += new
        System.IO.Ports.SerialDataReceivedEventHandler(
        DataReceived);

    //---display the available COM port on the computer---
    string[] portNames =
        System.IO.Ports.SerialPort.GetPortNames();
    for (int i = 0; i <= portNames.Length - 1; i++)
    {
        cbbCOMPorts.Items.Add(portNames[i]);
    }
```

```
    //---Load the WebBrowser control with the Virtual Earth
    // map---
    string fileContents;
    //---remember to set the Copy to Output Directory
    // property of Map.html to "Copy if newer"---
    fileContents = System.IO.File.ReadAllText(
        Application.StartupPath + "\\Map.html");
    WebBrowser1.DocumentText = fileContents;
    WebBrowser1.ObjectForScripting = this;
}
```

You can now test the application to see whether the map is able to load correctly. Press F5, and you should see the map as shown in Figure 2-25.

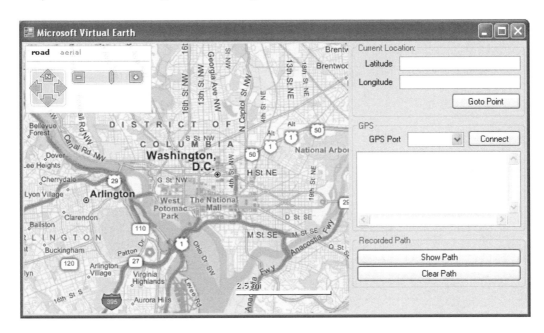

Figure 2-25. *Loading the map onto the WebBrowser control*

TESTING THE C# CODE

For the C# version of the code, before you press F5 to test the code, you need to comment out the following section of the code because the DataReceived() event handler has not been defined yet:

```
//---set the event handler for the DataReceived event---
// serialPort.DataReceived += new
// System.IO.Ports.SerialDataReceivedEventHandler(
// DataReceived);
```

Displaying the Coordinates of the Map

When you use the mouse to drag the map, notice that the map will move and pan. You can also use the dashboard to pan the map and use the slider to change the zoom level of the map (see Figure 2-26).

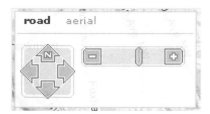

Figure 2-26. *The dashboard and the zoom slider*

When you double-click a particular location of the map, the map will zoom in and display the selected location in the center of the map.

■**Tip** You can also zoom in and out of the map by clicking the map and then using the wheel on your wheel mouse.

It is useful to display the latitude and longitude of the selected location on the map. As a matter of fact, when you click the map, the onClick event of the VE Map control is fired. And as you recall in the Map.html page, you attached the updatePosition() event handler to the following events:

```
map.AttachEvent("onendcontinuouspan", updatePosition); // when spanning is done
map.AttachEvent("onendzoom", updatePosition); // when zooming is done
map.AttachEvent("onclick", updatePosition); // when the map is clicked
```

The updatePosition() JavaScript event handler calls an external (as indicated by the window.external object) method named mapPositionChange():

```
// Update the position of the map in the TextBox controls
function updatePosition(e)
{
    window.external.mapPositionChange(
        e.view.latlong.latitude,e.view.latlong.longitude);
}
```

Therefore, in the code-behind for Form1, let's now add a mapPositionChange() subroutine so you can display the latitude and longitude of the selected location in the TextBox controls.

Visual Basic 2005

```
'---update the latitude and longitude on the TextBox controls---
Public Sub mapPositionChange( _
   ByVal lat As Double, ByVal lng As Double)
    txtLatitude.Text = lat
    txtLongitude.Text = lng
End Sub
```

C# 2005

```
//---update the latitude and longitude on the TextBox
// controls---
public void mapPositionChange(double lat, double lng)
{
    txtLatitude.Text = Convert.ToString(lat);
    txtLongitude.Text = Convert.ToString(lng);
}
```

This subroutine simply takes two input parameters (latitude and longitude) and then displays them in the appropriate TextBox controls you created earlier.

Alternatively, users can also enter a set of coordinates and click the Goto Point button to bring them directly to the specified location. You accomplish this using the event handler for the Goto Point button.

Visual Basic 2005

```
'---set the map to a particular location---
Private Sub btnGotoPoint_Click( _
   ByVal sender As System.Object, _
   ByVal e As System.EventArgs) _
   Handles btnGotoPoint.Click
    Dim lat, lng As Double

    '---get the latitude and longitude---
    lat = txtLatitude.Text
    lng = txtLongitude.Text
    gotoPosition(lat, lng, False, "")
End Sub
```

C# 2005

```
//---set the map to a particular location---
private void btnGotoPoint_Click(object sender, EventArgs e)
{
    double lat, lng;

    //---get the latitude and longitude---
    lat = Convert.ToDouble(txtLatitude.Text);
    lng = Convert.ToDouble(txtLongitude.Text);
```

```
       gotoPosition(lat, lng, false, "");
}
```

The event handler for the Goto Point button first extracts the latitude and longitude from the TextBox controls and then calls the gotoPosition() subroutine.

Visual Basic 2005

```
'---go to a particular location on the map---
Private Sub gotoPosition( _
   ByVal lat As Double, ByVal lng As Double, _
   ByVal showPushpin As Boolean, ByVal pushPinText As String)

    '---display map at specific location---
    Dim param() As Object = New Object() {lat, lng}
    WebBrowser1.Document.InvokeScript("goto_map_position", param)

    '---if need to insert pushpin---
    If showPushpin Then
        '---set the pushpin---
        param = New Object() {pushpin, pushPinText, lat, lng}
        WebBrowser1.Document.InvokeScript("addPushpin", param)
        pushpin += 1
    End If
End Sub
```

C# 2005

```
//---go to a particular location on the map---
private void gotoPosition(
   double lat, double lng,
   bool showPushpin, string pushPinText)
{
    //---display map at specific location---
    object[] param = new object[] { lat, lng };
    WebBrowser1.Document.InvokeScript("goto_map_position",
       param);

    //---if need to insert pushpin---
    if (showPushpin)
    {
        //---set the pushpin---
        param = new object[]
           { pushpin, pushPinText, lat, lng };
        WebBrowser1.Document.InvokeScript("addPushpin",
           param);
        pushpin += 1;
    }
}
```

The gotoPosition() subroutine first gets the map to display a particular location by calling the JavaScript function (using the InvokeScript method of the Document object) goto_map_position(). It then determines whether it needs to insert a pushpin into the specified location. The gotoPosition() subroutine is also used later to plot traveled paths.

Connecting to a GPS Receiver

If you have a GPS receiver paired to the computer running the application, you can connect to it using a serial connection and then retrieve your positioning information. When the application is loaded, it lists all the available COM ports on your computer (see Figure 2-27).

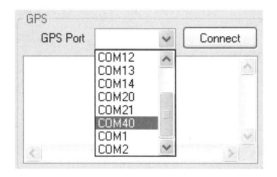

Figure 2-27. *Listing all the available COM ports on your computer*

Assuming you have paired your computer with a Bluetooth-enabled GPS receiver, you then select the serial port associated with your GPS device and click Connect to establish a connection to the serial port. You accomplish this process with the following event handler.

Visual Basic 2005

```
'---connect to a serial port to communicate with the GPS
' receiver---
Private Sub btnConnect_Click( _
    ByVal sender As System.Object, _
    ByVal e As System.EventArgs) _
    Handles btnConnect.Click
    If btnConnect.Text = "Connect" Then
        btnConnect.Text = "Disconnect"

        '---close the serial port if it is open---
        If serialPort.IsOpen Then
            serialPort.Close()
        End If
        Try
            '---configure the parameters of the serial port---
            With serialPort
                .PortName = cbbCOMPorts.Text
                .BaudRate = 9600
```

```vb
                    .Parity = IO.Ports.Parity.None
                    .DataBits = 8
                    .StopBits = IO.Ports.StopBits.One
                End With

                '---open the serial port---
                serialPort.Open()
                lblMessage.Text = cbbCOMPorts.Text & " connected."
            Catch ex As Exception
                MsgBox(ex.ToString)
            End Try
        Else
            '---close the serial port---
            btnConnect.Text = "Connect"
            serialPort.Close()
        End If
End Sub
```

C# 2005

```csharp
//---connect to a serial port to communicate with the GPS
// receiver---
private void btnConnect_Click(object sender, EventArgs e)
{
    if (btnConnect.Text == "Connect")
    {
        btnConnect.Text = "Disconnect";

        //---close the serial port if it is open---
        if (serialPort.IsOpen)
        {
            serialPort.Close();
        }
        try
        {
            //---configure the parameters of the serial
            // port---
            serialPort.PortName = cbbCOMPorts.Text;
            serialPort.BaudRate = 9600;
            serialPort.Parity = System.IO.Ports.Parity.None;
            serialPort.DataBits = 8;
            serialPort.StopBits =
                System.IO.Ports.StopBits.One;

            //---open the serial port---
            serialPort.Open();
            lblMessage.Text = cbbCOMPorts.Text + "
```

```
                connected.";
        }
        catch (Exception ex)
        {
            MessageBox.Show(ex.ToString());
        }
    }
    else
    {
        //---close the serial port---
        btnConnect.Text = "Connect";
        serialPort.Close();
    }
}
```

With the GPS connected to your application via the selected serial port, you must now stand by for incoming data from the GPS receiver. Generally, most GPS receivers support the NMEA standard. Table 2-5 lists some common NMEA data sentences.

Table 2-5. *Common NMEA Data Sentences and Their Meanings*

Sentence	Description
$GPGGA	Global positioning system fixed data
$GPGLL	Geographic position: latitude/longitude
$GPGSA	GNSS DOP and active satellites
$GPGSV	GNSS satellites in view
$GPRMC	Recommended minimum specific GNSS data
$GPVTG	Course over ground and ground speed

A typical stream of GPS data looks like this:

```
$GPVTG,,T,,M,,N,,K,N*2C
$GPGGA,001431.092,0118.2653,N,10351.1359,E,0,00,,-19.6,M,4.1,M,,0000*5B
$GPGSA,A,1,,,,,,,,,,,,,,,,*1E
$GPGSV,3,1,12,20,00,000,,10,00,000,,25,00,000,,27,00,000,*79
$GPGSV,3,2,12,03,00,000,,31,00,000,,24,00,000,,15,00,000,*78
$GPGSV,3,3,12,16,00,000,,05,00,000,,01,00,000,,26,00,000,*7D
$GPRMC,001431.092,V,0118.2653,N,10351.1359,E,,,070805,,,N*72
$GPVTG,,T,,M,,N,,K,N*2C
$GPGGA,001432.092,0118.2653,N,10351.1359,E,0,00,,-19.6,M,4.1,M,,0000*58
$GPRMC,001432.092,V,0118.2653,N,10351.1359,E,,,070805,,,N*71
$GPVTG,,T,,M,,N,,K,N*2C
$GPGGA,001433.106,0118.2653,N,10351.1359,E,0,00,,-19.6,M,4.1,M,,0000*55
$GPRMC,001433.106,V,0118.2653,N,10351.1359,E,,,070805,,,N*7C
```

■**Tip** You can learn more about GPS NMEA sentences at `http://www.commlinx.com.au/`
`NMEA_sentences.htm`. Table 2-5 is extracted from the previous website.

For the example application, you would be interested only in knowing your geographical
location, that is, latitude and longitude. Therefore, you need to look out for sentences beginning with $GPGGA.

Table 2-6 shows the breakdown of a typical $GPGGA sentence.

Table 2-6. *The Fields in a $GPGGA Sentence*

Field	Sample	Description
0	$GPGGA	Sentence prefix
1	001431.092	UTC time (in *hhmmss.sss* format)
2	0118.2653	Latitude (in *ddmm.mmmm* format)
3	N	(N)orth or (S)outh
4	10351.1359	Longitude (in *dddmm.mmmm* format)
5	E	(E)ast or (W)est
6	0	Position Fix (0 is invalid, 1 is valid, 2 is valid DGPS, 3 is valid PPS)
7	04	Satellites used
8		Horizontal dilution of precision
9	–19.6	Altitude (unit specified in next field)
10	M	M is meter
11	4.1	Geoid separation (unit specified in next field)
12	M	M is meter
13		Age of DGPS data (in seconds)
14	0000	DGPS station ID
15	*5B	Checksum
15	CRLF	Terminator

As you can see from Table 2-6, you need to look in fields 2 and 4 to obtain the latitude and
longitude of a position.

To receive incoming data on the serial port, create the DataReceived event.

Visual Basic 2005

```
Private Sub DataReceived( _
   ByVal sender As Object, _
   ByVal e As System.IO.Ports.SerialDataReceivedEventArgs) _
   Handles serialPort.DataReceived
   '---invoke the delegate to display the received data---
```

```
        txtDataReceived.BeginInvoke(New _
            myDelegate(AddressOf updateTextBox), _
            New Object() {})
End Sub
```

C# 2005

```csharp
private void DataReceived(object sender,
    System.IO.Ports.SerialDataReceivedEventArgs e)
{
    //---invoke the delegate to display the received data---
    txtDataReceived.BeginInvoke(new
        myDelegate(updateTextBox));
}
```

When incoming data is detected, the DataReceived event will be fired, and it will then call a delegate to display the data on the TextBox control.

Visual Basic 2005

```vbnet
Public Delegate Sub myDelegate()
Public Sub updateTextBox()
    Try
        With txtDataReceived
            '---read all data from serial port---
            Dim Data As String = serialPort.ReadExisting

            '---append the data to the TextBox control---
            .AppendText(Data)
            .ScrollToCaret()

            '---extract the second last line---
            Dim GPSData As String = txtDataReceived.Lines( _
                txtDataReceived.Lines.Length - 2)

            '---process only lines starting with $GPGGA---
            If GPSData.StartsWith("$GPGGA") Then
                If Not processGPSData(GPSData) Then
                    lblMessage.Text = "No fix..."
                End If
            End If
        End With
    Catch ex As Exception
        Console.WriteLine(ex.ToString)
    End Try
End Sub
```

C# 2005

```csharp
public delegate void myDelegate();
public void updateTextBox()
{
    try
    {
        //---read all data from serial port---
        string Data = serialPort.ReadExisting();

        //---append the data to the TextBox control---
        txtDataReceived.AppendText(Data);
        txtDataReceived.ScrollToCaret();

        //---extract the second last line---
        string GPSData =
            txtDataReceived.Lines[txtDataReceived.Lines.Length
            - 2];

        //---process only lines starting with $GPGGA---
        if (GPSData.StartsWith("$GPGGA"))
        {
            if (!(processGPSData(GPSData)))
            {
                lblMessage.Text = "No fix...";
            }
        }
    }
    catch (Exception ex)
    {
        Console.WriteLine(ex.ToString());
    }
}
```

Incoming data is appended to the end of the TextBox control. One important point you need to be aware of is that the GPS receiver may not necessarily send incoming data as a complete sentence. For example, the following sentence:

$GPGGA,000000.053,0118.2653,N,10351.1359,E,0,00,,-19.6,M,4.1,M,,0000*51

might be sent in three separate blocks:

$GPGGA,000000.053,0118.2
653,N,10351.1359,E,0,00,
,-19.6,M,4.1,M,,0000*51

In this case, each block of data received by the serialPort.ReadExisting() method is incomplete, and you must wait until the whole $GPGGA sentence is received before you can parse it for the data you need. One easy way to solve this is to extract the $GPGGA sentence from the TextBox control (txtDataReceived). Because all incoming data is appended to the end of the TextBox control and the last line may contain a partial sentence, you should thus always extract the second-to-last line to extract the location information (see Figure 2-28). Programmatically, you can extract the second-to-last line of a TextBox control by subtracting 2 from its length. For example, if a TextBox contains five lines (with index from 0 to 4), then the index of the second-to-last line will be 5 minus 2, which is 3.

■ **Note** Ideally, you should use the `serialPort.ReadLine()` method to read each line of incoming data. However, the current implementation causes an exception to be thrown during runtime.

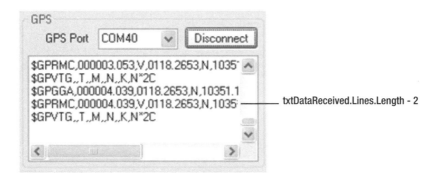

txtDataReceived.Lines.Length - 2

Figure 2-28. *The second-to-last line contains a complete sentence.*

CONVERTING LATITUDE AND LONGITUDE VALUES

Both the latitude and longitude values represented in the NMEA data sentence are presented in degrees, minutes, and decimal minutes. Both latitude and longitude are represented as *ddmm.mmmm*. The directions of latitude and longitude are indicated as a single character in the next field (N for north, S for south, E for east, and W for west).

However, most mapping applications require latitude and longitude information to be represented as signed decimal degrees, with negative latitude for south and negative longitude for west. You can use the formula shown in the following illustration to convert latitude (or longitude) information from the "degrees, minutes, and decimal minutes" format to the "decimal degree" format:

$$\left| \frac{ddmm.mmmm}{100} \right| + \frac{ddmm.mmmm - \left| \frac{ddmm.mmmm}{100} \right| \cdot 100}{60}$$

The vertical bars represent integer division.

Hence, if the second-to-last line begins with the $GPGGA word, you will call the `processGPSData()` function to process the sentence, which is defined as follows.

Visual Basic 2005

```vb
Private Function processGPSData(ByVal str As String) As Boolean
    Try
        '---separate the GPS data into various fields---
        Dim field() As String
        field = str.Split(",")
        Dim lat, lng As Double
        Dim rawLatLng As Double
        If field.Length < 15 Then Return False

        '---latitude---
        rawLatLng = Convert.ToDouble(field(2))
        lat = (rawLatLng \ 100) + _
            ((rawLatLng - ((rawLatLng \ 100) * 100)) / 60)

        '---latitude is negative if South---
        If field(3) = "S" Then
            lat *= -1.0
        End If

        '---longitude---
        rawLatLng = Convert.ToDouble(field(4))
        lng = (rawLatLng \ 100) + _
            ((rawLatLng - ((rawLatLng \ 100) * 100)) / 60)

        '---longitude is negative if West---
        If field(5) = "W" Then
            lng *= -1.0
        End If

        '---update map---
        If str.StartsWith("$") Then
            '---live data from GPS---
            gotoPosition(lat, lng, False, "")
        Else
            '---recorded path---
            gotoPosition(lat, lng, True, "X")
        End If
        lblMessage.Text = "Latitude: " & lat & " Longitude: " & _
            lng
        Return True
    Catch
        Return False
    End Try
End Function
```

C# 2005

```csharp
private bool processGPSData(string str)
{
    try
    {
        //---separate the GPS data into various fields---
        string[] field;
        field = str.Split(',');
        double lat;
        double lng;
        double rawLatLng;
        if (field.Length < 15)
        {
            return false;
        }

        //---latitude---
        rawLatLng = Convert.ToDouble(field[2]);
        lat = ((int)(rawLatLng / 100)) +
            ((rawLatLng - (((int)(rawLatLng / 100)) * 100)) / 60);

        //---latitude is negative if South---
        if (field[3] == "S")
        {
            lat *= -1;
        }

        //---longitude---
        rawLatLng = Convert.ToDouble(field[4]);
        lng = ((int)(rawLatLng / 100)) + ((rawLatLng -
            (((int)(rawLatLng / 100)) * 100)) / 60);

        //---longitude is negative if West---
        if (field[5] == "W")
        {
            lng *= -1;
        }

        //---update map---
        if (str.StartsWith("$"))
        {
            //---live data from GPS---
            gotoPosition(lat, lng, false, "");

        } else
        {
            //---recorded path---
```

```
            gotoPosition(lat, lng, true, "X");
        }
        lblMessage.Text = "Latitude: " + lat +
            " Longitude: " + lng;
        return true;
    }
    catch
    {
        return false;
    }
}
```

The processGPSData() function extracts the fields containing the latitude and longitude and then performs some simple processing. In particular, you need to convert them to the correct degree and minute format that VE can understand. Also, if the direction indicated is south, then the latitude must be negated. Similarly, the longitude is negated for west. Finally, the map is updated with the new position.

You can now test the application and see whether it is able to display your current location. Press F5, and select the serial port that is connected to your GPS receiver.

Tip Be sure you are connected to the Internet so that the map can be retrieved and updated.

Plotting Saved Path

Besides displaying the map in real time, you can also save the positional information reported by your GPS receiver to a text file and then feed it into the application to plot the path you have traveled.

Tip You can download a Pocket PC application that I have written to collect the data from a GPS receiver from the Source Code/Download section of the Apress website (http://www.apress.com).

To load a saved GPS data file, the user clicks the Show Path button (see Figure 2-29).

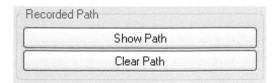

Figure 2-29. *The Show Path and Clear Path buttons*

The event handler for the Show Path button is as follows.

Visual Basic 2005

```vb
'---plot a path from a GPS data file---
Private Sub btnShowPath_Click( _
    ByVal sender As System.Object, _
    ByVal e As System.EventArgs) _
    Handles btnShowPath.Click

    Dim fileContents As String = String.Empty

    '---let user choose a file---
    Dim openFileDialog1 As New OpenFileDialog()
    openFileDialog1.InitialDirectory = "c:\"
    openFileDialog1.Filter = _
        "txt files (*.txt)|*.txt|All files (*.*)|*.*"
    openFileDialog1.FilterIndex = 2
    openFileDialog1.RestoreDirectory = True

    '---Load the content of the selected file---
    If openFileDialog1.ShowDialog() = _
        Windows.Forms.DialogResult.OK Then
            fileContents = My.Computer.FileSystem.ReadAllText( _
                openFileDialog1.FileName)
    End If

    '---split the content various lines using the $ as the
    ' delimiter---
    line = fileContents.Split("$")
    lineIndex = 0
    Timer1.Enabled = True
End Sub
```

C# 2005

```csharp
//---plot a path from a GPS data file---
private void btnShowPath_Click(object sender, EventArgs e)
{
    string fileContents = string.Empty;

    //---let user choose a file---
    OpenFileDialog openFileDialog1 = new OpenFileDialog();
    openFileDialog1.InitialDirectory = "c:\\";
    openFileDialog1.Filter =
        "txt files (*.txt)|*.txt|All files (*.*)|*.*";
```

```
    openFileDialog1.FilterIndex = 2;
    openFileDialog1.RestoreDirectory = true;

    //---Load the content of the selected file---
    if (openFileDialog1.ShowDialog() == DialogResult.OK)
    {
        fileContents =
            System.IO.File.ReadAllText(
            openFileDialog1.FileName);
    }

    //---split the content various lines using the $ as the
    // delimiter---
    line = fileContents.Split('$');
    lineIndex = 0;
    Timer1.Enabled = true;
}
```

It prompts the user to select a saved GPS data file and then splits (using $ as the delimiter) its content into an array called line. The content of a typical GPS data file may look like this:

```
$GPGGA,001409.105,0118.2653,N,10351.1359,E,0,00,,-19.6,M,4.1,M,,0000*5F
$GPRMC,001409.105,V,0118.2653,N,10351.1359,E,,,070805,,,N*76
$GPVTG,,T,,M,,N,,K,N*2C
$GPGGA,001410.091,0118.2653,N,10351.1359,E,0,00,,-19.6,M,4.1,M,,0000*5B
$GPRMC,001410.091,V,0118.2653,N,10351.1359,E,,,070805,,,N*72
$GPVTG,,T,,M,,N,,K,N*2C
$GPGGA,001411.091,0118.2653,N,10351.1359,E,0,00,,-19.6,M,4.1,M,,0000*5A
$GPGSA,A,1,,,,,,,,,,,,,,*1E
$GPGSV,3,1,12,20,00,000,,10,00,000,,25,00,000,,27,00,000,*79
$GPGSV,3,2,12,03,00,000,,31,00,000,,24,00,000,,15,00,000,*78
$GPGSV,3,3,12,16,00,000,,05,00,000,,01,00,000,,26,00,000,*7D
$GPRMC,001411.091,V,0118.2653,N,10351.1359,E,,,070805,,,N*73
$GPVTG,,T,,M,,N,,K,N*2C
$GPGGA,001412.106,0118.2653,N,10351.1359,E,0,00,,-19.6,M,4.1,M,,0000*56
$GPRMC,001412.106,V,0118.2653,N,10351.1359,E,,,070805,,,N*7F
$GPVTG,,T,,M,,N,,K,N*2C
$GPGGA,001413.091,0118.2653,N,10351.1359,E,0,00,,-19.6,M,4.1,M,,0000*58
$GPRMC,001413.091,V,0118.2653,N,10351.1359,E,,,070805,,,N*71
$GPVTG,,T,,M,,N,,K,N*2C
$GPGGA,001414.091,0118.2653,N,10351.1359,E,0,00,,-19.6,M,4.1,M,,0000*5F
```

Figure 2-30 shows the content of the line array after the split.

```
Line(0) → ""
Line(1) → "GPGGA,001409.105,0118.2653,N,10351.1359,E,0,00,,-19.6,M,4.1,M,,0000*5F"
Line(2) → "GPRMC,001409.105,V,0118.2653,N,10351.1359,E,,,070805,,,N*76"
Line(3) → "GPVTG,,T,,M,,N,,K,N*2C"
Line(4) → "GPGGA,001410.091,0118.2653,N,10351.1359,E,0,00,,-19.6,M,4.1,M,,0000*5B"
Line(5) → "GPRMC,001410.091,V,0118.2653,N,10351.1359,E,,,070805,,,N*72"
Line(6) → "GPVTG,,T,,M,,N,,K,N*2C"
Line(7) → "GPGGA,001411.091,0118.2653,N,10351.1359,E,0,00,,-19.6,M,4.1,M,,0000*5A"
Line(8) → "GPGSA,A,1,,,,,,,,,,,,,,*1E"
Line(9) → "GPGSV,3,1,12,20,00,000,,10,00,000,,25,00,000,,27,00,000,*79"
Line(10) → "GPGSV,3,2,12,03,00,000,,31,00,000,,24,00,000,,15,00,000,*78"
```

Figure 2-30. *The content of the line array*

To animate the path taken, you use the Timer control to draw each point every second. You do this by setting the Enabled property of the Timer control to true.

Every second, the Timer1_Tick event will fire. This is where you examine the data in the line array to extract the latitude and longitude of the current position.

Visual Basic 2005

```
'---for plotting a path---
Private Sub Timer1_Tick( _
    ByVal sender As System.Object, _
    ByVal e As System.EventArgs) _
    Handles Timer1.Tick

    If lineIndex = 0 Then pointCounter = 1

    '---plot a point in the path---
    While (lineIndex <= line.Length - 1)
        If line(lineIndex).StartsWith("GPGGA") AndAlso _
            processGPSData(line(lineIndex)) Then
            lblMessage.Text = "Updating map...point " & _
                pointCounter
            pointCounter += 1
            Exit While
        End If
        lineIndex += 1
    End While
    lineIndex += 1

    '---stop the Timer control when the end of the path is
    ' reached---
```

```
        If lineIndex > line.Length - 1 Then
            Timer1.Enabled = False
            lblMessage.Text = "Plotting completed."
        End If
    End Sub
End Sub
```

C# 2005

```csharp
//---for plotting a path---
private void Timer1_Tick(object sender, EventArgs e)
{
    if (lineIndex == 0)
    {
        pointCounter = 1;
    }

    //---plot a point in the path---
    while ((lineIndex <= line.Length - 1))
    {
        if (line[lineIndex].StartsWith("GPGGA") &&
            processGPSData(line[lineIndex]))
        {
            lblMessage.Text = "Updating map...point " +
                pointCounter;
            pointCounter += 1;
            break;
        }
        lineIndex += 1;
    }
    lineIndex += 1;

    //---stop the Timer control when the end of the path is
    // reached---
    if (lineIndex > line.Length - 1)
    {
        Timer1.Enabled = false;
        lblMessage.Text = "Plotting completed.";
    }
}
```

In essence, you keep looking for lines beginning with the word *GPGGA* and then use the latitude and longitude to update the position on the map. The Tick event will keep on firing every second until you explicitly turn it off when the number of lines to process has reached the end. Each location on the map is shown with a pushpin (marked with an *x*; see Figure 2-31).

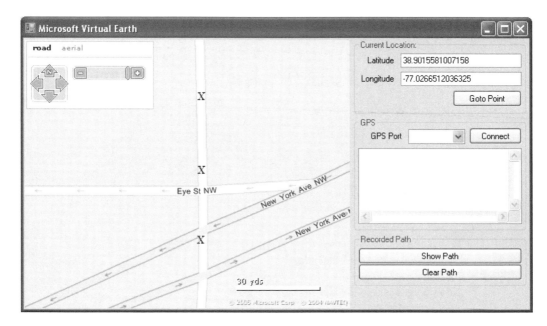

Figure 2-31. *Displaying the traveled path with pushpins*

To clear the path just shown on the map, click the Clear Path button. The following event handler handles this.

Visual Basic 2005

```
'---clear the plotted path by removing all pushpins---
Private Sub btnClearPath_Click( _
   ByVal sender As System.Object, _
   ByVal e As System.EventArgs) _
   Handles btnClearPath.Click
    '---removing all the pushpins---
    For i As Integer = 0 To pushpin
        removePushpin(i)
    Next
End Sub
```

C# 2005

```
//---clear the plotted path by removing all pushpins---
private void btnClearPath_Click(object sender, EventArgs e)
{
```

```
    //---removing all the pushpins---
    for (int i = 0; i <= pushpin; i++)
    {
        removePushpin(i);
    }
}
```

It calls the removePushPin() subroutine repeatedly until all the pushpins are removed.

Visual Basic 2005

```
'---remove a pushpin---
Private Sub removePushpin(ByVal id As Integer)
    Dim param() As Object = New Object() {id}
    WebBrowser1.Document.InvokeScript("removePushpin", param)
End Sub
```

C# 2005

```
//---remove a pushpin---
private void removePushpin(int id)
{
    object[] param = new object[] { id };
    WebBrowser1.Document.InvokeScript("removePushpin", param);
}
```

Summary

In this chapter, you built three projects using the SerialPort class. As you can see, the SerialPort class has greatly simplified your life by encapsulating much of the functionality you need. In the first project, you used serial communication to enable two PCs to communicate. You can use the same application to control a mobile phone via a Bluetooth connection. In the second project, you ported the first project to the Windows Mobile 5.0 platform; using this project, two Pocket PCs can communicate wirelessly over Bluetooth (which supports the serial profile). In the last project, you saw how to pipe GPS data to your PC via a serial port (over Bluetooth) and how to use the data to display a map using a mapping application such as Microsoft Virtual Earth.

CHAPTER 3

■■■

Incorporating Fingerprint Recognition into Your .NET Application

Biometric recognition is one of the most reliable ways to confirm the identity of an individual. And by now, most people should be familiar with the Microsoft Fingerprint Reader (`http://www.microsoft.com/hardware/mouseandkeyboard/productdetails.aspx?pid=036`; see also Figure 3-1).

Figure 3-1. *The Microsoft Fingerprint Reader*

Using the Microsoft Fingerprint Reader, you can now log in to your computer by placing your finger on the reader. You can also use the application provided by the Fingerprint Reader to save your user IDs and passwords for websites that require them for authentication. You can then use your fingerprint as a key to retrieve the user IDs and passwords for logging into these sites securely. The Microsoft Fingerprint Reader removes the hassle of remembering different passwords for different sites.

However, that's all you can do with the Fingerprint Reader. Microsoft does not provide a SDK to allow developers to incorporate the Fingerprint Reader into their applications. For this, you have to rely on third-party solution providers. Fortunately, one such provider exists: Griaule (http://griaule.com/).

Griaule provides the GrFinger Fingerprint SDK (http://griaule.com/page/en-us/grfinger_sdk), a fingerprint recognition SDK that supports existing fingerprint readers; it works with Microsoft Fingerprint Reader, Digital Persona U.are.U 4000, SecuGen Hamster FDU02, Geomok (Testech) Bio-I, and Crossmatch USB Fingerprint Reader.

In this chapter, I will show you how you can use the GrFinger Fingerprint SDK to integrate the Microsoft Fingerprint Reader into your .NET 2.0 Windows applications. In particular, you will build a visitor identification system whereby users visiting your office can register at the reception desk (see Figure 3-2). Once a user is registered, the next time the user visits the office, he can simply scan his fingerprint, and the system will register his visit. Schools can also adapt this application for attendance-taking purposes, such as in big lecture theaters where attendance must be taken rapidly and efficiently.

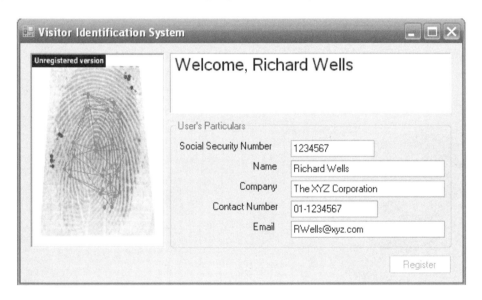

Figure 3-2. *The visitor identification system application you will build in this chapter*

Using the GrFinger SDK

Two editions of the GrFinger Fingerprint SDK exist: light and full (http://www.griaule.com/page/en-us/grfinger_sdk). Consult Griaule's website for full pricing information for each edition. For this chapter's examples, I have used the full edition of the GrFinger SDK 4.2. You can apply for a free 90-day trial license to test the SDK (http://www.griaule.com/page/en-us/downloads).

Creating the Application

Once you have the GrFinger SDK installed, you are ready to create the application. Using Visual Studio 2005, create a new Windows application (select either Visual Basic or C#), and name it **Fingerprintreader**.

First, you need to add the GrFingerXCtrl control (an ActiveX control representing the GrFinger component) to your Toolbox. Right-click the Toolbox, and select Add/Remove Items. On the COM Components tab, check the GrFingerXCtrl Class item (see Figure 3-3), and click OK.

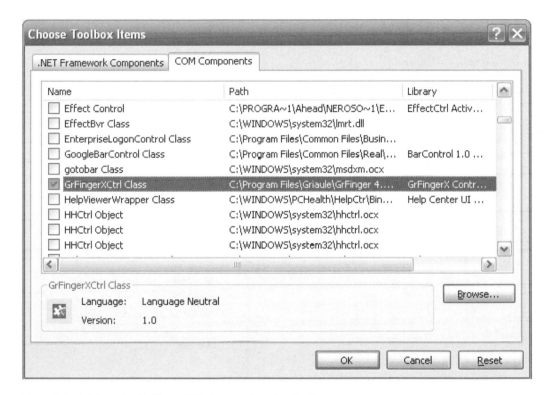

Figure 3-3. *Adding the GrFingerXCtrl control to the Toolbox*

The GrFingerXCtrl control will now appear in the Toolbox (see Figure 3-4).

Figure 3-4. *The GrFingerXCtrl control in the Toolbox*

In the default Form1, populate it with the following controls (see Figure 3-5):

- PictureBox
- AxGrFingerXCtrl
- Label
- TextBox
- Button
- GroupBox
- Timer

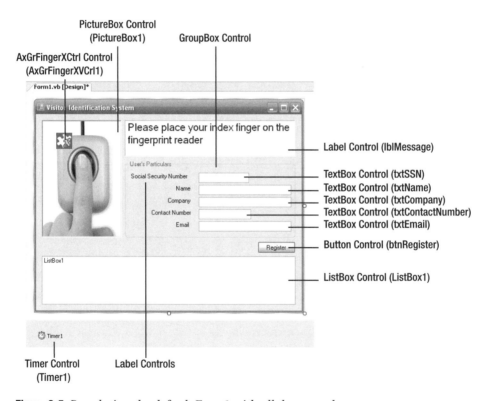

Figure 3-5. *Populating the default Form1 with all the controls*

ACTIVEX CONTROL BUG IN VISUAL STUDIO 2005

Because of a bug in Visual Studio 2005, you may encounter an error message when you try to drag and drop the AxGrFingerXCtrl control from the Toolbox onto the Windows form. The typical error message is "Failed to import the ActiveX control. Please ensure it is properly registered." This error usually arises when you try to add third-party ActiveX controls to your Windows application.

To solve this error, after the error message, go to the `obj\Debug` folder in the application, and delete the file named `Interop.GrFingerXLib.dll`. Once you've deleted the file, perform the drag and drop one more time. This time, you should be able to add the ActiveX control successfully.

Set the image of the PictureBox control by clicking the ellipsis (…) icon in the `Image` property of the PictureBox control in the Properties window. Click the Import button to load an image named *fingerprintreader* (see Figure 3-6). Click OK.

■**Tip** Download the sample code from the Source Code/Download section of the Apress website (`http://www.apress.com`).

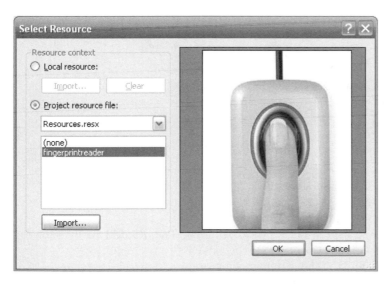

Figure 3-6. *Selecting a picture resource*

Also, set the `Interval` property of the Timer control to 5000. This will cause the Timer control to fire an event every five seconds.

Coding the Application

The GrFinger Fingerprint SDK comes with a sample application written in different languages: Visual Basic 6, Java, C++, Visual Basic .NET (for Visual Studio .NET 2003), Visual Basic 2005 (for Visual Studio 2005), and so on. For the Visual Basic 2005 and C# 2005 versions of this sample, Griaule has provided two useful libraries: DBClass.vb/DBClass.cs and Util.vb/Util.cs.

The DBClass.vb (or DBClass.cs) library contains routines to add/retrieve user's information to/from a database. The Util.vb (or Util.cs) library contains all the necessary routines to use the GrFingerXCtrl control and other supporting Win32 APIs. For this reason (rather than reinventing the wheel), you will use these libraries in this application.

Hence, add the DBClass.vb (or DBClass.cs) and Util.vb (or Util.cs) files to the project (see Figure 3-7; right-click Solution Explorer, and then select Add ➤ Existing Item). You can add the two files from the default installation directory: C:\Program Files\Griaule\GrFinger 4.2\samples\Visual Basic.NET 2005\GrFingerX (or C:\Program Files\Griaule\GrFinger 4.2\samples\C# 2005\GrFingerX).

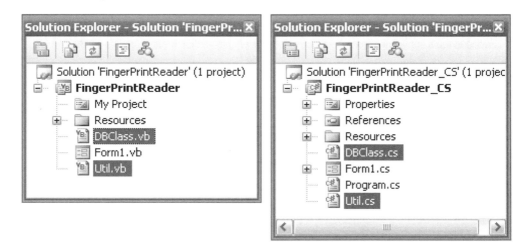

Figure 3-7. *Adding the two useful libraries provided by Griaule*

Listing 3-1 and Listing 3-2 (later in the chapter) show the full source of Util.vb (and Util.cs) and DBClass.vb (and DBClass.cs). You will also modify the sample application provided by Griaule to suit the purpose of this application.

To keep the code in the DBClass.vb (or DBClass.cs) library intact, you will use the sample Access database provided by Griaule. The original Access database is named GrFingerSample.mdb (you can find this in the default directory, C:\Program Files\Griaule\GrFinger 4.2\samples\), and it contains one single table called *enroll*. The original enroll table contains only two fields: ID and template (for storing the fingerprint image). For this application, you will add five more fields to the enroll table. They are SSN, Name, Company, ContactNumber, and Email (see Figure 3-8).

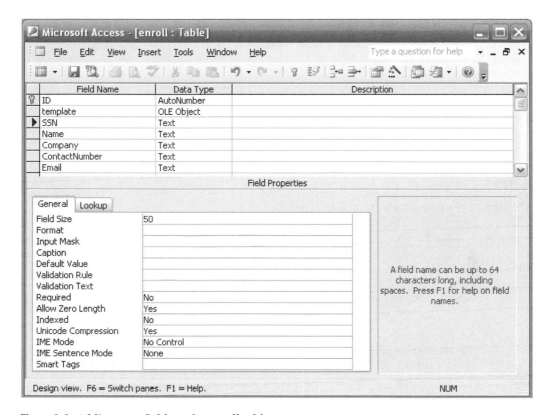

Figure 3-8. *Adding new fields to the enroll table*

Save the changes to the database, and add it to the project (right-click Solution Explorer, and select Add ➤ Existing Items). Figure 3-9 shows the GrFingerSample.mdb database added to the project.

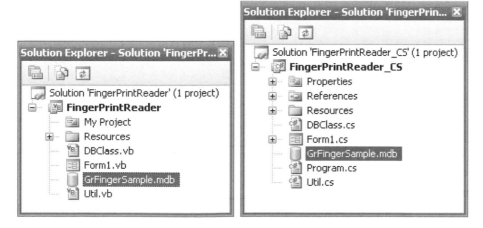

Figure 3-9. *Adding the GrFingerSample.mdb database to the project*

Wiring Up All the Controls

Let's now switch to the code-behind of Form1 and write the code to wire up all the controls. First, import the GrFingerXLib namespace.

Visual Basic 2005

```
Imports GrFingerXLib
```

C# 2005

```
using GrFingerXLib;
```

Declare the following constants and member variables.

Visual Basic 2005

```
Public Class Form1
    '---name of the database---
    Const DBFile = "GrFingerSample.mdb"
    Const Logfile = "C:\Log.csv"
    Const ConnectionString = "Provider=Microsoft.Jet.OLEDB.4.0; " & _
        "Data Source="

    '---for an instance of the Util.vb class---
    Private myUtil As Util
    '---for storing user's ID---
    Private _UserID As Integer
    '---database connection---
    Private connection As System.Data.OleDb.OleDbConnection
```

C# 2005

```
//---name of the database---
const string DBFile = "GrFingerSample.mdb";
const string Logfile = "C:\\Log.csv";
const string ConnectionString =
    "Provider=Microsoft.Jet.OLEDB.4.0;Data Source=";

//---for an instance of the Util.vb class---
Util myUtil;
//---for storing user's ID---
int _UserID;

//---database connection---
System.Data.OleDb.OleDbConnection connection;
```

In the Form1_Load event, code the following.

Visual Basic 2005

```vbnet
Private Sub Form1_Load( _
    ByVal sender As System.Object, _
    ByVal e As System.EventArgs) _
    Handles MyBase.Load
     Dim err As Integer

      '---initialize Util class---
      myUtil = New Util(ListBox1, PictureBox1, AxGrFingerXCtrl1)

      '---Initialize GrFingerX Library---
      err = myUtil.InitializeGrFinger()

      '---Print result in log---
      If err < 0 Then
          myUtil.WriteError(err)
          Exit Sub
      Else
          myUtil.WriteLog( _
              "**GrFingerX Initialized Successfully**")
      End If

      '---create a log file---
      If Not System.IO.File.Exists(Logfile) Then
          System.IO.File.Create(Logfile)
      End If
End Sub
```

C# 2005

```csharp
private void Form1_Load(object sender, EventArgs e)
{
    int err;

    //---initialize util class---
    myUtil = new Util(ListBox1, PictureBox1, null, null,
        null, null, null, null);

    //---wire up all the event handlers for the reader---
    axGrFingerXCtrl1.SensorPlug += new
        AxGrFingerXLib.
            _IGrFingerXCtrlEvents_SensorPlugEventHandler(
        axGrFingerXCtrl1_SensorPlug);
    axGrFingerXCtrl1.SensorUnplug += new
        AxGrFingerXLib.
            _IGrFingerXCtrlEvents_SensorUnplugEventHandler(
        axGrFingerXCtrl1_SensorUnplug);
```

```
axGrFingerXCtrl1.FingerDown += new
    AxGrFingerXLib.
        _IGrFingerXCtrlEvents_FingerDownEventHandler(
    axGrFingerXCtrl1_FingerDown);
axGrFingerXCtrl1.FingerUp += new
    AxGrFingerXLib.
        _IGrFingerXCtrlEvents_FingerUpEventHandler(
    axGrFingerXCtrl1_FingerUp);
axGrFingerXCtrl1.ImageAcquired += new
    AxGrFingerXLib.
        _IGrFingerXCtrlEvents_ImageAcquiredEventHandler(
    axGrFingerXCtrl1_ImageAcquired);

//---Initialize GrFingerX Library---
err = myUtil.InitializeGrFinger(axGrFingerXCtrl1);

//---Print result in log---
if ((err < 0))
{
    myUtil.WriteError((GRConstants)err);
    return;
}
else
{
    myUtil.WriteLog(
        "**GrFingerX Initialized Successfully**");
}

//---create a log file---
if (!System.IO.File.Exists(Logfile))
{
    System.IO.File.Create(Logfile);
}
}
```

Here, you create an instance of the Util class. The constructor of the Visual Basic version of the Util class takes three arguments: the ListBox control to display the status of the GrFingerXCtrl control, a PlctureBox control to display the captured fingerprint image, and finally the GrFingerXCtrl control. The C# version of the Util class takes eight arguments, but only the first two are relevant in this case: the ListBox control to display the status of the GrFingerXCtrl control and the PictureBox control to display the captured fingerprint image. The rest of the arguments are related to the sample example shipped with the Fingerprint SDK, and hence you will just ignore them here by sending a null value.

Note For the C# code, you need to wire up the event handlers for the axGrFingerXCtrl1 control.

You then initialize the GrFingerX library and create a log file (if it is not already present). This log file is a comma-separated values (CSV) file that contains the user's ID and login time.

Next, service all the necessary events of the GrFingerXCtrl control.

Visual Basic 2005

```
' ----------------------------------------------------------------------------
' GrFingerX events
' ----------------------------------------------------------------------------
'---A fingerprint reader was plugged on system---
Private Sub AxGrFingerXCtrl1_SensorPlug( _
   ByVal sender As System.Object, _
   ByVal e As _
   AxGrFingerXLib._IGrFingerXCtrlEvents_SensorPlugEvent) _
   Handles AxGrFingerXCtrl1.SensorPlug
    myUtil.WriteLog("Sensor: " & e.idSensor & ". Event: Plugged.")
    AxGrFingerXCtrl1.CapStartCapture(e.idSensor)
End Sub

'---A fingerprint reader was unplugged from system---
Private Sub AxGrFingerXCtrl1_SensorUnplug( _
   ByVal sender As System.Object, _
   ByVal e As _
      AxGrFingerXLib._IGrFingerXCtrlEvents_SensorUnplugEvent) _
   Handles AxGrFingerXCtrl1.SensorUnplug
    myUtil.WriteLog("Sensor: " & e.idSensor & _
       ". Event: Unplugged.")
    AxGrFingerXCtrl1.CapStopCapture(e.idSensor)
End Sub

'---A finger was placed on reader---
Private Sub AxGrFingerXCtrl1_FingerDown( _
   ByVal sender As System.Object, _
   ByVal e As _
      AxGrFingerXLib._IGrFingerXCtrlEvents_FingerDownEvent) _
   Handles AxGrFingerXCtrl1.FingerDown
    myUtil.WriteLog("Sensor: " & e.idSensor & _
       ". Event: Finger Placed.")
End Sub

'---A finger was removed from reader---
Private Sub AxGrFingerXCtrl1_FingerUp( _
   ByVal sender As System.Object, _
   ByVal e As AxGrFingerXLib._IGrFingerXCtrlEvents_FingerUpEvent) _
   Handles AxGrFingerXCtrl1.FingerUp
    myUtil.WriteLog("Sensor: " & e.idSensor & _
       ". Event: Finger removed.")
End Sub
```

C# 2005

```
//-------------------------------------------------------------
//  GrFingerX events
//-------------------------------------------------------------
//---A fingerprint reader was plugged on system---
private void axGrFingerXCtrl1_SensorPlug(object sender,
    AxGrFingerXLib._IGrFingerXCtrlEvents_SensorPlugEvent e)
{
    myUtil.WriteLog((("Sensor: "
        + (e.idSensor + ". Event: Plugged."))));
    axGrFingerXCtrl1.CapStartCapture(e.idSensor);
}

//---A fingerprint reader was unplugged from system---
private void axGrFingerXCtrl1_SensorUnplug(object sender,
    AxGrFingerXLib._IGrFingerXCtrlEvents_SensorUnplugEvent e)
{
    myUtil.WriteLog((("Sensor: "
        + (e.idSensor + ". Event: Unplugged."))));
    axGrFingerXCtrl1.CapStopCapture(e.idSensor);
}

//---A finger was placed on reader---
private void axGrFingerXCtrl1_FingerDown(object sender,
    AxGrFingerXLib._IGrFingerXCtrlEvents_FingerDownEvent e)
{
    myUtil.WriteLog((("Sensor: "
        + (e.idSensor + ". Event: Finger Placed."))));
}

//---A finger was removed from reader---
private void axGrFingerXCtrl1_FingerUp(object sender,
    AxGrFingerXLib._IGrFingerXCtrlEvents_FingerUpEvent e)
{
    myUtil.WriteLog((("Sensor: "
        + (e.idSensor + ". Event: Finger removed."))));
}
```

These events are raised when the following happens:

- A fingerprint reader is plugged or unplugged from the computer.

- A finger is placed or removed from the fingerprint reader.

Also, you need to service the ImageAcquired event of the GrFingerXCtrl control. This event is fired whenever a fingerprint image is acquired. Once the image is acquired, you call the ExtractTemplate() function (explained after this) and then the IdentifyFingerprint() subroutine to identify the user's fingerprint.

Visual Basic 2005

```vb
'---An image was acquired from reader---
Private Sub AxGrFingerXCtrl1_ImageAcquired( _
    ByVal sender As System.Object, _
    ByVal e As _
    AxGrFingerXLib._IGrFingerXCtrlEvents_ImageAcquiredEvent) _
    Handles AxGrFingerXCtrl1.ImageAcquired

    '---Copying acquired image---
    myUtil.raw.height = e.height
    myUtil.raw.width = e.width
    myUtil.raw.res = e.res
    myUtil.raw.img = e.rawImage

    '---Signaling that an Image Event occurred.---
    myUtil.WriteLog("Sensor: " & e.idSensor & _
        ". Event: Image captured.")

    '---display fingerprint image---
    myUtil.PrintBiometricDisplay(False, _
        GRConstants.GR_DEFAULT_CONTEXT)

    '---extract the template from the fingerprint scanned---
    ExtractTemplate()

    '---identify who the user is---
    _UserID = IdentifyFingerprint()
    If _UserID > 0 Then
        '---user found---
        Beep()
        btnRegister.Enabled = False

        '---display user's information---
        GetUserInfo()

        '---writes to log file---
        WriteToLog(_UserID)
    Else
        '---user not found---
        ClearDisplay()
        btnRegister.Enabled = True
        Beep()
        lblMessage.Text = "User not found! Please register " & _
            "your information below"
    End If
End Sub
```

C# 2005

```
//---An image was acquired from reader---
private void axGrFingerXCtrl1_ImageAcquired(object sender,
    AxGrFingerXLib._IGrFingerXCtrlEvents_ImageAcquiredEvent e)
{
    //---Copying acquired image---
    myUtil._raw.height = e.height;
    myUtil._raw.width = e.width;
    myUtil._raw.Res = e.res;
    myUtil._raw.img = e.rawImage;

    //---Signaling that an Image Event occurred.---
    myUtil.WriteLog(("Sensor: "
        + (e.idSensor + ". Event: Image captured.")));

    //---display fingerprint image---
    myUtil.PrintBiometricDisplay(false, _
        GRConstants.GR_DEFAULT_CONTEXT);

    //---extract the template from the fingerprint scanned---
    ExtractTemplate();

    //---identify who the user is---
    _UserID = IdentifyFingerprint();
    if ((_UserID > 0))
    {
        //---user found---
        btnRegister.Enabled = false;
        GetUserInfo();

        //---writes to log file---
        WriteToLog(_UserID.ToString());
    }
    else
    {
        //---user not found---
        ClearDisplay();
        btnRegister.Enabled = true;
        lblMessage.Text = "User not found! Please " & _
            "register your information below";
    }
}
```

Once the user's identity is found, you will display the user's particulars by calling the GetUserInfo() subroutine. You will also write an entry to the log file by calling the WriteToLog() subroutine.

Once a fingerprint image is captured, you need to extract some characteristic points from the image, called *minutiae*. One regular fingerprint has some 50 minutiae. To identify a user, you need about 13 of them. When all the minutiae are extracted, they are put together into a structure called a *template*, which is the joining of all the extracted minutiae in a fingerprint. According to Griaule, the identification is made by a triangulation process and geometrical relation between the minutiae only, not the entire image. You accomplish this process by using the ExtractTemplate() function.

Visual Basic 2005

```
'---Extract a template from a fingerprint image---
Private Function ExtractTemplate() As Integer
    Dim ret As Integer

    '---extract template---
    ret = myUtil.ExtractTemplate()

    '---write template quality to log---
    If ret = GRConstants.GR_BAD_QUALITY Then
        myUtil.WriteLog("Template extracted successfully. " & _
            "Bad quality.")
    ElseIf ret = GRConstants.GR_MEDIUM_QUALITY Then
        myUtil.WriteLog("Template extracted successfully. " & _
            "Medium quality.")
    ElseIf ret = GRConstants.GR_HIGH_QUALITY Then
        myUtil.WriteLog("Template extracted successfully. " & _
            "High quality.")
    End If

    If ret >= 0 Then
        '---if no error, display minutiae/segments/directions
        ' into the image---
        myUtil.PrintBiometricDisplay(True, _
            GRConstants.GR_NO_CONTEXT)
    Else
        '---write error to log---
        myUtil.WriteError(ret)
    End If
    Return ret
End Function
```

C# 2005

```
//---Extract a template from a fingerprint image---
private int ExtractTemplate()
{
    int ret;
```

```
    //---extract template---
    ret = myUtil.ExtractTemplate();

    //---write template quality to log---
    if ((GRConstants)ret == GRConstants.GR_BAD_QUALITY)
    {
        myUtil.WriteLog(
            "Template extracted successfully. Bad quality.");
    }
    else if ((GRConstants)ret ==
      GRConstants.GR_MEDIUM_QUALITY)
    {
        myUtil.WriteLog(
            "Template extracted successfully. Medium quality.");
    }
    else if ((GRConstants)ret == GRConstants.GR_HIGH_QUALITY)
    {
        myUtil.WriteLog(
            "Template extracted successfully. High quality.");
    }
    if ((ret >= 0))
    {
        //---if no error, display minutiae/segments/directions
        // into the image---
        myUtil.PrintBiometricDisplay(true,
            GRConstants.GR_NO_CONTEXT);
    }
    else
    {
        //---write error to log---
        myUtil.WriteError((GRConstants)ret);
    }
    return ret;
}
```

The IdentifyFingerprint() function locates the identity of the user by calling the Identify() method located in the Util.vb (or Util.cs) class. It returns the ID of the identified user.

Visual Basic 2005

```
'---Identify a fingerprint; returns the ID of the user---
Private Function IdentifyFingerprint() As Integer
    Dim ret As Integer, score As Integer
    score = 0

    '---identify it---
    ret = myUtil.Identify(score)
```

```vbnet
    '---write result to log---
    If ret > 0 Then
        myUtil.WriteLog("Fingerprint identified. ID = " & ret & _
            ". Score = " & score & ".")
        myUtil.PrintBiometricDisplay(True, _
            GRConstants.GR_DEFAULT_CONTEXT)
    ElseIf ret = 0 Then
        myUtil.WriteLog("Fingerprint not Found.")
    Else
        myUtil.WriteError(ret)
    End If
    Return ret
End Function
```

C# 2005

```csharp
//---Identify a fingerprint; returns the ID of the user---
private int IdentifyFingerprint()
{
    int ret;
    int score;
    score = 0;

    //---identify it---
    ret = myUtil.Identify(ref score);

    //---write result to log---
    if ((ret > 0))
    {
        myUtil.WriteLog((("Fingerprint identified. ID = "
            + (ret + (". Score = " + (score + "."))))));
        myUtil.PrintBiometricDisplay(true,
            GRConstants.GR_DEFAULT_CONTEXT);
    }
    else if ((ret == 0))
    {
        myUtil.WriteLog("Fingerprint not Found.");
    }
    else
    {
        myUtil.WriteError((GRConstants)ret);
    }
    return ret;
}
```

The GetUserInfo() subroutine retrieves the user's particulars using the value of the UserID variable.

Visual Basic 2005

```vb
'---get user's information---
Public Sub GetUserInfo()
    Dim filePath As String
    Try
        filePath = Application.StartupPath() & "\" & DBFile
        connection = New OleDb.OleDbConnection(ConnectionString _
            & filePath)
        connection.Open()
        Dim reader As OleDb.OleDbDataReader
        Dim command As OleDb.OleDbCommand = New OleDb.OleDbCommand
        command.Connection = connection

        '---retrieve user's particulars---
        command.CommandText = "SELECT * FROM Enroll WHERE ID=" & _
          _UserID
        reader = _
            command.ExecuteReader(CommandBehavior.CloseConnection)
        reader.Read()

        '---display user's particulars---
        lblMessage.Text = "Welcome, " & reader("name")
        txtSSN.Text = reader("SSN")
        txtName.Text = reader("Name")
        txtCompany.Text = reader("Company")
        txtContactNumber.Text = reader("ContactNumber")
        txtEmail.Text = reader("Email")

        '---reset the timer to another five seconds---
        Timer1.Enabled = False
        Timer1.Enabled = True
    Catch ex As Exception
        MsgBox(ex.ToString)
    Finally
        connection.Close()
    End Try
End Sub
```

C# 2005

```csharp
//---get user's information---
public void GetUserInfo()
{
    string filePath;
    try
    {
```

```
        filePath = (Application.StartupPath + ("\\" +
            DBFile));
        connection = new System.Data.OleDb.OleDbConnection((
            ConnectionString + filePath));
        connection.Open();
        System.Data.OleDb.OleDbDataReader reader;
        System.Data.OleDb.OleDbCommand command = new
            System.Data.OleDb.OleDbCommand();
        command.Connection = connection;

        //---retrieve user's particulars---
        command.CommandText = (
            "SELECT * FROM Enroll WHERE ID=" + _UserID);
        reader =
            command.ExecuteReader(
            CommandBehavior.CloseConnection);
        reader.Read();

        //---display user's particulars---
        lblMessage.Text = ("Welcome, " + reader["name"]);
        txtSSN.Text = reader["SSN"].ToString();
        txtName.Text = reader["Name"].ToString();
        txtCompany.Text = reader["Company"].ToString();
        txtContactNumber.Text =
            reader["ContactNumber"].ToString();
        txtEmail.Text = reader["Email"].ToString();

        //---reset the timer to another five seconds---
        Timer1.Enabled = false;
        Timer1.Enabled = true;
    }
    catch (Exception ex)
    {
        MessageBox.Show(ex.ToString(), "Error");
    }
    finally
    {
        connection.Close();
    }
}
```

When a fingerprint is not recognized, the user can register the fingerprint by filling in his particulars. This is accomplished by the Register button, which first adds the fingerprint to the database (via the EnrollFingerprint() function) and then adds the particulars of the user using the AddNewUser() subroutine.

Visual Basic 2005

```vb
'---Register button---
Private Sub btnRegister_Click( _
    ByVal sender As System.Object, _
    ByVal e As System.EventArgs) _
    Handles btnRegister.Click

    '---first add the fingerprint---
    _UserID = EnrollFingerprint()

    '---then add the particulars---
    AddNewUser()

    '---clears the display---
    ClearDisplay()

    '---writes to log file---
    WriteToLog(_UserID)
End Sub
```

C# 2005

```csharp
//---Register button---
private void btnRegister_Click(
    object sender,
    System.EventArgs e)
{
    //---first add the fingerprint---
    _UserID = EnrollFingerprint();

    //---then add the particulars---
    AddNewUser();

    //---clears the display---
    ClearDisplay();

    //---writes to log file---
    WriteToLog(_UserID.ToString());
}
```

The EnrollFingerprint() function enrolls a finger in the database using the Enroll() method defined in the Util.vb (or Util.cs) class.

Visual Basic 2005

```vb
'---adds a fingerprint to the database; returns the ID of the
' user---
Private Function EnrollFingerprint() As Integer
    Dim id As Integer
```

```
    '---add fingerprint---
    id = myUtil.Enroll()

    '---write result to log---
    If id >= 0 Then
        myUtil.WriteLog("Fingerprint enrolled with id = " & id)
    Else
        myUtil.WriteLog("Error: Fingerprint not enrolled")
    End If
    Return id
End Function
```

C# 2005

```
//---adds a fingerprint to the database; returns the ID of
// the user---
private int EnrollFingerprint()
{
    int id;
    //---add fingerprint---
    id = myUtil.Enroll();

    //---write result to log---
    if ((id >= 0))
    {
        myUtil.WriteLog(("Fingerprint enrolled with id = " +
            id));
    }
    else
    {
        myUtil.WriteLog("Error: Fingerprint not enrolled");
    }
    return id;
}
```

The AddNewUser() subroutine saves the user's particulars in the database.

Visual Basic 2005

```
'---Add a new user's information to the database---
Public Sub AddNewUser()
    Dim filePath As String
    Try
        filePath = Application.StartupPath() & "\" & DBFile
        connection = New OleDb.OleDbConnection(ConnectionString _
            & filePath)
        connection.Open()
        Dim command As OleDb.OleDbCommand = New OleDb.OleDbCommand
```

```
            command.Connection = connection

            '---set the user's particulars in the table---
            Dim sql As String = "UPDATE enroll SET SSN='" & _
                txtSSN.Text & "', " & _
                "Name='" & txtName.Text & "', " & _
                "Company='" & txtCompany.Text & "', " & _
                "ContactNumber='" & txtContactNumber.Text & "', " & _
                "Email='" & txtEmail.Text & "' " & _
                " WHERE ID=" & _UserID
            command.CommandText = sql
            command.ExecuteNonQuery()
            MsgBox("User added successfully!")
        Catch ex As Exception
            MsgBox(ex.ToString)
        Finally
            connection.Close()
        End Try
    End Sub
```

C# 2005

```
//---Add a new user's information to the database---
public void AddNewUser()
{
    string filePath;
    try
    {
        filePath = (Application.StartupPath + ("\\" +
            DBFile));
        connection = new System.Data.OleDb.OleDbConnection((
            ConnectionString + filePath));
        connection.Open();
        System.Data.OleDb.OleDbCommand command = new
            System.Data.OleDb.OleDbCommand();
        command.Connection = connection;

        //---set the user's particulars in the table---
        string sql = ("UPDATE enroll SET SSN=\'"
            + (txtSSN.Text + ("\', " + ("Name=\'"
            + (txtName.Text + ("\', " + ("Company=\'"
            + (txtCompany.Text + ("\', " +
            ("ContactNumber=\'"
            + (txtContactNumber.Text + ("\', " + ("Email=\'"
            + (txtEmail.Text + ("\' " + (" WHERE ID=" +
            _UserID))))))))))))))));
        command.CommandText = sql;
```

```
        command.ExecuteNonQuery();
        MessageBox.Show("User added successfully!", "Error");
        connection.Close();
    }
    catch (Exception ex)
    {
        MessageBox.Show(ex.ToString(), "Error");
    }
    finally
    {
        connection.Close();
    }
}
```

The ClearDisplay() subroutine clears the information displayed in the various TextBox controls.

Visual Basic 2005

```
'---Clears the user's particulars---
Public Sub ClearDisplay()
    lblMessage.Text = _
        "Please place your index finger on the fingerprint reader"
    PictureBox1.Image = My.Resources.fingerprintreader

    txtSSN.Text = String.Empty
    txtName.Text = String.Empty
    txtCompany.Text = String.Empty
    txtContactNumber.Text = String.Empty
    txtEmail.Text = String.Empty
End Sub
```

C# 2005

```
//---Clears the user's particulars---
public void ClearDisplay()
{
    lblMessage.Text =
        "Please place your index finger on the fingerprint" +
        " reader";
    PictureBox1.Image = FingerPrintReader_CS.
        Properties.Resources.fingerprintreader;
    txtSSN.Text = String.Empty;
    txtName.Text = String.Empty;
    txtCompany.Text = String.Empty;
    txtContactNumber.Text = String.Empty;
    txtEmail.Text = String.Empty;
}
```

When the Timer1_Tick event is fired (every five seconds), call the ClearDisplay() subroutine to clear the display.

Visual Basic 2005

```
'---the Timer control---
Private Sub Timer1_Tick( _
    ByVal sender As System.Object, _
    ByVal e As System.EventArgs) _
    Handles Timer1.Tick
    ClearDisplay()
    Timer1.Enabled = False
End Sub
```

C# 2005

```
private void Timer1_Tick(object sender, EventArgs e)
{
    ClearDisplay();
    Timer1.Enabled = false;
}
```

The WriteToLog() subroutine writes to the log file an entry containing the user's ID and the current time.

Visual Basic 2005

```
Public Sub WriteToLog(ByVal ID As String)
    '---write to a log file---
    Dim sw As New System.IO.StreamWriter( _
        Logfile, True, System.Text.Encoding.ASCII)
    sw.WriteLine(id & "," & Now.ToString)
    sw.Close()
End Sub
```

C# 2005

```
public void WriteToLog(string ID)
{
    //---write to a log file---
    System.IO.StreamWriter sw = new
        System.IO.StreamWriter(
        Logfile, true, System.Text.Encoding.ASCII);
    sw.WriteLine((ID + ("," +
        System.DateTime.Now.ToString())));
    sw.Close();
}
```

Testing the Application

You are now ready to test the application. Press F5 in Visual Studio 2005, and you will see the application shown in Figure 3-10.

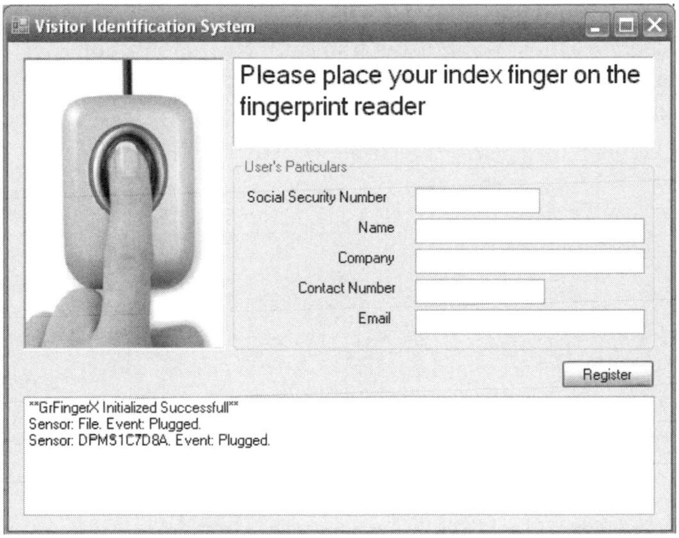

Figure 3-10. *Testing the application*

Place your index finger on the reader, and you should be prompted to register with your particulars. Once registered, your particulars will be cleared after five seconds. You can now try placing the same finger to check whether you can be identified correctly. If so, you will see your information displayed, as shown in Figure 3-11.

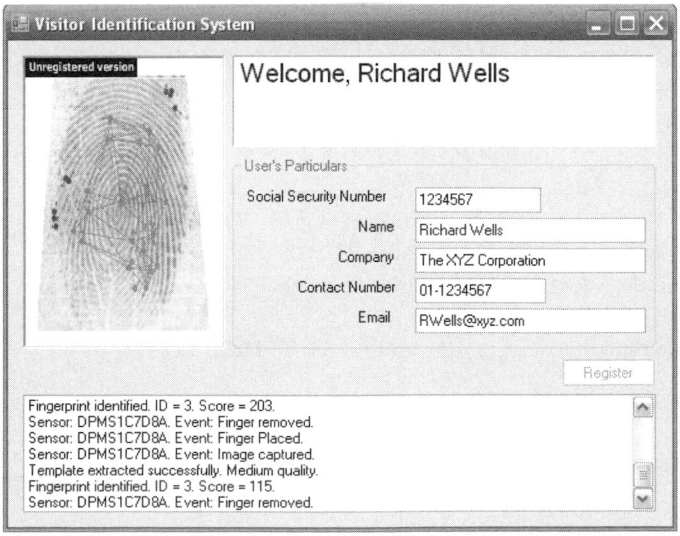

Figure 3-11. *Displaying the information of an identified user*

Note that sometimes your fingerprint may not be correctly identified. This is likely due to the incorrect positioning of your finger. Try again, and it should be identified correctly.

Summary

In this chapter, you saw how to integrate a fingerprint reader into your .NET application. Although the example shown in this chapter was simple, you can easily extend it to more complex scenarios, such as video rental applications, payment services, and so on. If you have not started evaluating biometric authentication for your projects, this is a good time to start!

Listing 3-1. Util.vb

Visual Basic 2005

```
'-------------------------------------------------------------------------------
'GrFinger Sample
'(c) 2005 Griaule Tecnologia Ltda.
'http://www.griaule.com
'-------------------------------------------------------------------------------
'
'This sample is provided with "GrFinger Fingerprint Recognition Library" and
'can't run without it. It's provided just as an example of using GrFinger
'Fingerprint Recognition Library and should not be used as basis for any
'commercial product.
'
'Griaule Tecnologia makes no representations concerning either the merchantability
'of this software or the suitability of this sample for any particular purpose.
'
'THIS SAMPLE IS PROVIDED BY THE AUTHOR "AS IS" AND ANY EXPRESS OR
'IMPLIED WARRANTIES, INCLUDING, BUT NOT LIMITED TO, THE IMPLIED WARRANTIES
'OF MERCHANTABILITY AND FITNESS FOR A PARTICULAR PURPOSE ARE DISCLAIMED.
'IN NO EVENT SHALL GRIAULE BE LIABLE FOR ANY DIRECT, INDIRECT,
'INCIDENTAL, SPECIAL, EXEMPLARY, OR CONSEQUENTIAL DAMAGES (INCLUDING, BUT
'NOT LIMITED TO, PROCUREMENT OF SUBSTITUTE GOODS OR SERVICES; LOSS OF USE,
'DATA, OR PROFITS; OR BUSINESS INTERRUPTION) HOWEVER CAUSED AND ON ANY
'THEORY OF LIABILITY, WHETHER IN CONTRACT, STRICT LIABILITY, OR TORT
'(INCLUDING NEGLIGENCE OR OTHERWISE) ARISING IN ANY WAY OUT OF THE USE OF
'THIS SOFTWARE, EVEN IF ADVISED OF THE POSSIBILITY OF SUCH DAMAGE.
'
'You can download the free version of GrFinger directly from Griaule website.
'
'These notices must be retained in any copies of any part of this
'documentation and/or sample.
'
'-------------------------------------------------------------------------------

'-------------------------------------------------------------------------------
```

```vb
' Support and fingerprint management routines
' --------------------------------------------------------------------------------

Imports GrFingerXLib
Imports Microsoft.VisualBasic

' Raw image data type.
Public Structure RawImage
    ' Image data.
    Public img As Object
    ' Image width.
    Public width As Long
    ' Image height.
    Public height As Long
    ' Image resolution.
    Public res As Long
End Structure

Public Class Util

    ' Some constants to make our code cleaner
    Public Const ERR_CANT_OPEN_BD As Integer = -999
    Public Const ERR_INVALID_ID As Integer = -998
    Public Const ERR_INVALID_TEMPLATE As Integer = -997

    ' Importing necessary HDC functions
    Private Declare Function GetDC Lib "user32" (ByVal hwnd As Int32) As Int32
    Private Declare Function ReleaseDC Lib "user32" _
        (ByVal hwnd As Int32, ByVal hdc As Int32) As Int32

    ' The last acquired image.
    Public raw As RawImage
    ' The template extracted from last acquired image.
    Public template As New TTemplate
    ' Database class.
    Public DB As DBClass
    ' Reference to main form log.
    Private _lbLog As ListBox
    ' Reference to main form Image.
    Private _pbPic As PictureBox
    ' GrFingerX component
    Private _GrFingerX As AxGrFingerXLib.AxGrFingerXCtrl


    ' --------------------------------------------------------------------------
    ' Support functions
    ' --------------------------------------------------------------------------
```

```vbnet
' This class creates an Util class with some functions
' to help us to develop our GrFinger Application
Public Sub New(ByRef lbLog As ListBox, _
    ByRef pbPic As PictureBox, _
    ByRef GrFingerX As AxGrFingerXLib.AxGrFingerXCtrl)
    _lbLog = lbLog
    _pbPic = pbPic
    _GrFingerX = GrFingerX
End Sub

' Write a message in box.
Public Sub WriteLog(ByVal message As String)
    _lbLog.Items.Add(message)
    _lbLog.SelectedIndex = _lbLog.Items.Count - 1
    _lbLog.ClearSelected()
End Sub

' Write and describe an error.
Public Sub WriteError(ByVal errorCode As Integer)
    Select Case errorCode
        Case GRConstants.GR_ERROR_INITIALIZE_FAIL
            WriteLog("Fail to Initialize GrFingerX. (Error:" & errorCode & ")")
        Case GRConstants.GR_ERROR_NOT_INITIALIZED
            WriteLog("The GrFingerX Library is not initialized. (Error:" & _
                errorCode & ")")
        Case GRConstants.GR_ERROR_FAIL_LICENSE_READ
            WriteLog( _
                "License not found. See manual for troubleshooting. (Error:" _
                & errorCode & ")")
            MessageBox.Show( _
                "License not found. See manual for troubleshooting.")
        Case GRConstants.GR_ERROR_NO_VALID_LICENSE
            WriteLog( _
                "The license is not valid. See manual for " & _
                "troubleshooting. (Error:" & errorCode & ")")
            MessageBox.Show( _
                "The license is not valid. See manual for troubleshooting.")
        Case GRConstants.GR_ERROR_NULL_ARGUMENT
            WriteLog("The parameter have a null value. (Error:" & _
                errorCode & ")")
        Case GRConstants.GR_ERROR_FAIL
            WriteLog("Fail to create a GDI object. (Error:" & errorCode & ")")
        Case GRConstants.GR_ERROR_ALLOC
            WriteLog("Fail to create a context. Cannot " & _
                "allocate memory. (Error:" & errorCode & ")")
        Case GRConstants.GR_ERROR_PARAMETERS
            WriteLog("One or more parameters are out of " & _
```

```
                "bound. (Error:" & errorCode & ")")
    Case GRConstants.GR_ERROR_WRONG_USE
        WriteLog("This function cannot be called at " & _
            "this time. (Error:" & errorCode & ")")
    Case GRConstants.GR_ERROR_EXTRACT
        WriteLog("Template Extraction failed. (Error:" & errorCode & ")")
    Case GRConstants.GR_ERROR_SIZE_OFF_RANGE
        WriteLog("Image is too larger or too short.  (Error:" & _
            errorCode & ")")
    Case GRConstants.GR_ERROR_RES_OFF_RANGE
        WriteLog("Image have too low or too high resolution. (Error:" & _
            errorCode & ")")
    Case GRConstants.GR_ERROR_CONTEXT_NOT_CREATED
        WriteLog("The Context could not be created. (Error:" & _
            errorCode & ")")
    Case GRConstants.GR_ERROR_INVALID_CONTEXT
        WriteLog("The Context does not exist. (Error:" & errorCode & ")")

        ' Capture error codes

    Case GRConstants.GR_ERROR_CONNECT_SENSOR
        WriteLog("Error while connection to sensor. (Error:" & _
            errorCode & ")")
    Case GRConstants.GR_ERROR_CAPTURING
        WriteLog("Error while capturing from sensor. (Error:" & _
            errorCode & ")")
    Case GRConstants.GR_ERROR_CANCEL_CAPTURING
        WriteLog("Error while stop capturing from sensor. (Error:" & _
            errorCode & ")")
    Case GRConstants.GR_ERROR_INVALID_ID_SENSOR
        WriteLog("The idSensor is invalid. (Error:" & errorCode & ")")
    Case GRConstants.GR_ERROR_SENSOR_NOT_CAPTURING
        WriteLog("The sensor is not capturing. (Error:" & errorCode & ")")
    Case GRConstants.GR_ERROR_INVALID_EXT
        WriteLog("The File have a unknown extension. (Error:" & _
            errorCode & ")")
    Case GRConstants.GR_ERROR_INVALID_FILENAME
        WriteLog("The filename is invalid. (Error:" & errorCode & ")")
    Case GRConstants.GR_ERROR_INVALID_FILETYPE
        WriteLog("The file type is invalid. (Error:" & errorCode & ")")
    Case GRConstants.GR_ERROR_SENSOR
        WriteLog("The sensor raise an error. (Error:" & errorCode & ")")

        ' Our error codes

    Case ERR_INVALID_TEMPLATE
        WriteLog("Invalid Template. (Error:" & errorCode & ")")
```

```vbnet
            Case ERR_INVALID_ID
                WriteLog("Invalid ID. (Error:" & errorCode & ")")
            Case ERR_CANT_OPEN_BD
                WriteLog("Unable to connect to DataBase. (Error:" & errorCode & ")")
            Case Else
                WriteLog("Error:" & errorCode)
        End Select
    End Sub

    ' Check if we have a valid template
    Private Function TemplateIsValid() As Boolean
        ' Check template size
        Return template.Size > 0
    End Function

    ' -----------------------------------------------------------------------
    ' Main functions for fingerprint recognition management
    ' -----------------------------------------------------------------------

    ' Initializes GrFinger ActiveX and all necessary utilities.
    Public Function InitializeGrFinger() As Integer
        Dim err As Integer

        DB = New DBClass
        ' Open DataBase
        If DB.OpenDB() = False Then Return ERR_CANT_OPEN_BD
        ' Create a new Template
        template.Size = 0
        ' Create a new raw image
        raw.img = Nothing
        raw.width = 0
        raw.height = 0
        ' Initializing library
        err = _GrFingerX.Initialize()
        If err < 0 Then Return err
        Return _GrFingerX.CapInitialize()
    End Function

    ' Finalizes and close the DB.
    Public Sub FinalizeGrFinger()
        ' finalize library
        _GrFingerX.Finalize()
        _GrFingerX.CapFinalize()

        ' close DB
        DB.closeDB()
        DB = Nothing
    End Sub
```

```vbnet
' Display fingerprint image on screen
Public Sub PrintBiometricDisplay( _
    ByVal biometricDisplay As Boolean, ByVal context As Integer)

    ' handle to finger image
    Dim handle As System.Drawing.Image = Nothing

    ' screen HDC
    Dim hdc As Integer = GetDC(0)

    If biometricDisplay Then
        ' get image with biometric info
        _GrFingerX.BiometricDisplay( _
            template.tpt, raw.img, raw.width, raw.height, _
            raw.res, hdc, handle, context)
    Else
        ' get raw image
        _GrFingerX.CapRawImageToHandle( _
            raw.img, raw.width, raw.height, hdc, handle)
    End If

    ' draw image on picture box
    If Not (handle Is Nothing) Then
        _pbPic.Image = handle
        _pbPic.Update()
    End If
    ' release screen HDC
    ReleaseDC(0, hdc)
End Sub

' Add a fingerprint template to database
Public Function Enroll() As Integer
    ' Checking if template is valid.
    If TemplateIsValid() Then
        ' Adds template to database and gets ID.
        Return DB.AddTemplate(template)
    Else
        Return -1
    End If
End Function

' Extract a fingerprint template from current image
Function ExtractTemplate() As Integer
    Dim ret As Integer

    ' set current buffer size for extract template
    template.Size = template.tpt.Length
```

```vbnet
        ret = _GrFingerX.Extract( _
            raw.img, raw.width, raw.height, raw.res, template.tpt, template.Size, _
                GRConstants.GR_DEFAULT_CONTEXT)
        ' if error, set template size to 0
        ' Result < 0 => extraction problem
        If ret < 0 Then template.Size = 0
        Return ret
    End Function


    ' Identify current fingerprint on our database
    Public Function Identify(ByRef score As Integer) As Integer
        Dim ret As Integer
        Dim i As Integer

        ' Checking if template is valid.
        If Not TemplateIsValid() Then Return ERR_INVALID_TEMPLATE

        ' Starting identification process and supplying query template.

        Dim tmpTpt As Array = Array.CreateInstance(GetType(Byte), template.Size)
        Array.Copy(template.tpt, tmpTpt, template.Size)
        ret = _GrFingerX.IdentifyPrepare(tmpTpt, GRConstants.GR_DEFAULT_CONTEXT)
        ' error?
        If ret < 0 Then Return ret
        ' Getting enrolled templates from database.
        Dim templates As TTemplates() = DB.getTemplates()
        ' Iterate over all templates in database
        For i = 1 To templates.Length
            ' Comparing the current template.
            If Not (templates(i - 1).template Is Nothing) Then
                Dim tempTpt As Array = _
                    Array.CreateInstance(GetType(Byte), _
                    templates(i - 1).template.Size)
                Array.Copy(templates(i - 1).template.tpt, tempTpt, _
                    templates(i - 1).template.Size)
                ret = _GrFingerX.Identify(tempTpt, score, _
                    GRConstants.GR_DEFAULT_CONTEXT)
            End If
            ' Checking if query template and reference template match.
            If ret = GRConstants.GR_MATCH Then
                Return templates(i - 1).ID
            End If
            If ret < 0 Then Return ret
        Next
        ' end of database, return "no match" code
        Return GRConstants.GR_NOT_MATCH
    End Function
```

```vb
' Check current fingerprint against another one in our database
Public Function Verify(ByVal id As Integer, ByRef score As Integer) As Integer
    Dim tptref As System.Array

    ' Checking if template is valid.
    If Not (TemplateIsValid()) Then Return ERR_INVALID_TEMPLATE
    ' Getting template with the supplied ID from database.
    tptref = DB.getTemplate(id)
    ' Checking if ID was found.
    If tptref Is Nothing Then Return ERR_INVALID_ID
    ' Comparing templates.
    Dim tempTpt As Array = Array.CreateInstance(GetType(Byte), template.Size)
    Array.Copy(template.tpt, tempTpt, template.Size)
    Return _GrFingerX.Verify(tempTpt, tptref, score, _
        GRConstants.GR_DEFAULT_CONTEXT)
End Function

' Show GrFinger version and type
Public Sub MessageVersion()
    Dim majorVersion As Integer = 0
    Dim minorVersion As Integer = 0
    Dim result As GRConstants
    Dim vStr As String = ""

    result = _GrFingerX.GetGrFingerVersion(majorVersion, minorVersion)
    If result = GRConstants.GRFINGER_FULL Then vStr = "FULL"
    If result = GRConstants.GRFINGER_LIGHT Then vStr = "LIGHT"
    If result = GRConstants.GRFINGER_FREE Then vStr = "FREE"
    MessageBox.Show("The GrFinger DLL version is " & majorVersion & _
            "." & minorVersion & "." & vbCrLf & _
      "The license type is '" & vStr & "'.", "GrFinger Version")
End Sub

End Class
```

C# 2005

```csharp
/*
--------------------------------------------------------------------------------
GrFinger Sample
(c) 2005 Griaule Tecnologia Ltda.
http://www.griaule.com
--------------------------------------------------------------------------------

This sample is provided with "GrFinger Fingerprint Recognition Library" and
can't run without it. It's provided just as an example of using GrFinger
Fingerprint Recognition Library and should not be used as basis for any
commercial product.
```

Griaule Tecnologia makes no representations concerning either the merchantability
of this software or the suitability of this sample for any particular purpose.

THIS SAMPLE IS PROVIDED BY THE AUTHOR "AS IS" AND ANY EXPRESS OR
IMPLIED WARRANTIES, INCLUDING, BUT NOT LIMITED TO, THE IMPLIED WARRANTIES
OF MERCHANTABILITY AND FITNESS FOR A PARTICULAR PURPOSE ARE DISCLAIMED.
IN NO EVENT SHALL GRIAULE BE LIABLE FOR ANY DIRECT, INDIRECT,
INCIDENTAL, SPECIAL, EXEMPLARY, OR CONSEQUENTIAL DAMAGES (INCLUDING, BUT
NOT LIMITED TO, PROCUREMENT OF SUBSTITUTE GOODS OR SERVICES; LOSS OF USE,
DATA, OR PROFITS; OR BUSINESS INTERRUPTION) HOWEVER CAUSED AND ON ANY
THEORY OF LIABILITY, WHETHER IN CONTRACT, STRICT LIABILITY, OR TORT
(INCLUDING NEGLIGENCE OR OTHERWISE) ARISING IN ANY WAY OUT OF THE USE OF
THIS SOFTWARE, EVEN IF ADVISED OF THE POSSIBILITY OF SUCH DAMAGE.

You can download the free version of GrFinger directly from Griaule website.

These notices must be retained in any copies of any part of this
documentation and/or sample.

```
    --------------------------------------------------------------------------------
*/

// --------------------------------------------------------------------------------
// Support and fingerprint management routines
// --------------------------------------------------------------------------------

using GrFingerXLib;
using System;
using System.Drawing;
using System.Data.OleDb;
using System.Windows.Forms;
using System.Runtime.InteropServices;

// Raw image data type.
public struct TRawImage
{
    // Image data.
    public object img;
    // Image width.
    public int width;
    // Image height.
    public int height;
    // Image resolution.
    public int Res;
};

public class Util
{
```

```csharp
// Some constants to make our code cleaner
public const int ERR_CANT_OPEN_BD = -999;
public const int ERR_INVALID_ID = -998;
public const int ERR_INVALID_TEMPLATE = -997;


// ----------------------------------------------------------------------------
// Support functions
// ----------------------------------------------------------------------------

// This class creates an Util class with some functions
// to help us to develop our GrFinger Application
public Util(ListBox lbLog, PictureBox pbPic,
    Button btEnroll, Button btnExtract, Button btIdentify, Button btVerify,
    CheckBox cbAutoExtract, CheckBox  cbAutoIdentify)
{
    _lbLog = lbLog;
    _pbPic = pbPic;
    _btEnroll = btEnroll;
    _btExtract = btnExtract;
    _btIdentify = btIdentify;
    _btVerify = btVerify;
    _cbAutoExtract = cbAutoExtract;
    _cbAutoIdentify = cbAutoIdentify;
    _DB = null;
    _tpt = null;
}

~Util()
{
}

//  Write a message in log box.
public void WriteLog(String msg)
{
    _lbLog.Items.Add(msg);
    _lbLog.SelectedIndex = _lbLog.Items.Count - 1;
    _lbLog.ClearSelected();
}

// Write and describe an error.
public void WriteError(GrFingerXLib.GRConstants errorCode)
{
    switch ((int)errorCode)
    {
        case (int)GRConstants.GR_ERROR_INITIALIZE_FAIL:
            WriteLog("Fail to Initialize GrFingerX. (Error:" + errorCode + ")");
            return;
```

```
case (int)GRConstants.GR_ERROR_NOT_INITIALIZED:
   WriteLog("The GrFingerX Library is not initialized. (Error:" +
      errorCode + ")");
   return;
case (int)GRConstants.GR_ERROR_FAIL_LICENSE_READ:
   WriteLog("License not found. See manual for " +
      "troubleshooting. (Error:" + errorCode + ")");
   MessageBox.Show("License not found. See " +
      "manual for troubleshooting.");
   return;
case (int)GRConstants.GR_ERROR_NO_VALID_LICENSE:
   WriteLog("The license is not valid. See manual for " +
      "troubleshooting. (Error:" + errorCode + ")");
   MessageBox.Show("The license is not valid. See " +
      "manual for troubleshooting.");
   return;
case (int)GRConstants.GR_ERROR_NULL_ARGUMENT:
   WriteLog("The parameter have a null value. (Error:" +
      errorCode + ")");
   return;
case (int)GRConstants.GR_ERROR_FAIL:
   WriteLog("Fail to create a GDI object. (Error:" + errorCode + ")");
   return;
case (int)GRConstants.GR_ERROR_ALLOC:
   WriteLog("Fail to create a context. Cannot allocate " +
      "memory. (Error:" + errorCode + ")");
   return;
case (int)GRConstants.GR_ERROR_PARAMETERS:
   WriteLog("One or more parameters are out of bound. (Error:" +
      errorCode + ")");
   return;
case (int)GRConstants.GR_ERROR_WRONG_USE:
   WriteLog("This function cannot be called at this time. (Error:" +
      errorCode + ")");
   return;
case (int)GRConstants.GR_ERROR_EXTRACT:
   WriteLog("Template Extraction failed. (Error:" + errorCode + ")");
   return;
case (int)GRConstants.GR_ERROR_SIZE_OFF_RANGE:
   WriteLog("Image is too larger or too short.  (Error:" +
      errorCode + ")");
   return;
case (int)GRConstants.GR_ERROR_RES_OFF_RANGE:
   WriteLog("Image have too low or too high resolution. (Error:" +
      errorCode + ")");
   return;
case (int)GRConstants.GR_ERROR_CONTEXT_NOT_CREATED:
```

```
        WriteLog("The Context could not be created. (Error:" +
            errorCode + ")");
        return;
    case (int)GRConstants.GR_ERROR_INVALID_CONTEXT:
        WriteLog("The Context does not exist. (Error:" + errorCode + ")");
        return;


        // Capture error codes

    case (int)GRConstants.GR_ERROR_CONNECT_SENSOR:
        WriteLog("Error while connection to sensor. (Error:" +
            errorCode + ")");
        return;
    case (int)GRConstants.GR_ERROR_CAPTURING:
        WriteLog("Error while capturing from sensor. (Error:" +
            errorCode + ")");
        return;
    case (int)GRConstants.GR_ERROR_CANCEL_CAPTURING:
        WriteLog("Error while stop capturing from sensor. (Error:" +
            errorCode + ")");
        return;
    case (int)GRConstants.GR_ERROR_INVALID_ID_SENSOR:
        WriteLog("The idSensor is invalid. (Error:" + errorCode + ")");
        return;
    case (int)GRConstants.GR_ERROR_SENSOR_NOT_CAPTURING:
        WriteLog("The sensor is not capturing. (Error:" + errorCode + ")");
        return;
    case (int)GRConstants.GR_ERROR_INVALID_EXT:
        WriteLog("The File have a unknown extension. (Error:" +
            errorCode + ")");
        return;
    case (int)GRConstants.GR_ERROR_INVALID_FILENAME:
        WriteLog("The filename is invalid. (Error:" + errorCode + ")");
        return;
    case (int)GRConstants.GR_ERROR_INVALID_FILETYPE:
        WriteLog("The file type is invalid. (Error:" + errorCode + ")");
        return;
    case (int)GRConstants.GR_ERROR_SENSOR:
        WriteLog("The sensor raise an error. (Error:" + errorCode + ")");
        return;

        // Our error codes
    case ERR_INVALID_TEMPLATE:
        WriteLog("Invalid Template. (Error:"+errorCode+")");
        return;
    case ERR_INVALID_ID:
        WriteLog("Invalid ID. (Error:"+errorCode+")");
        return;
```

```
            case ERR_CANT_OPEN_BD:
                WriteLog("Unable to connect to DataBase. (Error:"+errorCode+")");
                return;

            default:
                WriteLog("Error:" + errorCode);
                return;
        }
    }

// Check if we have a valid template
    private bool TemplateIsValid() {
        // Check the template size and data
        return ((_tpt._size > 0) && (_tpt._tpt != null));
    }

    // ---------------------------------------------------------------------------
    // Main functions for fingerprint recognition management
    // ---------------------------------------------------------------------------

    // Initializes GrFinger ActiveX and all necessary utilities.
    public int InitializeGrFinger(AxGrFingerXLib.AxGrFingerXCtrl grfingerx)
    {
        GRConstants result;

        _grfingerx = grfingerx;
        //Check DataBase Class.
        if (_DB == null)
            _DB = new DBClass();
        //Open DataBase
        if(_DB.openDB()==false)
        {
            return ERR_CANT_OPEN_BD;
        }

        //Create a new Template
        if (_tpt == null)
            _tpt = new TTemplate();

        //Create a new raw image
        _raw = new TRawImage();

        //Initialize library
        result = (GRConstants)_grfingerx.Initialize();
        if (result < 0) return (int)result;
        return (int)_grfingerx.CapInitialize();
    }
```

```
//  Finalizes library and close DB.
public void FinalizeUtil() {
    // finalize library
    _grfingerx.Finalize();
    _grfingerx.CapFinalize();
    // close DB
    _DB.closeDB();
    _raw.img = null;
    _tpt = null;
    _DB = null;
}

// Display fingerprint image on screen
public void PrintBiometricDisplay(bool isBiometric,
    GrFingerXLib.GRConstants contextId)
{
    // handle to finger image
    System.Drawing.Image handle = null;
    // screen HDC
    IntPtr hdc = GetDC(System.IntPtr.Zero);

    if (isBiometric) {
      // get image with biometric info
        _grfingerx.BiometricDisplay(ref _tpt._tpt,
            ref _raw.img,_raw.width,_raw.height,_raw.Res,hdc.ToInt32(),
            ref handle,(int)contextId);
    } else {
      // get raw image
        _grfingerx.CapRawImageToHandle(ref _raw.img,_raw.width,
            _raw.height, hdc.ToInt32(), ref handle);
    }

    // draw image on picture box
    if (handle != null)
    {
        _pbPic.Image = handle;
        _pbPic.Update();
    }

    // release screen HDC
    ReleaseDC(System.IntPtr.Zero,hdc);
}

// Add a fingerprint template to database
public int Enroll()
{
    int id = 0;
```

```
        // Checks if template is valid.
        if (TemplateIsValid())
        {
            // Adds template to database and returns template ID.
            _DB.addTemplate(_tpt, ref id);
            return id;
        }
        else
        {
            return -1;
        }
    }

    // Extract a fingerprint template from current image
    public int ExtractTemplate()
    {
        int result;

        // set current buffer size for the extract template
        _tpt._size = (int)GRConstants.GR_MAX_SIZE_TEMPLATE;
        result = (int)_grfingerx.Extract(
            ref _raw.img, _raw.width, _raw.height, _raw.Res,
            ref _tpt._tpt,ref _tpt._size,
            (int)GRConstants.GR_DEFAULT_CONTEXT);
        // if error, set template size to 0
        if (result < 0)
        {
            // Result < 0 => extraction problem
            _tpt._size = 0;
        }
        return result;
    }

    // Identify current fingerprint on our database
    public int Identify(ref int score) {
        GRConstants result;
        int id;
        OleDbDataReader rs;
        TTemplate tptRef;

        // Checking if template is valid.
        if(!TemplateIsValid()) return ERR_INVALID_TEMPLATE;
        // Starting identification process and supplying query template.
        result = (GRConstants) _grfingerx.IdentifyPrepare(ref _tpt._tpt,
            (int)GRConstants.GR_DEFAULT_CONTEXT);
        // error?
        if (result < 0) return (int)result;
```

```csharp
    // Getting enrolled templates from database.
    rs = _DB.getTemplates();
    while(rs.Read())
    {
        // Getting current template from recordset.
        tptRef = _DB.getTemplate(rs);

        // Comparing current template.
        result = (GRConstants) _grfingerx.Identify(ref tptRef._tpt,
            ref score,(int)GRConstants.GR_DEFAULT_CONTEXT);

        // Checking if query template and the reference template match.
        if(result == GRConstants.GR_MATCH)
        {
            id = _DB.getId(rs);
            rs.Close();
            return id;
        }
        else if (result < 0)
        {
            rs.Close();
            return (int)result;
        }
    }

    // Closing recordset.
    rs.Close();
    return (int)GRConstants.GR_NOT_MATCH;
}

// Check current fingerprint against another one in our database
public int Verify(int id, ref int score) {
    TTemplate tptRef;

    // Checking if template is valid.
    if(!TemplateIsValid()) return ERR_INVALID_TEMPLATE;

    // Getting template with the supplied ID from database.
    tptRef = _DB.getTemplate(id);

    // Checking if ID was found.
    if ((tptRef._tpt==null) || (tptRef._size == 0))
    {
        return ERR_INVALID_ID;
    }

    // Comparing templates.
```

```
        return (int) _grfingerx.Verify(ref _tpt._tpt,ref tptRef._tpt,
            ref score, (int)GRConstants.GR_DEFAULT_CONTEXT);
    }

    // Show GrFinger version and type
    public void MessageVersion()
    {
        byte majorVersion=0,minorVersion=0;
        GRConstants result;
        string vStr = "";

        result = (GRConstants)_grfingerx.GetGrFingerVersion(ref majorVersion,
            ref minorVersion);
        if(result == GRConstants.GRFINGER_FULL)
            vStr = "FULL";
        else if(result == GRConstants.GRFINGER_LIGHT)
            vStr = "LIGHT";
        else if(result == GRConstants.GRFINGER_FREE)
            vStr = "FREE";

        MessageBox.Show("The GrFinger DLL version is " +
            majorVersion + "." + minorVersion + ". \n" +
            "The license type is '" + vStr + "'.","GrFinger Version");
    }

    //Importing necessary HDC functions
    [DllImport("user32.dll",EntryPoint="GetDC")]
    public static extern IntPtr GetDC(IntPtr ptr);

    [DllImport("user32.dll",EntryPoint="ReleaseDC")]
    public static extern IntPtr ReleaseDC(IntPtr hWnd,IntPtr hDc);

    // Database class.
    public DBClass _DB;
    // The last acquired image.
    public TRawImage _raw;
    // Reference to main form Image.
    public PictureBox _pbPic;

    // The template extracted from last acquired image.
    private TTemplate _tpt;
    // Reference to main form log.
    private ListBox _lbLog;
      //references Main form Auto Extract Check Box
    private CheckBox _cbAutoExtract;
      //references Main form Auto Identify Check Box
    private CheckBox _cbAutoIdentify;
```

```
    //references Main form enroll button
    Button _btEnroll;
    //references Main form extract button
    Button _btExtract;
    //references Main form identify button
    Button _btIdentify;
    //references Main form verify button
    Button _btVerify;
    // GrFingerX component
    AxGrFingerXLib.AxGrFingerXCtrl _grfingerx;
};
```

Listing 3-2. DBClass.vb

Visual Basic 2005

```
'-----------------------------------------------------------------------------
'GrFinger Sample
'(c) 2005 Griaule Tecnologia Ltda.
'http://www.griaule.com
'-----------------------------------------------------------------------------
'
'This sample is provided with "GrFinger Fingerprint Recognition Library" and
'can't run without it. It's provided just as an example of using GrFinger
'Fingerprint Recognition Library and should not be used as basis for any
'commercial product.
'
'Griaule Tecnologia makes no representations concerning either the merchantability
'of this software or the suitability of this sample for any particular purpose.
'
'THIS SAMPLE IS PROVIDED BY THE AUTHOR "AS IS" AND ANY EXPRESS OR
'IMPLIED WARRANTIES, INCLUDING, BUT NOT LIMITED TO, THE IMPLIED WARRANTIES
'OF MERCHANTABILITY AND FITNESS FOR A PARTICULAR PURPOSE ARE DISCLAIMED.
'IN NO EVENT SHALL GRIAULE BE LIABLE FOR ANY DIRECT, INDIRECT,
'INCIDENTAL, SPECIAL, EXEMPLARY, OR CONSEQUENTIAL DAMAGES (INCLUDING, BUT
'NOT LIMITED TO, PROCUREMENT OF SUBSTITUTE GOODS OR SERVICES; LOSS OF USE,
'DATA, OR PROFITS; OR BUSINESS INTERRUPTION) HOWEVER CAUSED AND ON ANY
'THEORY OF LIABILITY, WHETHER IN CONTRACT, STRICT LIABILITY, OR TORT
'(INCLUDING NEGLIGENCE OR OTHERWISE) ARISING IN ANY WAY OUT OF THE USE OF
'THIS SOFTWARE, EVEN IF ADVISED OF THE POSSIBILITY OF SUCH DAMAGE.
'
'You can download the free version of GrFinger directly from Griaule website.
'
'These notices must be retained in any copies of any part of this
'documentation and/or sample.
'
'-----------------------------------------------------------------------------
```

```vb
' -------------------------------------------------------------------------------
' Database routines
' -------------------------------------------------------------------------------

Imports System.Data.OleDb
Imports System.Runtime.InteropServices

' Template data
Public Class TTemplate
    ' Template itself
    Public tpt As System.Array = Array.CreateInstance(GetType(Byte), _
       GrFingerXLib.GRConstants.GR_MAX_SIZE_TEMPLATE)



    ' Template size
    Public Size As Long
End Class

' Template list
Public Structure TTemplates
    ' ID
    Public ID As Integer
    ' Template itself
    Public template As TTemplate
End Structure

Public Class DBClass

    ' the database we'll be connecting to
    Const DBFile As String = "GrFingerSample.mdb"
    Const ConnectionString As String = _
       "Provider=Microsoft.Jet.OLEDB.4.0;Data Source="

    ' the connection object
    Dim connection As New OleDbConnection

    ' Open connection
    Public Function OpenDB() As Boolean
        Dim filePath As String
        Try
            filePath = Application.StartupPath() & "\" & DBFile
            connection = New OleDb.OleDbConnection(ConnectionString & filePath)
            Return True
        Catch
            Return False
        End Try
    End Function
```

```vb
' Close conection
Public Sub closeDB()
    connection.Close()
End Sub

' Clear database
Public Sub clearDB()
    Dim sqlCMD As OleDbCommand = _
        New OleDbCommand("DELETE FROM enroll", connection)
    ' run "clear" query
    sqlCMD.Connection.Open()
    sqlCMD.ExecuteNonQuery()
    sqlCMD.Connection.Close()
End Sub

' Add template to database. Returns added template ID.
Public Function AddTemplate(ByRef template As TTemplate) As Long
    Dim da As New OleDbDataAdapter("select * from enroll", connection)

    ' Create SQL command containing ? parameter for BLOB.
    da.InsertCommand = New OleDbCommand( _
        "INSERT INTO enroll (template) Values(?)", connection)
    da.InsertCommand.CommandType = CommandType.Text
    da.InsertCommand.Parameters.Add("@template", _
        OleDbType.Binary, template.Size, "template")

    ' Open connection
    connection.Open()

    ' Fill DataSet.
    Dim enroll As DataSet = New DataSet
    da.Fill(enroll, "enroll")

    ' Add a new row.
    ' Create parameter for ? contained in the SQL statement.
    Dim newRow As DataRow = enroll.Tables("enroll").NewRow()
    newRow("template") = template.tpt
    enroll.Tables("enroll").Rows.Add(newRow)

    ' Include an event to fill in the Autonumber value.
    AddHandler da.RowUpdated, _
        New OleDbRowUpdatedEventHandler(AddressOf OnRowUpdated)

    ' Update DataSet.
    da.Update(enroll, "enroll")
    connection.Close()
```

```
        ' return ID
        Return newRow("ID")
End Function

' Event procedure for OnRowUpdated
Private Sub OnRowUpdated(ByVal sender As Object, _
    ByVal args As OleDbRowUpdatedEventArgs)
        ' Include a variable and a command to retrieve identity value
        ' from Access database.
        Dim newID As Integer = 0
        Dim idCMD As OleDbCommand = _
            New OleDbCommand("SELECT @@IDENTITY", connection)

        If args.StatementType = StatementType.Insert Then
            ' Retrieve identity value and store it in column
            newID = CInt(idCMD.ExecuteScalar())
            args.Row("ID") = newID
        End If
End Sub

' Returns a DataTable with all enrolled templates from database.
Public Function getTemplates() As TTemplates()
        Dim ds As New DataSet
        Dim da As New OleDbDataAdapter("select * from enroll", connection)
        Dim ttpts As TTemplates()
        Dim i As Integer

        ' Get query response
        da.Fill(ds)
        Dim tpts As DataRowCollection = ds.Tables(0).Rows
        ' Create response array
        ReDim ttpts(tpts.Count)
        ' No results?
        If tpts.Count = 0 Then Return ttpts
        ' get each template and put results in our array
        For i = 1 To tpts.Count
            ttpts(i).template = New TTemplate
            ttpts(i).ID = tpts.Item(i - 1).Item("ID")
            ttpts(i).template.tpt = tpts.Item(i - 1).Item("template")
            ttpts(i).template.Size = ttpts(i).template.tpt.Length
        Next
        Return ttpts
End Function

' Returns template with supplied ID.
Public Function getTemplate(ByVal id As Long) As Byte()
        Dim ds As New DataSet
```

```vb
        Dim da As New OleDbDataAdapter( _
            "select * from enroll where ID = " & id, connection)
        Dim tpt As New TTemplate

        ' Get query response
        da.Fill(ds)
        Dim tpts As DataRowCollection = ds.Tables(0).Rows
        ' No results?
        If tpts.Count <> 1 Then Return Nothing
        ' Deserialize template and return it
        Return tpts.Item(0).Item("template")
    End Function

End Class
```

C# 2005

```csharp
/*
--------------------------------------------------------------------------------
GrFinger Sample
(c) 2005 Griaule Tecnologia Ltda.
http://www.griaule.com
--------------------------------------------------------------------------------


This sample is provided with "GrFinger Fingerprint Recognition Library" and
can't run without it. It's provided just as an example of using GrFinger
Fingerprint Recognition Library and should not be used as basis for any
commercial product.

Griaule Tecnologia makes no representations concerning either the merchantability
of this software or the suitability of this sample for any particular purpose.

THIS SAMPLE IS PROVIDED BY THE AUTHOR "AS IS" AND ANY EXPRESS OR
IMPLIED WARRANTIES, INCLUDING, BUT NOT LIMITED TO, THE IMPLIED WARRANTIES
OF MERCHANTABILITY AND FITNESS FOR A PARTICULAR PURPOSE ARE DISCLAIMED.
IN NO EVENT SHALL GRIAULE BE LIABLE FOR ANY DIRECT, INDIRECT,
INCIDENTAL, SPECIAL, EXEMPLARY, OR CONSEQUENTIAL DAMAGES (INCLUDING, BUT
NOT LIMITED TO, PROCUREMENT OF SUBSTITUTE GOODS OR SERVICES; LOSS OF USE,
DATA, OR PROFITS; OR BUSINESS INTERRUPTION) HOWEVER CAUSED AND ON ANY
THEORY OF LIABILITY, WHETHER IN CONTRACT, STRICT LIABILITY, OR TORT
(INCLUDING NEGLIGENCE OR OTHERWISE) ARISING IN ANY WAY OUT OF THE USE OF
THIS SOFTWARE, EVEN IF ADVISED OF THE POSSIBILITY OF SUCH DAMAGE.

You can download the free version of GrFinger directly from Griaule website.

These notices must be retained in any copies of any part of this
documentation and/or sample.
```

```
    ---------------------------------------------------------------------------
*/

// ---------------------------------------------------------------------------
// Database routines
// ---------------------------------------------------------------------------

using System;
using System.Data;
using System.Data.OleDb;
using GrFingerXLib;
using System.Runtime.InteropServices;

// the template class
public class TTemplate
{
    // Template data.
    public System.Array _tpt;
    // Template size
    public int _size;

    public TTemplate(){
        // Create a byte buffer for the template
        _tpt = new byte[(int)GRConstants.GR_MAX_SIZE_TEMPLATE];
        _size = 0;
    }
}

// the database class
public class DBClass{

    // the connection object
    private OleDbConnection _connection;

    // temporary template for retrieving data from DB
    private TTemplate tptBlob;

    // the database we'll be connecting to
    public readonly string CONNECTION_STRING =
        "Provider=Microsoft.Jet.OLEDB.4.0;Data Source=GrFingerSample.mdb";

    public DBClass(){
    }

    // Open connection
    public bool openDB()
    {
```

```
        _connection = new OleDbConnection();
        _connection.ConnectionString = CONNECTION_STRING;
        try{
            _connection.Open();
        }
        catch{
            return false;
        }
        tptBlob = new TTemplate();
        return true;
}//END

// Close conection
public bool closeDB()
{
    if(_connection.State != ConnectionState.Closed)
      _connection.Close();
    return true;
}

// Clear database
public bool clearDB()
{
    OleDbCommand cmdClear = null;
    cmdClear = new OleDbCommand("DELETE FROM enroll", _connection);

    // run "clear" query
    if(_connection.State == ConnectionState.Open)
        cmdClear.ExecuteNonQuery();

    return true;
}


// Add template to database. Returns added template ID.
public bool addTemplate(TTemplate tpt,ref int id)
{
    OleDbCommand cmdInsert = null;
    OleDbParameter dbParamInsert = null;
    OleDbCommand cmdSelect =  null;

    try{
        // Create SQL command containing ? parameter for BLOB.
        cmdInsert = new OleDbCommand(
            "INSERT INTO enroll(template) values(?) ", _connection);
        // Create parameter for ? contained in the SQL statement.
        System.Byte [] temp = new System.Byte[tpt._size + 1];
```

```
            System.Array.Copy(tpt._tpt, 0, temp, 0, tpt._size);

            dbParamInsert = new OleDbParameter("@template",
                OleDbType.VarBinary, tpt._size,
                ParameterDirection.Input, false, 0, 0,"ID",
                DataRowVersion.Current, temp);
            cmdInsert.Parameters.Add(dbParamInsert);

            //execute query
            if(_connection.State == ConnectionState.Open)
                cmdInsert.ExecuteNonQuery();
        }
        catch{
            return false;
        }

        try{
            // Create SQL command containing ? parameter for BLOB.
            cmdSelect = new OleDbCommand(
                "SELECT top 1 ID FROM enroll ORDER BY ID DESC", _connection);

            id = System.Convert.ToInt32(cmdSelect.ExecuteScalar());
        }
        catch {
            return false;
        }

        return true;
    }

    // Returns an OleDbDataReader with all enrolled templates from database.
    public OleDbDataReader  getTemplates()
    {
        OleDbCommand   cmdGetTemplates;
        OleDbDataReader   rs;

        //setting up command
        cmdGetTemplates =  new OleDbCommand("SELECT * FROM enroll", _connection);
        rs = cmdGetTemplates.ExecuteReader();

        return rs;
    }


    // Returns template with the supplied ID.
    public TTemplate getTemplate(int id)
    {
```

```csharp
        OleDbCommand cmd = null;
        OleDbDataReader dr = null;
        tptBlob._size = 0;
        try
        {
            cmd =  new OleDbCommand(System.String.Concat(
                "SELECT * FROM enroll WHERE ID = ",
                System.Convert.ToString((int)id)), _connection);
            dr = cmd.ExecuteReader();
            // Get query response
            dr.Read();
            getTemplate(dr);
            dr.Close();
        }
        catch{
            dr.Close();
        }
        return tptBlob;
    }


    // Return template data from an OleDbDataReader
    public TTemplate getTemplate(OleDbDataReader rs)
    {
        long readedBytes;
        tptBlob._size = 0;
        // alloc space
        System.Byte[] temp = new System.Byte[
            (int)GRConstants.GR_MAX_SIZE_TEMPLATE];
        // get bytes
        readedBytes = rs.GetBytes(1, 0, temp, 0,temp.Length);
        // copy to structure
        System.Array.Copy(temp, 0, tptBlob._tpt,0,(int)readedBytes);
        // set real size
        tptBlob._size = (int)readedBytes;

        return tptBlob;
    }


    // Return enrollment ID from an OleDbDataReader
    public int getId(OleDbDataReader rs)
    {
        return rs.GetInt32(0);
    }
}
```

CHAPTER 4

■ ■ ■

Infrared Programming

With all the buzz around WiFi, Bluetooth, and other wireless technologies, it's easy to overlook one of the simplest and most common forms of wireless communications—infrared. Anyone who has ever used a remote control has used it! Infrared uses the invisible spectrum of light just beyond red in the visible spectrum. You can use it in applications for short-range, point-to-point data transfer. Because it uses light, line-of-sight is a prerequisite for infrared. Despite this limitation, infrared is increasingly popular in devices such as digital cameras, PDAs, and notebook computers.

In this chapter, I will show you how to build an application that allows two devices (as well as computers) to communicate wirelessly using infrared. You can adapt the programming technique illustrated in this chapter for other programming tasks, such as writing wireless network games, and so on.

Introducing IrDA

Founded in 1993 as a nonprofit organization, the Infrared Data Association (IrDA) is an international organization that creates and promotes interoperable, low-cost infrared data interconnection standards that allow users to point one device at another and have it work. The Infrared Data Association standards support a broad range of appliances, computing, and communication devices.

The term *IrDA* also refers to the protocols for infrared communications, not exclusively to the nonprofit body. Currently four versions of IrDA exist, with their differences mainly being transfer speed:

- Serial Infrared (SIR) is the original standard with transfer speeds of up to 115Kbps.

- Medium Infrared (MIR) has improved transfer speeds of 1.152Mbps. This is not widely implemented.

- Fast Infrared (FIR) has speeds of up to 4Mbps. Most new computers implement this standard.

- Very Fast Infrared (VFIR) has speeds of up to 16Mbps. This is not widely implemented yet.

Future versions of the IrDA will boost speeds to 50Mbps. When two devices with two different IrDA implementations communicate with each other, they'll both step down to the lower transfer speed.

In terms of operating range, infrared devices can communicate up to 1–2 meters (3–7 feet). Depending on the implementation, if a device uses a lower power version, the range can be stepped down to a mere 20–30 centimeters (8–12 inches). This is crucial for low-power devices.

All data packets exchanged are protected using a cyclic redundancy check (CRC), which uses a number derived from the transmitted data to verify its integrity. CRC-16 is used for speeds up to 1.152Mbps, and CRC-32 is used for speeds up to 4Mbps. The IrDA also defines bidirectional communication for infrared communications.

Creating Infrared Communications Between Windows Mobile Devices

The first application you will build in this chapter is a Pocket PC application that allows two Pocket PCs to communicate with each other using the built-in infrared port. Although this doesn't have much practical usage in the real world (who would want to point their Pocket PCs at each other and then type on their Pocket PCs instead of talking face to face?), this application serves as a good foundation for you to learn how to build a robust application that persistently listens for incoming infrared data and at the same time allows you to send data via infrared. You can easily adapt this application for other uses, such as file transfer using infrared, wireless network games, or any other cool applications you can think of that use infrared.

What You Need

For this project, you need a Windows Mobile 5.0 Pocket PC device with an infrared port. For my testing, I used a Dopod 838 (see Figure 4-1).

Figure 4-1. *The Dopod 838*

Creating the Project

To begin creating the application, launch Microsoft Visual Studio 2005, and create a Windows Mobile 5.0 Pocket PC project, as shown in Figure 4-2. Name the project **IRChat**.

■**Tip** By default, Visual Studio 2005 does not come with the Windows Mobile 5.0 Pocket PC project template. You need to download the Windows Mobile 5.0 SDK for Pocket PC by going to http://www.microsoft.com/ downloads/ and searching for *Windows Mobile 5.0 for Pocket PC SDK*.

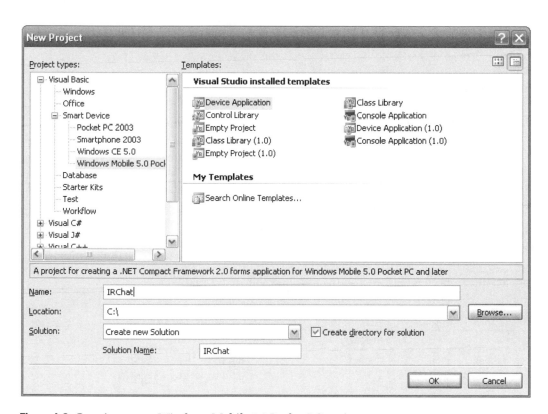

Figure 4-2. *Creating a new Windows Mobile 5.0 Pocket PC project*

You will start by first building the interface of the chat application. Populate the default Form1 with the following controls (see also Figure 4-3 and name the controls as shown):

- TextBox
- StatusBar
- MainMenu

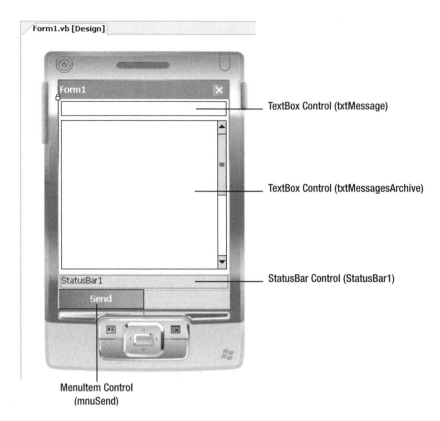

TextBox Control (txtMessage)

TextBox Control (txtMessagesArchive)

StatusBar Control (StatusBar1)

MenuItem Control
(mnuSend)

Figure 4-3. *Populating the default Form1 with the various controls*

Set the properties for the various controls as shown in Table 4-1.

Table 4-1. *Setting the Properties for the Various Controls*

Control	Property	Value
txtMessage	Anchor	Top, Bottom, Left, Right
txtMessagesArchive	Anchor	Top, Bottom, Left, Right
txtMessagesArchive	MultiLine	True
txtMessagesArchive	ScrollBars	Vertical

Coding the Application

You are now ready to code the application. Switch to the code-behind of Form1, and add the following namespaces.

Visual Basic 2005

```
Imports System.Net
Imports System.IO
Imports System.Net.Sockets
```

C# 2005

```
using System.Net;
using System.IO;
using System.Net.Sockets;
```

To use the relevant libraries in the .NET Compact Framework for infrared communications, you need to add a reference to the System.Net.IrDa library to the project. Right-click the project name (IRChat) in Solution Explorer, and select Add Reference. Double-click the System.Net.IrDa component, and click OK.

■**Note** All the infrared functions are located in the System.Net.Sockets namespace.

Next, declare the following constants and member variables.

Visual Basic 2005

```
Public Class Form1
    Inherits System.Windows.Forms.Form

    '---define the constants---
    Const MAX_MESSAGE_SIZE As Integer = 1024
    Const MAX_TRIES As Integer = 3

    '---define the member variables---
    Private ServiceName As String = "default"
```

C# 2005

```
public partial class Form1 : Form
{

    //---define the constants---
    const int MAX_MESSAGE_SIZE = 1024;
    const int MAX_TRIES = 3;

    //---define the member variables---
    private string ServiceName = "default";
```

The MAX_MESSAGE_SIZE constant is the maximum size of a message exchanged, and MAX_TRIES is the maximum number of times to try sending a message before giving up. The ServiceName variable is a unique identifier for an infrared communication session.

Receiving Messages

When the application is loaded, it needs to start listening for messages in the background. And so, in the Form1_Load event, invoke the ReceiveLoop() method on a separate thread to continuously listen for incoming messages.

■**Note** Henceforth in this chapter, to make Visual Studio 2005 automatically create the event handler for a control (such as a form's Load event or a button's Click event), double-click the control to create the event handler.

Visual Basic 2005

```
Private Sub Form1_Load( _
    ByVal sender As System.Object, _
    ByVal e As System.EventArgs) Handles MyBase.Load

    txtMessage.Focus()

    '---receive incoming messages as a separate thread---
    Dim t1 As System.Threading.Thread
    t1 = New Threading.Thread(AddressOf ReceiveLoop)
    t1.Start()
End Sub
```

C# 2005

```
private void Form1_Load(object sender, EventArgs e)
{
    txtMessage.Focus();

    //---receive incoming messages as a separate thread---
    System.Threading.Thread t1;
    t1 = new System.Threading.Thread(ReceiveLoop);
    t1.Start();
}
```

Essentially, I've spun off a separate thread to invoke the ReceiveLoop() method. The aim here is to listen for messages in the background so you can send messages at any time. The code for the ReceiveLoop() subroutine is as follows.

Visual Basic 2005

```
Public Sub ReceiveLoop()
    Dim strReceived As String

    strReceived = ReceiveMessage()
```

```
    '---keep on listening for new message---
    While True
        If strReceived <> String.Empty Then
            txtMessagesArchive.BeginInvoke( _
            New myDelegate(AddressOf UpdateTextBox), _
            New Object() {strReceived})
        End If
        strReceived = ReceiveMessage()
    End While
End Sub
```

C# 2005

```
public void ReceiveLoop()
{
    string strReceived;
    strReceived = ReceiveMessage();

    //---keep on listening for new message---
    while (true)
    {
        if (strReceived != string.Empty)
        {
            txtMessagesArchive.BeginInvoke(
                new myDelegate(UpdateTextBox),
                new object[] { strReceived });
        }
        strReceived = ReceiveMessage();
    }
}
```

The main use of the ReceiveLoop() subroutine is to repeatedly invoke the ReceiveMessage() function. The ReceiveMessage() function returns the message received from the infrared port. The code for the ReceiveMessage() method is as follows.

Visual Basic 2005

```
Private Function ReceiveMessage() As String
    Dim bytesRead As Integer = 0
    Dim listener As IrDAListener = New IrDAListener(ServiceName)
    Dim client As IrDAClient = Nothing
    Dim stream As System.IO.Stream = Nothing
    Dim Buffer(MAX_MESSAGE_SIZE - 1) As Byte
    Dim str As String = String.Empty
    Try
        listener.Start()

        '---blocking call---
```

```
            client = listener.AcceptIrDAClient()
            stream = client.GetStream()
            bytesRead = stream.Read(Buffer, 0, Buffer.Length)

            '---format the received message---
            str = ">" & _
                System.Text.ASCIIEncoding.ASCII.GetString( _
                Buffer, 0, bytesRead)
        Catch ex As SocketException
            '---ignore error---
        Catch e As Exception
            StatusBar1.BeginInvoke( _
                New myDelegate(AddressOf UpdateStatus), New Object() _
                {e.ToString})
        Finally
            If (Not stream Is Nothing) Then stream.Close()
            If (Not client Is Nothing) Then client.Close()
            listener.Stop()
        End Try
        Return str
End Function
```

C# 2005

```
private string ReceiveMessage()
{
    int bytesRead = 0;
    IrDAListener listener = new IrDAListener(ServiceName);
    IrDAClient client = null;
    System.IO.Stream stream = null;
    byte[] Buffer = new byte[MAX_MESSAGE_SIZE - 1];
    string str = string.Empty;
    try
    {
        listener.Start();

        //---blocking call---
        client = listener.AcceptIrDAClient();
        stream = client.GetStream();
        bytesRead = stream.Read(Buffer, 0, Buffer.Length);
        //---format the received message---
        str = ">" +
            System.Text.ASCIIEncoding.ASCII.GetString(
            Buffer, 0, bytesRead);
    }
    catch (SocketException ex)
    {
```

```
        //---ignore error---
    }
    catch (Exception e)
    {
        StatusBar1.BeginInvoke(new myDelegate(UpdateStatus),
            new object[] { e.ToString() });
    }
    finally
    {
        if ((!(stream == null)))
        {
            stream.Close();
        }
        if ((!(client == null)))
        {
            client.Close();
        }
        listener.Stop();
    }
    return str;
}
```

Let's spend some time going through this function. First, you set up the relevant variables for this function. In particular, you created an IrDAListener object. The IrDAListener object listens for incoming data through the infrared port. It takes the ServiceName argument.

Tip Two devices communicating through infrared must have the same service name.

You also created an IrDAClient object for sending and receiving data from the other device. The IrDAListener object starts listening for incoming data and returns an IrDAClient object when data is received. You then use a Stream object to read the data on the stream and format it for display.

Finally, the ReceiveMessage() function returns the data formatted in a fashion ready to be displayed on the form.

Displaying the Received Messages

Since Windows Forms controls aren't thread-safe, accessing Windows controls from another thread will have unpredictable results. As such, you need to use a delegate method to call the UpdateTextBox() method to update the TextBox control with the received message.

Visual Basic 2005

```
Private Delegate Sub myDelegate(ByVal str As String)
```

C# 2005

```
private delegate void myDelegate(string str);
```

The UpdateTextBox() subroutine displays the received message in a TextBox control.

Visual Basic 2005

```
Private Sub UpdateTextBox(ByVal str As String)
    '---delegate to update the TextBox control---
    txtMessagesArchive.Text = str & vbCrLf & _
        txtMessagesArchive.Text
End Sub
```

C# 2005

```
private void UpdateTextBox(string str)
{
    //---delegate to update the TextBox control---
    txtMessagesArchive.Text = str + "\r\n" +
        txtMessagesArchive.Text;
}
```

The UpdateStatus() subroutine displays status information on the StatusBar control.

Visual Basic 2005

```
Private Sub UpdateStatus(ByVal str As String)
    '---delegate to update the StatusBar control---
    StatusBar1.Text = str
End Sub
```

C# 2005

```
private void UpdateStatus(string str)
{
    //---delegate to update the StatusBar control---
    StatusBar1.Text = str;
}
```

Sending Messages

Now that you've seen how to receive messages, you will write the code for sending messages.
When the Send menu item is clicked, you will invoke the SendMessage() subroutine.

Visual Basic 2005

```
Private Sub mnuSend_Click( _
   ByVal sender As System.Object, _
   ByVal e As System.EventArgs) _
   Handles mnuSend.Click
    mnuSend.Enabled = False
    sendMessage(MAX_TRIES, txtMessage.Text)
    mnuSend.Enabled = True
    txtMessage.Text = String.Empty
    txtMessage.Focus()
End Sub
```

C# 2005

```
private void mnuSend_Click(object sender, EventArgs e)
{
    mnuSend.Enabled = false;
    SendMessage(MAX_TRIES, txtMessage.Text);
    mnuSend.Enabled = true;
    txtMessage.Text = string.Empty;
    txtMessage.Focus();
}
```

The SendMessage() subroutine first tries to establish a connection with the other device until the number of retries is exceeded. Once a connection is established, it writes to the other device using an I/O Stream object. Finally, it closes the stream and the connection.

Visual Basic 2005

```
Private Sub SendMessage( _
   ByVal NumRetries As Integer, ByVal str As String)
   Dim client As IrDAClient = Nothing
   Dim CurrentTries As Integer = 0

   '---try to establish a connection---
   Do
       Try
           client = New IrDAClient(ServiceName)
       Catch se As Exception
           If (CurrentTries >= NumRetries) Then
               Throw se
           End If
       End Try
       CurrentTries = CurrentTries + 1
   Loop While client Is Nothing And CurrentTries < NumRetries

   '---timeout occurred---
   If (client Is Nothing) Then
```

```vb
        StatusBar1.BeginInvoke( _
            New myDelegate(AddressOf UpdateStatus), New Object() _
            {"Error establishing contact"})
        Return
    End If

    '---send the message over a stream object---
    Dim stream As System.IO.Stream = Nothing
    Try
        stream = client.GetStream()
        stream.Write( _
            System.Text.ASCIIEncoding.ASCII.GetBytes(str), 0, _
            str.Length)

        '---update the status bar---
        StatusBar1.BeginInvoke( _
            New myDelegate(AddressOf UpdateStatus), New Object() _
            {"Message sent!"})

        '---display the message that was sent---
        txtMessagesArchive.Text = str & vbCrLf & _
            txtMessagesArchive.Text
    Catch e As Exception
        StatusBar1.BeginInvoke( _
            New myDelegate(AddressOf UpdateStatus), New Object() _
            {"Error sending message."})
    Finally
        If (Not stream Is Nothing) Then stream.Close()
        If (Not client Is Nothing) Then client.Close()
    End Try
End Sub
```

C# 2005

```csharp
private void SendMessage(int NumRetries, string str)
{
    IrDAClient client = null;
    int CurrentTries = 0;
    //---try to establish a connection---
    do
    {
        try
        {
            client = new IrDAClient(ServiceName);
        }
        catch (Exception se)
        {
            if ((CurrentTries >= NumRetries))
```

```
            {
                throw se;
            }
        }
        CurrentTries = CurrentTries + 1;
    } while (client == null & CurrentTries < NumRetries);

    //---timeout occurred---
    if ((client == null))
    {
        StatusBar1.BeginInvoke(new myDelegate(UpdateStatus),
            new object[] { "Error establishing contact" });
        return;
    }

    //---send the message over a stream object---
    System.IO.Stream stream = null;
    try
    {
        stream = client.GetStream();
        stream.Write(
            System.Text.ASCIIEncoding.ASCII.GetBytes(str), 0,
            str.Length);

        //---update the status bar---
        StatusBar1.BeginInvoke(new myDelegate(UpdateStatus),
            new object[] { "Message sent!" });

        //---display the message that was sent---
        txtMessagesArchive.Text = str + "\r\n" +
            txtMessagesArchive.Text;
    }
    catch (Exception e)
    {
        StatusBar1.BeginInvoke(new myDelegate(UpdateStatus),
            new object[] { "Error sending message." });
    }
    finally
    {
        if (!(stream == null))
        {
            stream.Close();
        }
        if (!(client == null))
        {
            client.Close();
        }
    }
}
```

Compiling and Deploying the Application

That's it! To test the application, you need to install the application on two Windows Mobile 5.0 Pocket PCs. The easiest way to do this is to connect each Windows Mobile 5.0 device to the development machine and use Visual Studio 2005 to deploy the application on the device. When you press F5, the application will automatically be copied on to the device.

To start chatting using infrared, align the infrared port of each Pocket PC to face each other, and you can then start chatting. Figure 4-4 shows two Windows Mobile 5.0 Pocket PCs communicating using infrared.

Figure 4-4. *Testing the application using two Windows Mobile 5.0 Pocket PCs*

Creating Infrared Communications on the Desktop

In the previous project, you saw how to enable two Windows Mobile 5.0 Pocket PCs to communicate with each other using the infrared ports. Using infrared on the Pocket PC is easy using the System.Net.IrDA library available in the .NET Compact Framework. What about using infrared on a desktop computer? Unfortunately, the .NET Framework does not come with the System.Net.IrDA library, and hence you cannot directly use infrared using the .NET Framework.

Fortunately, Peter Foot (http://www.peterfoot.net/), a fellow MVP, has written the 32feet.NET library that makes infrared programming available on the desktop. 32feet.NET is a project that aims to make wireless networking (via Bluetooth and IrDA) much more easily accessible from .NET code, be it on mobile devices or on desktop computers. You can download the latest version of 32feet.NET (version 2.0.60828) from http://32feet.net/files/. Hence, in this project, you will port your Windows Mobile 5.0 application to the desktop and enable infrared programming using the 32feet.NET library.

What You Need

Most desktop computers and notebooks today do not come with infrared ports anymore. Hence, if you want to use infrared as a communication option, you need to equip your computer with one. The easiest way is to buy a USB infrared adapter (see Figure 4-5) that plugs into the USB port. Most adapters are plug and play; connect it to your computer, and Windows XP should be able to use it immediately.

Creating the Project

Using Visual Studio 2005, create a new Windows Application project, and name it **IRChat_Desktop**. Populate the default Form1 with the following controls (see also Figure 4-6, and name them accordingly):

Figure 4-5. *A USB infrared adapter*

- TextBox control

- Button control

- StatusStrip (add a StatusLabel control within it) control

Set the MultiLine and ReadOnly properties of the txtMessagesArchive control to True, and set its ScrollBars property to Vertical.

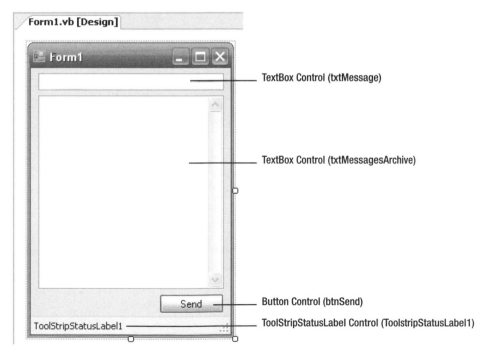

Figure 4-6 labels:
- TextBox Control (txtMessage)
- TextBox Control (txtMessagesArchive)
- Button Control (btnSend)
- ToolStripStatusLabel Control (ToolstripStatusLabel1)

Figure 4-6. *Populating the default Form1 with the various controls*

■**Note** You need to first download and install the `32feet.NET` library before coding the application.

Add a reference to the `InTheHand.Net.Personal` component to the project by right-clicking the project name in Solution Explorer and then selecting Add Reference. Select the `InTheHand.Net.Personal` component, and click OK (see Figure 4-7).

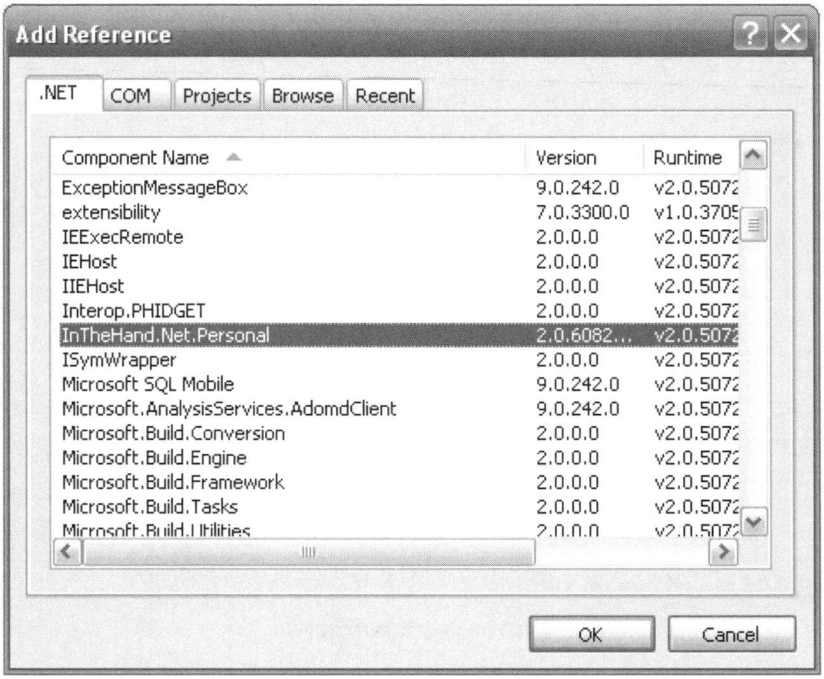

Figure 4-7. *Adding a reference to the InTheHand.Net.Personal component*

The next step is to begin coding the application. Because most of the code is similar to what you saw in the previous project, I will simply show you the code and point out the changes you need to make so you can use the libraries in the `InTheHand.Net.Personal` library.

Importing the Namespaces

In addition to importing the three namespaces as you did earlier, import the following namespace for use with the `InTheHand.Net.Personal` component.

Visual Basic 2005

```
Imports System.Net
Imports System.IO
Imports System.Net.Sockets
Imports InTheHand.Net.Sockets
```

C# 2005

```
using System.Net;
using System.IO;
using System.Net.Sockets;
using InTheHand.Net.Sockets;
```

Essentially, in the Windows Mobile 5.0 application, you are using the System.Net.IrDA library (in particular, the functions located in the System.Net.Sockets namespace) for all the infrared functionalities, whereas for the desktop version of the application, all the necessary infrared functionalities are fulfilled by the InTheHand.Net.Personal library (located within the InTheHand.Net.Sockets namespace). Because of this, there are almost no code changes for the infrared portion of the project.

Declaring the Constants and Member Variables

The following code shows how to declare the constants and member variables.

Visual Basic 2005

```
Public Class Form1
    '---define the constants---
    Const MAX_MESSAGE_SIZE As Integer = 1024
    Const MAX_TRIES As Integer = 3
    '---define the member variable---
    Private ServiceName As String = "default"
```

C# 2005

```
public partial class Form1 : Form
{
    //---define the constants---
    const int MAX_MESSAGE_SIZE = 1024;
    const int MAX_TRIES = 3;

    //---define the member variable---
    private string ServiceName = "default";
```

Coding the Form1_Load() Event

The following code shows the Form1_Load event.

Visual Basic 2005

```
Private Sub Form1_Load( _
   ByVal sender As System.Object, _
   ByVal e As System.EventArgs) _
   Handles MyBase.Load
```

```
    txtMessage.Focus()
    '---receive incoming messages as a separate thread---
    Dim t1 As System.Threading.Thread
    t1 = New Threading.Thread(AddressOf ReceiveLoop)
    t1.Start()
End Sub
```

C# 2005

```
private void Form1_Load(object sender, EventArgs e)
{
    txtMessage.Focus();

    //---receive incoming messages as a separate thread---
    System.Threading.Thread t1;
    t1 = new System.Threading.Thread(ReceiveLoop);
    t1.Start();
}
```

Coding the ReceiveLoop() Subroutine

The following code shows how to code the ReceiveLoop() subroutine.

Visual Basic 2005

```
Public Sub ReceiveLoop()
    Dim strReceived As String
    strReceived = ReceiveMessage()
    '---keep on listening for new message---
    While True
        If strReceived <> String.Empty Then
            txtMessagesArchive.BeginInvoke( _
            New myDelegate(AddressOf UpdateTextBox), _
                New Object() {strReceived})
        End If
        strReceived = ReceiveMessage()
    End While
End Sub
```

C# 2005

```
public void ReceiveLoop()
{
    string strReceived;
    strReceived = ReceiveMessage();

    //---keep on listening for new message---
    while (true)
    {
```

```
        if (strReceived != string.Empty)
        {
            txtMessagesArchive.BeginInvoke(new
                myDelegate(UpdateTextBox),
                new object[] { strReceived });
        }
        strReceived = ReceiveMessage();
    }
}
```

Coding the ReceiveMessage() Function

The following code shows how to code the ReceiveMessage() function.

Visual Basic 2005

```vb
Private Function ReceiveMessage() As String
    Dim bytesRead As Integer = 0
    Dim listener As IrDAListener = New IrDAListener(ServiceName)
    Dim client As IrDAClient = Nothing
    Dim stream As System.IO.Stream = Nothing
    Dim Buffer(MAX_MESSAGE_SIZE - 1) As Byte
    Dim str As String = String.Empty
    Try
        listener.Start()

        '---blocking call---
        client = listener.AcceptIrDAClient()
        stream = client.GetStream()
        bytesRead = stream.Read(Buffer, 0, Buffer.Length)

        '---display the received message---
        str = ">" & _
            System.Text.ASCIIEncoding.ASCII.GetString( _
            Buffer, 0, bytesRead)
    Catch ex As SocketException
        '---ignore error---
    Catch e As Exception
        txtMessagesArchive.BeginInvoke( _
            New myDelegate(AddressOf UpdateStatus), New Object() _
            {e.ToString})
    Finally
        If (Not stream Is Nothing) Then stream.Close()
        If (Not client Is Nothing) Then client.Close()
        listener.Stop()
    End Try
    Return str
End Function
```

C# 2005

```csharp
private string ReceiveMessage()
{
    int bytesRead = 0;
    IrDAListener listener = new IrDAListener(ServiceName);
    IrDAClient client = null;
    System.IO.Stream stream = null;
    byte[] Buffer = new byte[MAX_MESSAGE_SIZE - 1];
    string str = string.Empty;
    try
    {
        listener.Start();

        //---blocking call---
        client = listener.AcceptIrDAClient();
        stream = client.GetStream();
        bytesRead = stream.Read(Buffer, 0, Buffer.Length);

        //---format the received message---
        str = ">" +
            System.Text.ASCIIEncoding.ASCII.GetString(
            Buffer, 0, bytesRead);
    }
    catch (SocketException ex)
    {
        //---ignore error---
    }
    catch (Exception e)
    {
        txtMessagesArchive.BeginInvoke(new
            myDelegate(UpdateStatus),
            new object[] { e.ToString() });
    }
    finally
    {
        if (!(stream == null))
        {
            stream.Close();
        }
        if (!(client == null))
        {
            client.Close();
        }
        listener.Stop();
    }
    return str;
}
```

Coding the Delegate and the UpdateTextBox() and UpdateStatus() Subroutines

The following shows how to code the delegate and the UpdateTextBox() and UpdateStatus() subroutines.

Visual Basic 2005

```
Private Delegate Sub myDelegate(ByVal str As String)

Private Sub UpdateTextBox(ByVal str As String)
    '---delegate to update the TextBox control
    txtMessagesArchive.Text = str & vbCrLf & _
        txtMessagesArchive.Text
End Sub

Private Sub UpdateStatus(ByVal str As String)
    '---delegate to update the StatusBar control
    ToolStripStatusLabel1.Text = str
End Sub
```

C# 2005

```
private delegate void myDelegate(string str);

private void UpdateTextBox(string str)
{
    //---delegate to update the TextBox control---
    txtMessagesArchive.Text = str + Environment.NewLine +
        txtMessagesArchive.Text;
}

private void UpdateStatus(string str)
{
    //---delegate to update the StatusBar control---
    ToolStripStatusLabel1.Text = str;
}
```

Coding the SendMessage() Subroutine

The following shows how to code the SendMessage() subroutine.

Visual Basic 2005

```
Private Sub SendMessage( _
   ByVal NumRetries As Integer, ByVal str As String)
    Dim client As IrDAClient = Nothing
    Dim CurrentTries As Integer = 0
```

```vb
    '---try to establish a connection---
    Do
        Try
            client = New IrDAClient(ServiceName)
        Catch se As Exception
            If (CurrentTries >= NumRetries) Then
                Throw se
            End If
        End Try
        CurrentTries = CurrentTries + 1
    Loop While client Is Nothing And CurrentTries < NumRetries

    '---timeout occurred---
    If (client Is Nothing) Then
        txtMessagesArchive.BeginInvoke( _
            New myDelegate(AddressOf UpdateStatus), New Object() _
            {"Error establishing contact"})
        Return
    End If

    '---send the message over a stream object---
    Dim stream As System.IO.Stream = Nothing
    Try
        stream = client.GetStream()
        stream.Write( _
            System.Text.ASCIIEncoding.ASCII.GetBytes(str), 0, _
            str.Length)

        '---update the status bar---
        txtMessagesArchive.BeginInvoke( _
            New myDelegate(AddressOf UpdateStatus), New Object() _
            {"Message sent!"})

        '---display the message that was sent---
        txtMessagesArchive.Text = str & vbCrLf & _
            txtMessagesArchive.Text
    Catch e As Exception
        txtMessagesArchive.BeginInvoke( _
            New myDelegate(AddressOf UpdateStatus), New Object() _
            {"Error sending message."})
    Finally
        If (Not stream Is Nothing) Then stream.Close()
        If (Not client Is Nothing) Then client.Close()
    End Try
End Sub
```

C# 2005

```csharp
private void SendMessage(int NumRetries, string str)
{
    IrDAClient client = null;
    int CurrentTries = 0;

    //---try to establish a connection---
    do
    {
        try
        {
            client = new IrDAClient(ServiceName);
        }
        catch (Exception se)
        {
            if ((CurrentTries >= NumRetries))
            {
                throw se;
            }
        }
        CurrentTries = CurrentTries + 1;
    } while (client == null & CurrentTries < NumRetries);

    //---timeout occurred---
    if ((client == null))
    {
        txtMessagesArchive.BeginInvoke(new
            myDelegate(UpdateStatus),
            new object[] { "Error establishing contact" });
        return;
    }

    //---send the message over a stream object---
    System.IO.Stream stream = null;
    try
    {
        stream = client.GetStream();
        stream.Write(
            System.Text.ASCIIEncoding.ASCII.GetBytes(str), 0, _
            str.Length);

        //---update the status bar---
        txtMessagesArchive.BeginInvoke(new
            myDelegate(UpdateStatus),
            new object[] { "Message sent!" });
```

```
            //---display the message that was sent---
            txtMessagesArchive.Text = str + Environment.NewLine +
                txtMessagesArchive.Text;
        }
        catch (Exception e)
        {
            txtMessagesArchive.BeginInvoke(new
                myDelegate(UpdateStatus),
                new object[] { "Error sending message." });
        }
        finally
        {
            if (!(stream == null))
            {
                stream.Close();
            }
            if (!(stream == null)))))
            {
                client.Close();
            }
        }
    }
}
```

Coding the Send Button Control

The following shows how to code the Send button control.

Visual Basic 2005

```
Private Sub btnSend_Click( _
    ByVal sender As System.Object, _
    ByVal e As System.EventArgs) _
    Handles btnSend.Click
     btnSend.Enabled = False
     SendMessage(MAX_TRIES, txtMessage.Text)
     btnSend.Enabled = True
     txtMessage.Text = String.Empty
     txtMessage.Focus()
End Sub
```

C# 2005

```
private void btnSend_Click(object sender, EventArgs e)
{
    btnSend.Enabled = false;
    SendMessage(MAX_TRIES, txtMessage.Text);
    btnSend.Enabled = true;
    txtMessage.Text = string.Empty;
    txtMessage.Focus();
}
```

Testing the Application

Testing the application is straightforward. Follow these steps:

1. Connect the USB infrared adapter to your computer (if your computer does not have a built-in infrared port).

2. Press F5 in Visual Studio 2005 to run the application.

3. Using one of the Pocket PCs used in the first project, launch the IRChat application. The application is by default located in My Device/Program Files/IRChat (use the File Explorer in the Pocket PC to navigate to this directory, and launch the application by tapping on IRChat.exe).

4. Align the infrared port on the Pocket PC with the USB infrared adapter.

You can now start chatting!

Summary

In this chapter, I gave you a bit of background on infrared technology and showed you how to use Microsoft Visual Studio 2005 to develop infrared-enabled Pocket PC and desktop applications. Though the two sample applications are used for chatting, you should be able to easily adapt them for your own applications.

CHAPTER 5

■■■

Fun with RFID

Radio frequency identification (RFID) is one of the buzzwords receiving a lot of coverage in the IT world lately. An RFID system is an identification system that uses radio waves to retrieve data from a device called a *tag* or a *transponder*. RFID is all around us in our daily lives—in the supermarkets, libraries, bookstores, and so on. RFID provides a quick and efficient way to collect information, such as stocktaking in a warehouse or tracking of the whereabouts of items.

In this chapter, you will learn how to build a Windows application that incorporates RFID technology for data collection. You will use two RFID readers and understand their relative pros and cons.

Introducing RFID

At its bare minimum, an RFID system consists of two main components:

- Reader/writer

- Tags

An RFID reader/writer contains a *scanning antenna* and a *transceiver*. It uses the scanning antenna to send out radio frequency signals in a relatively short range. The radio frequency sent out is used to communicate and power the *tags* (also known as *transponders*; see Figure 5-1 for an example of a tag) that are within range, which will then transmit the data on the tag to the reader. The scanning antenna then picks up the information sent out by the tag. The data is then interpreted and decoded by the transceiver.

Two types of RFID tags exist: *active* and *passive*. Active RFID tags have their own power source, and hence they can transmit signals that travel farther. In contrast, passive RFID tags have

Figure 5-1. *An EPC RFID tag used for Wal-Mart (image courtesy of* http://en.wikipedia.org/wiki/Image:EPC-RFID-TAG.jpg*)*

no power source, and they have to rely solely on the signal sent from the scanning antenna to power them. Hence, the range supported by passive tag is limited. Active tags are much bigger in size than passive tags, and active tags have a limited life span. Passive tags, on the other hand, are much smaller in size and have a virtually unlimited life span.

RFID systems are categorized by their transmitting frequencies and are broadly grouped into three bands: low frequency (LF), high frequency (HF), and ultra high frequency (UHF). Table 5-1 shows the different frequencies used by the three bands and shows their characteristics.

Table 5-1. *Three Bands of RFID Systems**

Frequency Band	Common Frequency	Typical Communication Range	Maximum Communication Range	Data Rate	Reader Cost
LF	125kHz to 135kHz	20cm	100cm	Low	Low
HF	13.56Mhz	10cm	70cm	High	Medium
UHF	868Mhz to 928Mhz	3m	10m	Medium	Very High

* *Source:* http://www.atmel.com/dyn/resources/Prod_documents/secrerf_3_04.pdf

Note Note that 1 inch equals 2.54 centimeters, and 1 meter equals 39.3700787 inches.

Each RFID tag has a unique tag ID. Current tags carry no more than 2KB of data and can be used to store information such as history, location, and so on.

RFID AND BAR CODING

Some have criticized that RFID is simply a more expensive type of bar-coding technology (as well as a form of intrusion of a user's privacy), since the aim is to pick up a number stored on the tag (either an RFID tag or a bar-code label). However, RFID offers several advantages over bar coding:

- You don't need line of sight for RFID to work. For bar coding, you need to point the laser at the label before you can scan its ID.

- Each RFID tag ID is unique. A bar-code label does not uniquely identify a product—it just identifies a particular product type.

- RFID can track the whereabouts of goods. In places such as supermarkets, RFID readers can be deployed to track expensive goods. For example, if an item is removed from the shelf, an RFID reader could detect its absence and take the appropriate action.

Most common RFID applications use the tag ID transmitted by RFID tags as a key to information stored in databases. For example, an RFID tag attached to an employee pass contains only an RFID tag ID, which can be used to retrieve more detailed employee information stored in the organization databases. Although read-only RFID applications are cheaper, sometimes you may need to write data back to an RFID tag. These kinds of tags are known as *read-write* tags. Read-write RFID systems are deployed in situations where you need to write information back to the tag, like with stored value cards used in subways around the world.

■**Note** Some tags can be written only once.

Building an Attendance-Taking Application

Now that you have a good understanding of how RFID works, it is time to build the sample project for this chapter. For this chapter, you will build a simple attendance application that registers an employee when he reports for work. Figure 5-2 shows the user interface of the application.

When an employee scans his tag (assuming the tag is embedded in his employee pass), the application will display the employee information. The administrator can assign an unused tag to an employee by using the buttons on the right of the application. For security reasons, the employee information will be cleared after three seconds. To deploy this application in a real-life setting, the administrative functions could be hidden so that the user sees only the necessary information (see Figure 5-3).

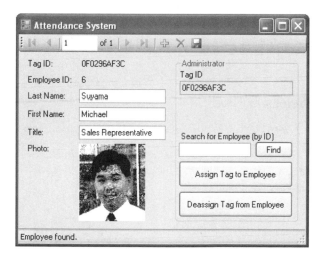

Figure 5-2. *The attendance system you will build in this chapter*

Figure 5-3. *Hiding the administrative functions in a deployed environment*

RFID Reader #1: Parallax's RFID Reader Module

The RFID reader you will be using in this example is the Parallax RFID Reader Module (http://www.parallax.com/detail.asp?product_id=28140). This low-cost ($39) RFID reader reads passive RFID transponder tags and uses serial communication to transmit the tag IDs. As you can see in Figure 5-4, the reader has four pins at the bottom (from left to right):

- VCC is for +5V DC power.

- /ENABLE is the enable (ground) or disable (+5V DC) pin.

- SOUT is the serial output.

- GND is the ground.

The effective read range of the Parallax RFID Reader Module is 1³/₄ inches to 3 inches (depending on the tag used). When a tag ID is acquired, the data is sent through the serial port using a 12-byte ASCII string. The linefeed (LF) serves as the Start byte, and the carriage return (CR) serves as the Stop byte. The ten digits contained within the LF and CR characters serve as the unique tag ID.

Figure 5-4. *The Parallax's RFID Reader Module*

RFID Tags

The Parallax RFID Reader Module reads the following tags:

- 54mm × 85mm Rectangle Tag (http://www.parallax.com/detail.asp?product_id=28141; $2.25 each)

- 50mm Round Tag (http://www.parallax.com/detail.asp?product_id=28142; $2.25 each), as shown in Figure 5-5

Figure 5-5. *The tags used for the Parallax reader*

Setting Up the Reader

To connect the reader to your computer, you need to perform a TTL-to-RS232 level shifting so the data can be read via a serial port. One way is to connect the reader to the RS-232 DCE AppMod (http://www. parallax.com/detail.asp?product_id=29120; $29; see Figure 5-6).

Alternatively, for those with a little electronic circuit board know-how, check out the following site that shows how to construct a low cost ($5) TTL-to-RS232 level shifter: http://www.zero-soft.com/HW/RS232/.

For my project, I used the Javelin Demo Board (http://www.parallax.com/detail.asp?product_id=550-00019; $119; see Figure 5-7) to connect to the reader.

Figure 5-6. *The RS-232 DCE AppMod*

Figure 5-7. *The Javelin Demo Board*

■**Tip** Either board will work well. I just happened to have the Javelin Demo Board, which is the more expensive option. If you are a modder, you can wire up the reader yourself using an RS-232 level shifting IC.

Figure 5-8 shows the wiring on the Javelin Demo Board. After that, you need to do the following:

1. Connect a 5V power source to the power connector.

2. Connect your RS-232 serial cable to the serial port at the top of the board.

3. Connect the reader module to the board using the pins shown in the diagram.

■**Tip** Be sure to use a "straight" serial cable to connect the board to your computer, or else you will not be able to get any data from the reader.

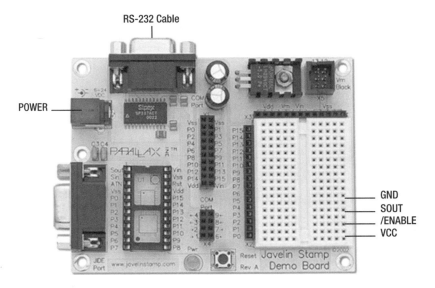

Figure 5-8. *The wiring on the Javelin Demo Board*

If you do not have a serial port on your computer, you can use a USB-to-serial converter to convert a USB connector into a serial port. You will also need a DB9 straight serial cable (see Figure 5-9).

Figure 5-9. *A USB-to-serial converter and a serial cable*

Figure 5-10 shows the assembled reader and board.

Figure 5-10. *The Parallax RFID Reader Module and the Javelin Demo Board connected and ready to go*

Building the Application User Interface

Using Visual Studio 2005, create a new Windows application, and name it **Attendance**. You will use the Northwind sample database provided by SQL Server 2000 in this example (see the "Installing the Sample Database" sidebar to learn how to install the SQL Server 2000 sample databases using SQL Express). To simplify data binding, you will use the drag and drop data-binding feature that is new in Visual Studio 2005.

INSTALLING THE SAMPLE DATABASE

Since SQL Server 2005 Express does not come with any sample databases, you need to install the sample databases.

You can install the pubs and Northwind sample databases by downloading their installation scripts at http://www.microsoft.com/downloads/details.aspx?familyid=06616212-0356-46a0-8da2-eebc53a68034&;displaylang=en.

Once the scripts are installed on your system, go to the Visual Studio 2005 command prompt (Start ➤ Programs ➤ Microsoft Visual Studio 2005 ➤ Visual Studio Tools ➤ Visual Studio 2005 Command Prompt), and change to the directory containing your installation scripts. Type the following to install the pubs and Northwind databases:

```
C:\SQL Server 2000 Sample Databases>sqlcmd -S .\SQLEXPRESS -i instpubs.sql
C:\SQL Server 2000 Sample Databases>sqlcmd -S .\SQLEXPRESS -i instnwnd.sql
```

In addition, you will also add a new TagID field to the Employees table in the Northwind database. To do so, follow these steps:

1. Go to Server Explorer (View ➤ Server Explorer).

2. Right-click Data Connections, and select Add Connection.

3. Select the Microsoft SQL Server (SqlClient) data source, and in the Server Name field, enter **.\SQLEXPRESS** (assuming you have SQL Express installed on your local computer). Select Northwind as the database name, and click OK.

4. In Server Explorer, expand the Northwind database and then the Tables item. Double-click Employees, and add the TagID field. For Data Type, select nchar(10), as shown in Figure 5-11.

■**Note** Ensure that the data source selected is Microsoft SQL Server (SqlClient). If it is not, click Change, and select Microsoft SQL Server.

Add a new data source to your project by selecting Data ➤ Add New Data Source. Using the Data Source Configuration Wizard, select Database, and click Next. Click the New Connection button to specify the database to use. You will see the Add Connection dialog box (see Figure 5-12). As before, enter **.\SQLEXPRESS** as the server name, and select Northwind as the database. Click OK.

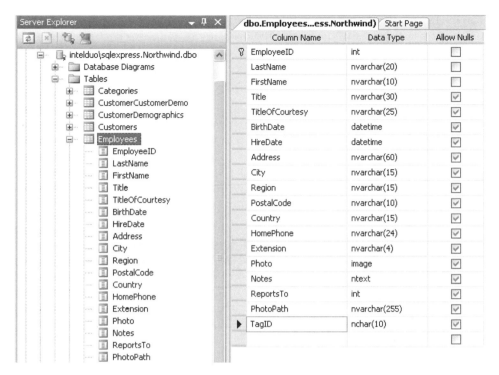

Figure 5-11. *Adding a new TagID field to the Employees table*

Figure 5-12. *Adding a new connection to the Northwind database*

Back in the Data Source Configuration Wizard, click Next. On the next screen, select the table and fields to use. Expand the Tables and Employees items, and then check the following fields (see also Figure 5-13):

- EmployeeID
- LastName
- FirstName
- Title
- Photo
- TagID

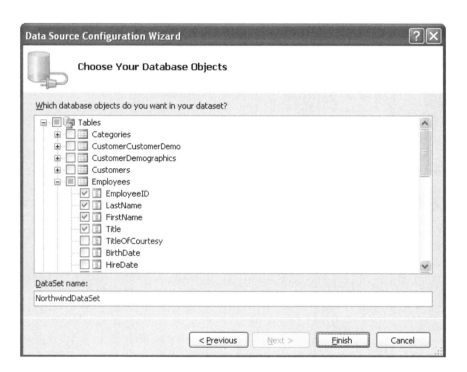

Figure 5-13. *Choosing the fields to use in the Employees table*

You can now view the newly added data source by selecting Data ➤ Show Data Sources. Figure 5-14 (left) shows the Employees data source. By default, the Employees table is bound to a DataGridView control, and all its fields (except the Photo field) are bound to TextBox controls. You should change the bindings to those shown in Table 5-2. The Employees data source should now look like the right of Figure 5-14.

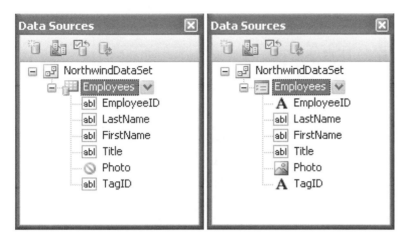

Figure 5-14. *The Employees data source*

Table 5-2. *Changing the Binding of the Employees Data Source*

Table/Fields	Binding
Employees	Details
Employee	Label
LastName	TextBox
FirstName	TextBox
Title	TextBox
Photo	PictureBox
TagID	Label

Drag and drop the Employees data source onto the default Form1. Figure 5-15 shows the controls that automatically populate the form. For the PictureBox control, set its Size property to 95,110, and set SizeMode to StretchImage.

■**Note** Move the TagID label and its accompanying Label control (on the right) to the top.

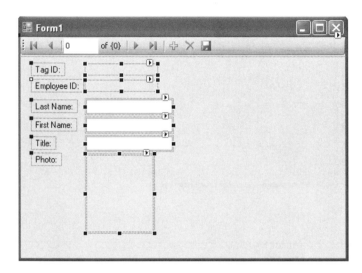

Figure 5-15. *The data-bound controls*

To test that the data binding works, you can now press F5 to debug the application. Figure 5-16 shows the application displaying the records in the Employees table.

Figure 5-16. *Testing to ensure that the data binding works*

The next part is to add controls to the form to allow an administrator to assign an RFID tag to a user. Figure 5-17 shows the controls to be added.

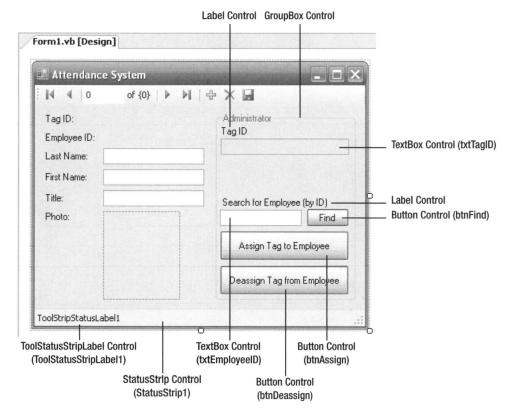

Figure 5-17. *Populating the form with the various controls*

For the txtTagID control, set both the ReadOnly and MultiLine properties to True.

In addition, drag and drop a Timer control from the Toolbox onto the form. This control will ensure that the employee record that is displayed will be cleared after three seconds.

Coding the Application

With the UI of the application out of the way, you can now focus on writing the code to wire up all the controls. Switch to the code-behind of Form1, and import the following namespaces.

Visual Basic 2005

```
Imports System.Data
Imports System.Data.SqlClient
Imports System.IO
```

C# 2005

```csharp
using System.Data;
using System.Data.SqlClient;
using System.IO;
```

Declare the following member variables and constants.

Visual Basic 2005

```vbnet
Public Class Form1
    '---serial port to listen to incoming data---
    Private WithEvents serialPort As New IO.Ports.SerialPort

    '---tag ID read from the reader---
    Private tagID As String = String.Empty

    '---the time that the tag ID was recorded---
    Private timeRecorded As DateTime = Now

    '---COM port to listen to---
    Const COM As String = "COM3"

    '---filename of the log file---
    Const FILE_NAME As String = "C:\Attendance.csv"

    '---the interval before the employee record is cleared
    ' from the screen (in seconds)---
    Const INTERVAL As Integer = 3
```

■**Note** For simplicity I have hard-coded the path for storing the log file. In a real-life application, you are better off using the `Application.ExecutablePath` property to retrieve the path of the application.

C# 2005

```csharp
public partial class Form1 : Form
{
    //---serial port to listen to incoming data---
    private System.IO.Ports.SerialPort serialPort =
        new System.IO.Ports.SerialPort();

    //---tag ID read from the reader---
    private string tagID = string.Empty;

    //---the time that the tag ID was recorded---
    private DateTime timeRecorded = System.DateTime.Today;
```

```
//---COM port to listen to---
const string COM = "COM3";

//---filename of the log file---
const string FILE_NAME = "C:\\Attendance.csv";

//---the interval before the employee record is cleared
// from the screen (in seconds)---
const int INTERVAL = 3;
```

When the form is loaded, you first clear the displayed employee by setting its filter to a nonexistent tag ID. The Timer control clears the displayed employee after a certain amount of time, and in this case you will set it to three seconds (as defined by the Interval constant). That is to say, when an employee is identified using his RFID tag, his information will be cleared from the screen after three seconds.

Because the Parallax RFID Reader Module uses a serial connection, you will use the SerialPort class (see Chapter 2 for a detailed description of the SerialPort class) to communicate with the reader.

Note For this example, I have assumed that COM3 is the port that is connected to the Parallax RFID Reader Module. You need to change it to the correct port number for your own use.

Code the Form1_Load event as follows.

Note Henceforth in this chapter, to make Visual Studio 2005 automatically create the event handler for a control (such as a form's Load event or a button's Click event), double-click the control to create the event handler.

Visual Basic 2005

```
Private Sub Form1_Load( _
    ByVal sender As System.Object, _
    ByVal e As System.EventArgs) Handles MyBase.Load

    'TODO: This line of code loads data into the
    ' 'NorthwindDataSet.Employees' table. You can move,
    ' or remove it, as needed.
    Me.EmployeesTableAdapter.Fill(Me.NorthwindDataSet.Employees)

    '---Clear the employee when the app is loaded---
    EmployeesBindingSource.Filter = "TAGID='xxxxxxxxxx'"
```

```
'---set the timer interval to clear the employee record---
Timer1.Interval = INTERVAL * 1000     'convert to milliseconds

'---open the serial port connecting to the reader---
If serialPort.IsOpen Then
    serialPort.Close()
End If

Try
    With serialPort
        .PortName = COM
        .BaudRate = 2400
        .Parity = IO.Ports.Parity.None
        .DataBits = 8
        .StopBits = IO.Ports.StopBits.One
        .Handshake = IO.Ports.Handshake.None
    End With
    serialPort.Open()
Catch ex As Exception
    MsgBox(ex.ToString)
End Try
End Sub
```

C# 2005

```
private void Form1_Load(object sender, EventArgs e)
{
    // TODO: This line of code loads data into the
    // northwindDataSet.Employees' table. You can move,
    // or remove it, as needed.
    this.employeesTableAdapter.Fill(
        this.northwindDataSet.Employees);

    serialPort.DataReceived += new
        System.IO.Ports.SerialDataReceivedEventHandler(
        DataReceived);

    //---Clear the employee when the app is loaded---
    employeesBindingSource.Filter = "TAGID='xxxxxxxxx'";

    //---set the timer interval to clear the employee
    // record---
    timer1.Interval = INTERVAL * 1000;

    //---open the serial port connecting to the reader---
    if (serialPort.IsOpen)
    {
```

```
            serialPort.Close();
        }

        try
        {
            serialPort.PortName = COM;
            serialPort.BaudRate = 2400;
            serialPort.Parity = System.IO.Ports.Parity.None;
            serialPort.DataBits = 8;
            serialPort.StopBits = System.IO.Ports.StopBits.One;
            serialPort.Handshake = System.IO.Ports.Handshake.None;
            serialPort.Open();
        }
        catch (Exception ex)
        {
            MessageBox.Show(ex.ToString());
        }
}
```

To receive incoming data from the SerialPort class, you need to service the DataReceived event. In this case, when incoming data is received, you will update the txtTagID control. Code the DataReceived event as follows.

Visual Basic 2005

```
Private Sub DataReceived( _
    ByVal sender As Object, _
    ByVal e As System.IO.Ports.SerialDataReceivedEventArgs) _
    Handles serialPort.DataReceived
        '---when incoming data is received, update the TagID
        ' textbox---
        txtTagID.BeginInvoke(New _
                    myDelegate(AddressOf updateTextBox), _
                    New Object() {})
End Sub
```

C# 2005

```
private void DataReceived(
    object sender,
    System.IO.Ports.SerialDataReceivedEventArgs e)
{
    //---when incoming data is received, update the TagID
    // textbox---
    txtTagID.BeginInvoke(new myDelegate(updateTextBox),
        new object[] { });
}
```

You need to define a delegate to call a routine to update the `txtTagID` control. Here, define the `myDelegate()` delegate and the `updateTextBox()` subroutine.

Visual Basic 2005

```
'---update the Tag ID textbox---
Public Delegate Sub myDelegate()
Public Sub updateTextBox()
    '---for receiving plain ASCII text---
    With txtTagID
        .AppendText(serialPort.ReadExisting)
        .ScrollToCaret()
    End With
End Sub
```

C# 2005

```
//---update the Tag ID textbox---
public delegate void myDelegate();
public void updateTextBox()
{
    //---for receiving plain ASCII text---
    txtTagID.AppendText(serialPort.ReadExisting());
    txtTagID.ScrollToCaret();
}
```

One important point you need to understand about RFID readers (at least for the RFID readers shown in this chapter) is that when a tag is scanned, it will continuously send the tag ID to the serial connection. For example, suppose a tag with an ID of 0F0296AF3C is placed near the reader. In this case, the reader will continuously send the value of 0F0296AF3C to the serial connection. For the Parallax RFID Reader Module, each value starts with the LF character (character 10: <10>) and ends with the CR character (character 13: <13>). To make matters complicated, using the `ReadExisting()` method of the `SerialPort` class does not guarantee you will read the complete tag ID in its entirety. This is because a value may be sent in four blocks, like this:

```
<10>0F
029
6AF3
C<13>
```

You may be tempted to use the `ReadLine()` method of the `SerialPort` class to read incoming data, but that will not work because the `ReadLine()` method will look for <13><10> at the end of the line. But since the incoming data does not end with <10>, this will cause the application to go into an infinite loop.

And if you don't clear the incoming data buffer fast enough, you may get a series of data queued up like this:

```
<10>
0F
029
6AF3
C
<13>
<10>
04
158D
C82B
<13>
```

Instead of writing elaborate logic to process the incoming data, an easy way is to append all incoming data to a TextBox control (with the MultiLine property set to True). Using the data just described, Figure 5-18 shows how it will look in the TextBox control.

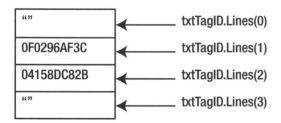

Figure 5-18. *Appending incoming data to a TextBox control*

As data is appended to the TextBox control, the first line contains the LF character (<10>), and hence the first line is always empty. As more data is appended to the control, the CR and LF characters (<13><10>) will force subsequent data to be appended to the new line of the control. The second-to-last line will hence always contain the tag ID you are interested in even if the last line is an empty string. In contrast, if the tag ID is only partially received, the state of the TextBox control will be as shown in Figure 5-19.

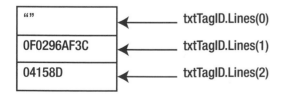

Figure 5-19. *The state of the TextBox control containing the last incomplete tag ID*

Because all incoming data is updated in the TextBox control, you can check whether the tag ID belongs to an employee whenever there are changes in the content of the TextBox control. You can detect this via the TextChanged event, which is defined next.

Visual Basic 2005

```
Private Sub txtTagID_TextChanged( _
   ByVal sender As System.Object, _
   ByVal e As System.EventArgs) _
   Handles txtTagID.TextChanged

    If txtTagID.Lines(txtTagID.Lines.Length - 1) = _
       String.Empty Then
         '---get the tag ID that is read---
         Dim temptagID As String = _
            txtTagID.Lines(txtTagID.Lines.Length - 2)

         '---get the time interval between the last read time
         ' and the current time---
         Dim tp As TimeSpan = Now.Subtract(timeRecorded)
         Dim timeInterval As Double = _
            tp.Ticks / TimeSpan.TicksPerSecond

         If (temptagID = tagID) And timeInterval < INTERVAL Then
             '---if it is the same tag and the time interval
             ' is less than 3 seconds, the tag won't be
             ' registered---
             Exit Sub
         End If

         '---the tag is saved---
         tagID = temptagID
         EmployeesBindingSource.RemoveFilter()

         '---find the employee associated with the tag---
         EmployeesBindingSource.Filter = "TAGID='" & tagID & "'"
         If EmployeesBindingSource.Count < 1 Then
             ToolStripStatusLabel1.Text = "Employee not found."
         Else
             ToolStripStatusLabel1.Text = "Employee found."

             '---write the employee information to log file---
             WriteToLog(EmployeeIDLabel1.Text, _
                LastNameTextBox.Text & ", " & _
                FirstNameTextBox.Text)
             '---reset the timer---
             Timer1.Enabled = False
             Timer1.Enabled = True
         End If
         '---save the time this tag was recorded---
         timeRecorded = Now
    End If
End Sub
```

C# 2005

```csharp
private void txtTagID_TextChanged(
    object sender,
    EventArgs e)
{
    //---get the tag ID that is read---
    if (txtTagID.Lines[txtTagID.Lines.Length - 1] ==
        string.Empty)
    {
        string temptagID =
            txtTagID.Lines[txtTagID.Lines.Length - 2];

        //---get the time interval between the last read time
        // and the current time---
        TimeSpan tp =
            System.DateTime.Today.Subtract(timeRecorded);
        double timeInterval =
            tp.Ticks / TimeSpan.TicksPerSecond;

        if ((temptagID == tagID) & timeInterval < INTERVAL)
        {
            //---if it is the same tag and the time interval
            // is less than 3 seconds, the tag won't be
            // registered---
            return;
        }

        //---the tag is saved---
        tagID = temptagID;
        employeesBindingSource.RemoveFilter();

        //---find the employee associated with the tag---
        employeesBindingSource.Filter = "TAGID='" + tagID +
            "'";
        if (employeesBindingSource.Count < 1)
        {
            ToolStripStatusLabel1.Text =
                "Employee not found.";
        }
        else
        {
            ToolStripStatusLabel1.Text = "Employee found.";

            //---write the employee information to log file---
            WriteToLog(employeeIDLabel1.Text,
                lastNameTextBox.Text +
                ", " + firstNameTextBox.Text);
```

```
                timer1.Enabled = false;
                timer1.Enabled = true;
        }

        //---save the time this tag was recorded---
        timeRecorded = System.DateTime.Today;
    }
}
```

In this event, you first examine whether the last line in the txtTagID control is an empty string; if it is, then you can find the scanned tag ID in the second-to-last line. Using this tag ID, you will check the time difference between the current time and the last time the tag ID was read. If it is less than three seconds and the tag ID is the same as the last read tag ID, it means it is the same user, and thus you can ignore the current tag ID. Using this implementation, the same user would be ignored for the next three seconds from the moment he first scanned his tag.

With the tag ID, you will apply a filter to the EmployeesBindingSource control to look for an employee with a matching tag ID. If an employee is found, an entry will be written to the log file using the WriteToLog() subroutine. The WriteToLog() subroutine is defined as follows.

Visual Basic 2005

```
Private Sub WriteToLog( _
   ByVal employeeID As String, _
   ByVal employeeName As String)
   '---write to log file---
   Dim str As String = employeeID & "," & _
                       employeeName & "," & Now & Chr(13)
   My.Computer.FileSystem.WriteAllText(FILE_NAME, str, True)
End Sub
```

C# 2005

```
private void WriteToLog(
   string employeeID, string employeeName)
{
   //---write to log file---
   string str = employeeID + "," + employeeName + "," +
      System.DateTime.Today.ToString() + Environment.NewLine;
   File.AppendAllText(FILE_NAME, str);
}
```

Figure 5-20 shows the content of a typical log file.

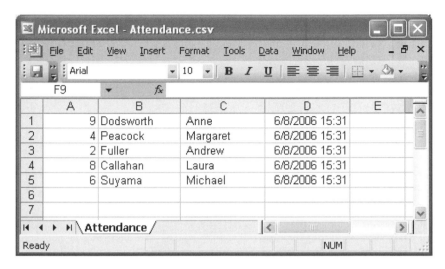

Figure 5-20. *The content of a typical log file*

The Timer control will fire off the Tick event every three seconds (as determined by the value set in its Interval property). Therefore, you need to service the Tick event so that every time it fires, you can clear the current employee information that is displayed. Here is the implementation of the Tick event.

Visual Basic 2005

```
Private Sub Timer1_Tick( _
   ByVal sender As System.Object, _
   ByVal e As System.EventArgs) _
   Handles Timer1.Tick
   '---clear the employee---
   EmployeesBindingSource.Filter = "TAGID='xxxxxxxxxx'"
   Timer1.Enabled = False
End Sub
```

C# 2005

```
private void timer1_Tick(object sender, EventArgs e)
{
    //---clear the employee---
    employeesBindingSource.Filter = "TAGID='xxxxxxxxxx'";
    timer1.Enabled = false;
}
```

If the tag ID that was just scanned does not belong to any user, the administrator can assign the tag ID to an employee. To do so, he can first click the Find button to find a user and then assign the tag ID to that user. The implementation of the Find button is as follows.

Visual Basic 2005

```vb
Private Sub btnFind_Click( _
   ByVal sender As System.Object, _
   ByVal e As System.EventArgs) _
   Handles btnFind.Click
    '---search for employee---
    If txtEmployeeID.Text = String.Empty Then
        EmployeesBindingSource.RemoveFilter()
    Else
        EmployeesBindingSource.Filter = _
            "EmployeeID='" & txtEmployeeID.Text & "'"
    End If
End Sub
```

C# 2005

```csharp
private void btnFind_Click(object sender, EventArgs e)
{
    //---search for employee---
    if (txtEmployeeID.Text == string.Empty)
    {
        employeesBindingSource.RemoveFilter();
    }
    else
    {
        employeesBindingSource.Filter =
            "EmployeeID='" + txtEmployeeID.Text + "'";
    }
}
```

Basically, you search for a user by applying a filter to the EmployeesBindingSource control. To assign a tag ID to the current employee, copy the tag ID onto the TagIDLabel1 control, and then save the changes. Here is the implementation of the Assign button.

Visual Basic 2005

```vb
Private Sub btnAssign_Click( _
   ByVal sender As System.Object, _
   ByVal e As System.EventArgs) _
   Handles btnAssign.Click
    '---obtain the tag ID that was read---
    If txtTagID.Lines.Length > 1 Then
        Dim tagID As String = _
            txtTagID.Lines(txtTagID.Lines.Length - 2)
    Else
        ToolStripStatusLabel1.Text = "No tag id scanned."
        Exit Sub
    End If
```

```
    If txtTagID.Text <> String.Empty Then
        '---assign the Tag ID to the current employee---
        TagIDLabel1.Text = tagID
        ToolStripStatusLabel1.Text = _
            "Tag associated with employee."

        '---save the record---
        Me.Validate()
        Me.EmployeesBindingSource.EndEdit()
        Me.EmployeesTableAdapter.Update( _
            Me.NorthwindDataSet.Employees)
    End If
End Sub
```

C# 2005

```
private void btnAssign_Click(object sender, EventArgs e)
{
    //---obtain the tag ID that was read---
    if (txtTagID.Lines.Length > 1)
    {
        string tagID = txtTagID.Lines[
            txtTagID.Lines.Length - 2];
    }
    else
    {
        ToolStripStatusLabel1.Text = "No tag id scanned.";
        return;
    }
    if (txtTagID.Text != string.Empty)
    {
        //---assign the Tag ID to the current employee---
        tagIDLabel1.Text = tagID;
        ToolStripStatusLabel1.Text =
            "Tag associated with employee.";

        //---save the record---
        this.Validate();
        this.employeesBindingSource.EndEdit();
        this.employeesTableAdapter.Update(
            this.northwindDataSet.Employees);
    }
}
```

The Deassign button allows a tag ID to be disassociated from an employee. You can easily accomplish this by setting the TagIDLabel1 control to an empty string. Here is the implementation of the Deassign button.

Visual Basic 2005

```vb
Private Sub btnDeassign_Click( _
   ByVal sender As System.Object, _
   ByVal e As System.EventArgs) _
   Handles btnDeassign.Click
    If Trim(TagIDLabel1.Text) = String.Empty Then
        ToolStripStatusLabel1.Text = _
            "Current employee has no tag ID."
        Exit Sub
    End If

    '---deassociate tag ID from employee---
    TagIDLabel1.Text = String.Empty

    '---save the record---
    Me.Validate()
    Me.EmployeesBindingSource.EndEdit()
    Me.EmployeesTableAdapter.Update(Me.NorthwindDataSet.Employees)
    ToolStripStatusLabel1.Text = "Tag deassociated from employee."
End Sub
```

C# 2005

```csharp
private void btnDeassign_Click(object sender, EventArgs e)
{
    if (tagIDLabel1.Text.Trim() == string.Empty)
    {
        ToolStripStatusLabel1.Text =
            "Current employee has no tag ID.";
        return;
    }

    //---deassociate tag ID from employee---
    tagIDLabel1.Text = string.Empty;

    //---save the record---
    this.Validate();
    this.employeesBindingSource.EndEdit();
    this.employeesTableAdapter.Update(
        this.northwindDataSet.Employees);
    ToolStripStatusLabel1.Text =
        "Tag deassociated from employee.";
}
```

Testing the Application

You are now ready to test the application. Press F5 to debug the application. Scan a tag using the RFID reader. The application should register your tag ID and show that no employee is found (see Figure 5-21).

Attendance System

Tag ID:
Employee ID:
Last Name:
First Name:
Title:
Photo:

Administrator
Tag ID
0101B67909

Search for Employee (by ID)
[   ] [Find]

[Assign Tag to Employee]

[Deassign Tag from Employee]

Employee not found.

Figure 5-21. *Scanning a tag that does not belong to any employee*

You can associate the tag ID with an employee by searching for an employee; enter the employee ID in the TextBox control, and click the Find button (or leave it empty, and it will return all records). Once you have located the employee you want, click the Assign Tag to Employee button to assign the tag ID to the employee.

The next time you scan the same tag, the employee will be shown!

RFID Reader #2: PhidgetRFID

The second RFID reader you will use is the PhidgetRFID reader (http://www.phidgetsusa.com/cat/viewproduct. asp?category=3000&subcategory=3100&SKU=1023; $59.95; see Figure 5-22) from Phidgets USA. The PhidgetRFID reader is also a read-only RFID reader that can read tags within a 3-inch proximity.

Unlike the Parallax RFID Reader Module, the PhidgetRFID reader uses a USB connection, which is actually easier for most people since almost all computers today support USB devices. And since it draws power from the USB connection, you don't need an external power source. Simply connect the PhidgetRFID reader to your computer, and you are ready to go.

Figure 5-22. *The PhidgetRFID*

RFID Tags

Instead of purchasing the stand-alone PhidgetRFID reader, I suggest you purchase the Phidget RFID kit (`http://www.phidgetsusa.com/cat/viewproduct.asp?category=3000&subcategory=3300&SKU=93001`; $88.95; see Figure 5-23), which comes with the following:

- Six 30mm disc RFID tags

- Two credit card–sized RFID tags

- Two key-fob RFID tags

- USB cable

Figure 5-23. *The PhidgetRFID kit*

The PhidgetRFID reads RFID tags that use the EM Marrin protocol, EM4102 (which is a 125kHz read-only protocol).

■**Tip** The PhidgetRFID reader also reads the tag I used for the Parallax RFID Reader Module. In fact, the tags described here also work with Parallax's reader.

Building the Sample Application

Rather than modify the application built in the previous sections to work with the PhidgetRFID reader (and have a lot of repetitive code snippets), I have opted to build a simpler application so you can learn the fundamentals without being bogged down with the details of the application.

■**Note** If you are interested in a copy of the attendance application that works with the PhidgetRFID reader, you can download it from the Source Code/Download section of the Apress website (`http://www.apress.com/`).

Using Visual Studio 2005, create a new Windows application, and populate the default form with the controls shown in Figure 5-24.

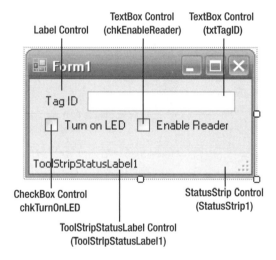

Figure 5-24. *Populating the form with the controls*

Using this application, you can view the tag ID that is being scanned, and you can also programmatically turn on/off the LED on the reader and enable/disable the reader.

Running the PhidgetRFID WebService

Phidget has made it easy for .NET programmers to use the PhidgetRFID reader. The Phidget WebService component actually controls the reader and interacts with your PhidgetRFID reader. The Phidget WebService component must be installed and running on the computer that has the PhidgetRFID reader connected. Once the Phidget WebService component is up and running, your program can then communicate with it in order to control the PhidgetRFID reader. You can obtain the Phidget library (containing the Phidget WebService component) from http://www.phidgetsusa.com (go to Downloads, click Phidget Library Files and Examples, and then choose Phidget21 Downloads) and download the PHIDGET.msi file.

■**Note** The use of the term *web service* is a little misleading here. The Phidget WebService component is not an XML web service like most people are familiar with. Rather, it is a Windows service that runs in the background.

When installed, you can find the Phidget WebService component in C:\Program Files\Phidgets. You can invoke the Phidget WebService Manager (a GUI version of the component) by running PhidgetWebServiceManger.exe from this directory. Once it is up and running, you can find it in the system tray (see Figure 5-25).

Figure 5-25. *Phidget WebService Manager in the system tray*

Double-click the icon to launch the Phidget WebService Manager. Using the manager, you can change the settings of the component as well as manage your Phidget devices (not just the PhidgetRFID reader). As shown in Figure 5-26, the Phidget WebService component is listening at port 5001 and requires the password *pass* (the default) in order to access it. With your PhidgetRFID reader attached to your computer, click Start. In my case, my reader has the serial number of 6207, which can be used to uniquely identify it.

One unique feature of the Phidget WebService component is that your client application does not necessarily need to be running on the same computer as the one with the reader connected. The client application uses sockets communication to talk to the Phidget WebService component, so this means a PhidgetRFID reader can be connected to one computer and the client application can be running on another computer (as long as they are accessible on the network). Figure 5-27 shows one possible scenario. The advantage of this approach is that your client can be running on mobile platform devices (such as a Pocket PC) as long as it can communicate with the host computer using sockets communication.

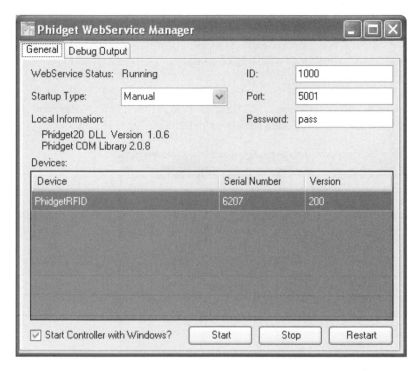

Figure 5-26. *The Phidget WebService Manager*

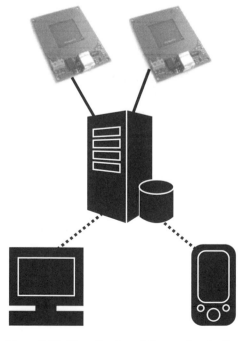

Figure 5-27. *The client and the reader don't need to be on the same computer.*

PhidgetRFID APIs

The functionalities of the PhidgetRFID reader are exposed as APIs located in the `PhidgetsNET.dll` library. This library is installed with the Phidget WebService component in `C:\Program Files\Phidgets\`.

To use the PhidgetRFID, first import the `PhidgetNET.dll` library into your application. Right-click the project name in Solution Explorer, and then select Add Reference. On the Browse tab, navigate to `C:\Program Files\Phidgets\`, and select `PhidgetsNET.dll` (see Figure 5-28).

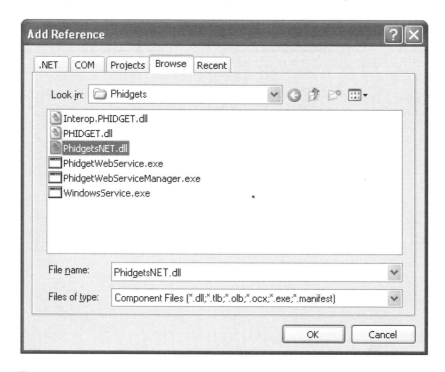

Figure 5-28. *Importing the* `PhidgetsNET.dll` *into your .NET application*

Coding the Application

Switch to the code-behind of Form1, and first declare a member variable representing the PhidgetRFID reader.

Visual Basic 2005

```
Public Class Form1
    Dim WithEvents RFIDReader As PhidgetsNET.PhidgetRFID
```

C# 2005

```
public partial class Form1 : Form
{
    PhidgetsNET.PhidgetRFID RFIDReader;
```

When the form is loaded, instantiate the PhidgetReader variable, and open a connection to the computer running the Phidget WebService component. You accomplish this by using the Form1_Load event (for the C# version of the code, you need to wire up the various event handlers for the PhidgetRFID class).

Visual Basic 2005

```
Private Sub Form1_Load( _
   ByVal sender As System.Object, _
   ByVal e As System.EventArgs) _
   Handles MyBase.Load
    RFIDReader = New PhidgetsNET.PhidgetRFID
    RFIDReader.OpenRemoteIP("localhost", 5001, -1, "pass")
    ToolStripStatusLabel1.Text = "Not Connected"
End Sub
```

C# 2005

```
private void Form1_Load(object sender, EventArgs e)
{
    RFIDReader = new PhidgetsNET.PhidgetRFID();

    //---wire up the various event handler for the PhidgetRFID
    // class---
    RFIDReader.Attach += new
       PhidgetsNET.AttachEventHandler(this.RFIDReader_Attach);
    RFIDReader.Detach += new
       PhidgetsNET.DetachEventHandler(this.RFIDReader_Detach);
    RFIDReader.Tag += new
       PhidgetsNET.TagEventHandler(this.RFIDReader_Tag);
    RFIDReader.Error += new
       PhidgetsNET.ErrorEventHandler(this.RFIDReader_Error);

    RFIDReader.OpenRemoteIP("localhost", 5001, -1, "pass");
    ToolStripStatusLabel1.Text = "Not Connected";
}
```

Note Notice that I used localhost because my reader is connected to my local computer. The port 5001 corresponds to the port number entered in the Phidget WebService Manager (see Figure 5-26). The -1 refers to the first device that is found in the Phidget WebService component. Alternatively, you can use 6207 (the device serial number). *pass* is the password (also set in the Phidget WebService Manager) you need.

For the PhidgetRFID reader, you need to service four important events:

Attach: Fired when a PhidgetRFID reader is attached to the computer running the Phidget WebService component

Detach: Fired when a PhidgetRFID reader is detached from the computer running the Phidget WebService component

Error: Fired when there is an error with the PhidgetRFID reader

Tag: Fired when a tag is scanned using the PhidgetRFID reader

In the Attach event, when a reader is connected, you will turn on the LED on the reader as well as enable the reader by using the SetOutputState() method of the PhidgetRFID class.

Visual Basic 2005

```vb
Private Sub RFIDReader_Attach( _
    ByVal sender As Object, _
    ByVal e As PhidgetsNET.AttachEventArgs) _
    Handles RFIDReader.Attach
    '---display the status---
    ToolStripStatusLabel1.Text = "Phidget RFID Reader Connected"

    '---Enable onboard LED---
    chkTurnOnLED.Checked = True
    RFIDReader.SetOutputState(2, True)

    '---Enable RFID Reader---
    chkEnableReader.Checked = True
    RFIDReader.SetOutputState(3, True)
End Sub
```

C# 2005

```csharp
private void RFIDReader_Attach(
    object sender,
    PhidgetsNET.AttachEventArgs e)
{
    //---display the status---
    ToolStripStatusLabel1.Text =
        "Phidget RFID Reader Connected";

    //---Enable onboard LED---
    chkTurnOnLED.Checked = true;
    RFIDReader.SetOutputState(2, true);

    //---Enable RFID Reader---
    chkEnableReader.Checked = true;
    RFIDReader.SetOutputState(3, true);
}
```

When a reader is detached, you simply update its status in the status bar.

Visual Basic 2005

```
Private Sub RFIDReader_Detach( _
   ByVal sender As Object, _
   ByVal e As PhidgetsNET.DetachEventArgs) _
   Handles RFIDReader.Detach
    '---display the status---
    ToolStripStatusLabel1.Text = _
       "Phidget RFID Reader Not Connected"
End Sub
```

C# 2005

```
private void RFIDReader_Detach(
   object sender,
   PhidgetsNET.DetachEventArgs e)
{
   //---display the status---
    ToolStripStatusLabel1.Text =
       "Phidget RFID Reader Not Connected";
}
```

The same goes for the Error event.

Visual Basic 2005

```
Private Sub RFIDReader_Error( _
   ByVal sender As Object, _
   ByVal e As PhidgetsNET.ErrorEventArgs) _
   Handles RFIDReader.Error
    '---display the error---
    ToolStripStatusLabel1.Text = e.getError
End Sub
```

C# 2005

```
private void RFIDReader_Error(
   object sender,
   PhidgetsNET.ErrorEventArgs e)
{
   //---display the error---
    ToolStripStatusLabel1.Text = e.getError();
}
```

For the Tag event, you will invoke a delegate to display the tag ID.

Visual Basic 2005

```
Private Sub RFIDReader_Tag( _
    ByVal sender As Object, _
    ByVal e As PhidgetsNET.TagEventArgs) _
    Handles RFIDReader.Tag
     '---when incoming data is received, update the TagID
     ' textbox---
    txtTagID.BeginInvoke(New _
                    myDelegate(AddressOf updateTextBox), _
                    New Object() {e.getTag})
End Sub
```

C# 2005

```
private void RFIDReader_Tag(
    object sender, PhidgetsNET.TagEventArgs e)
{
    //---when incoming data is received, update the TagID
    // textbox---
    txtTagID.BeginInvoke(new myDelegate(updateTextBox),
        new object[] { e.getTag() });
}
```

■**Note** Unlike the previous project using the Parallax's RFID reader, using the PhidgetRFID APIs eliminates the need to specially handle the incoming tag ID using a TextBox control. In this case, when a tag is scanned, you can obtain its tag ID via the Tag event.

The delegate and the subroutine to update the textbox with the tag ID is defined as follows.

Visual Basic 2005

```
'---update the Tag ID textbox---
Public Delegate Sub myDelegate(ByVal str As String)
Public Sub updateTextBox(ByVal str As String)
    '---update the textbox control---
    With txtTagID
        .Text = str
    End With
End Sub
```

C# 2005

```
//---update the Tag ID textbox---
public delegate void myDelegate(string str);
```

```
public void updateTextBox(string str)
{
    //---update the TextBox control---
    txtTagID.Text = str;
}
```

You can also turn on/off the LED on the reader during runtime. This is serviced by the CheckChanged event of the chkTurnOnLED control.

Visual Basic 2005

```
Private Sub chkTurnOnLED_CheckedChanged( _
   ByVal sender As System.Object, _
   ByVal e As System.EventArgs) _
   Handles chkTurnOnLED.CheckedChanged
    '---Enable/Disable onboard LED---
    RFIDReader.SetOutputState(2, chkTurnOnLED.Checked)
End Sub
```

C# 2005

```
private void chkTurnOnLED_CheckedChanged(
   object sender,
   EventArgs e)
{
    //---Enable/Disable onboard LED---
    RFIDReader.SetOutputState(2, chkTurnOnLED.Checked);
}
```

Similarly, you can enable/disable the reader by servicing the CheckChanged event of the chkEnableReader control.

Visual Basic 2005

```
Private Sub chkEnableReader_CheckedChanged( _
   ByVal sender As System.Object, _
   ByVal e As System.EventArgs) _
   Handles chkEnableReader.CheckedChanged
    '---Enable RFID Reader---
    RFIDReader.SetOutputState(3, chkEnableReader.Checked)
End Sub
```

C# 2005

```
private void chkEnableReader_CheckedChanged(
   object sender, EventArgs e)
{
    //---Enable RFID Reader---
    RFIDReader.SetOutputState(3, chkEnableReader.Checked);
}
```

Testing the Application

That's it! You can now press F5 to test the application. Ensure that your PhidgetRFID reader is enabled in the Phidget WebService Manager. Figure 5-29 shows a tag scanned successfully.

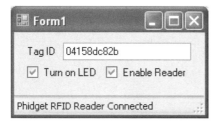

Figure 5-29. *A tag scanned successfully*

Figure 5-30 shows the reader with the LED turned on (top) and off (bottom).

Figure 5-30. *Turning the onboard LED on and off*

Comparing the Two RFID Readers

You have seen two types of RFID readers; so, which one should you buy? Here are some factors you can consider.

Cost

In terms of cost, the Parallax RFID Reader Module is very affordable at $39. However, you need to factor in the additional cost of wiring up the unit. You need to buy a power adapter (output 5V DC), a serial cable, and the additional hardware needed to convert the signal to serial output. In contrast, the PhidgetRFID reader costs about $58, and you don't need to worry about any additional costs.

Ease of Use

In terms of use, the PhidgetRFID reader is truly plug and play. Just make sure you download the Phidget WebService component, and you can start coding straightaway. The Parallax RFID Reader Module takes some effort to set up, especially if you are not familiar with electronics and worry about causing damage to the unit.

Flexibility

If you simply want to connect an RFID reader to your computer, then the PhidgetRFID reader is one clear option. However, the beauty of the Parallax RFID Reader Module is that it allows you to connect the unit to devices other than a PC, such as an embedded controller. Using the Parallax RFID Reader Module, you can embed it in a door and write your own code to authenticate users.

■**Tip** At the moment, you can't really use the .NET Framework (or the .NET Compact Framework) to write code for an embedded controller; however, I am really looking forward to the new .NET Micro Framework (http://www.aboutnetmf.com/entry.asp) to do the job in the near future.

Dimension

Both readers are similar in size and are flat enough to be hidden from view.

Summary

In this chapter, you saw how RFID works and then went on to build a Windows application that uses two RFID readers—one from Parallax and one from Phidget USA. Depending on your needs, both low-cost readers offer a lot of exciting possibilities for integrating RFID capabilities into your projects. If you have not tried RFID yet, this is a good time to begin!

CHAPTER 6

∎∎∎

Interfacing with External Devices

Today, a webcam is a common peripheral that most people can easily afford; and it's used most often for video conferencing. But what can you do with your webcam besides video conferencing? For .NET developers, the answer is plenty; and you will be glad to know that integrating a webcam with a Windows application is not as difficult as you might imagine.

Besides integrating a webcam with your application, you can connect your Windows application to an external device such as a sensor to monitor the movements of the surroundings.

In this chapter, you will build a security system by interfacing a Windows application with an external sensor and a webcam so you can monitor for unwanted activities. You will be able to detect the proximity of an intruder and use the webcam to record the intruder's movements. Figure 6-1 shows the application you will build in this chapter.

Figure 6-1. *The application you will build in this chapter*

Components Used

You'll use two components in this chapter:

- An ultrasonic sensor that is able to precisely measure distance

- A webcam you can use for your Windows Live Messenger or other instant messaging (IM) software

Sensor

The sensor, the PING ultrasonic sensor (http://www.parallax.com/detail.asp?product_id=28015; see Figure 6-2), is able to provide a precise measurement of distances ranging from 2 centimeters to 3 meters (0.79 inch to 9.84 feet). It works by emitting a short ultrasonic burst and then measuring the time it takes the burst to bounce back when it hits an object. By timing this process, it is able to calculate the exact distance between the sensor and the object. The PING sensor has a three-pin connector: GND, 5V DC, and a signal line. The signal line will return the distance measured in *pulses* (I will talk more about this in the "Programming the PING Sensor" section).

Figure 6-2. *The PING sensor*

■**Note** The PING sensor costs $24.95.

Webcam

You can use any webcam you already have. As long as it is recognized by Windows, it will be all right. For my case, I used the Logitech QuickCam for Notebooks Deluxe webcam (see Figure 6-3), which connects to my computer directly using a USB cable.

■Note Some webcams are plug and play in Windows, while others require you to install the drivers that came with them.

Figure 6-3. *The Logitech QuickCam for Notebooks Deluxe webcam*

Connecting the Sensor to the PC

Unlike the webcam, the PING sensor cannot be directly connected to the serial/USB port of the PC. The sensor is not designed for connecting to RS-232 serial (or USB) ports; a PC serial port works on RS-232 voltages and serial communication, while the PING sensor runs at 5V (TTL) and uses pulse-trigger and pulse-width to trigger. Hence, you would need a microcontroller to connect to the sensor and then use the microcontroller to return the results to the PC via a serial/USB connection.

For this purpose, I used the BASIC Stamp 2 (BS2) module (http://www.parallax.com/ detail.asp?product_id=BS2-IC), also from Parallax. The BS2 is a microcontroller that runs at 20MHz and can execute approximately 4,000 instructions per second.

■Note The BS2 costs $49.

You also need a board to house the BS2 module. I used Parallax's USB Board of Education (BoE) development board ($65; `http://www.parallax.com/detail.asp?product_id=28850`; see Figure 6-4).

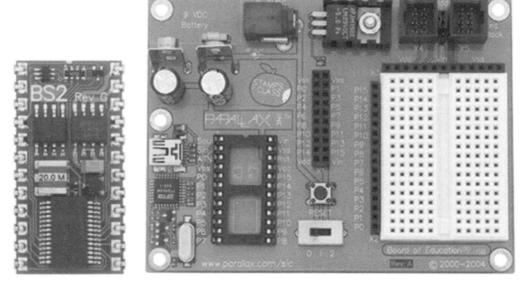

Figure 6-4. *Parallax's BS2 module and the USB BoE board*

The BoE board has two versions: serial and USB. I recommend you get the USB version because this saves you the trouble of buying a USB-to-serial adapter if you do not have a serial port on your computer (this especially applies to notebooks). Technically, the USB version is the same as the serial version—when you connect the USB cable to the BoE and your PC, you will notice that it is actually a serial port connection (the BoE actually performs a serial-to-USB conversion internally). To the .NET programmer, this is good news because you can now communicate with the BoE using serial connections (via the `SerialPort` class in the .NET Framework 2.0).

■**Tip** If cost is a concern, you might want to consider the Parallax HomeWork Board (`http://www.parallax.com/detail.asp?product_id=28158`; see Figure 6-5), which has the BS2 built onto the BoE board. The HomeWork Board costs $400 In quantities of ten, which is ideal if you have a few friends willing to share the pack. The price of $40 is cheaper than the combined cost of $114 for the BS2 and the BoE board.

Figure 6-5. *The Parallax HomeWork Board*

Connecting the PING Sensor

For the PING sensor, you will connect it to the built-in breadboard on the BoE board. Using jumper wires, connect the points as shown in Figure 6-6. For the PING sensor, you can directly plug in its three-pin connection to the breadboard. Specifically, GND connects to V_{ss}, 5V connects to V_{dd}, and SIG connects to P15 (pin 15).

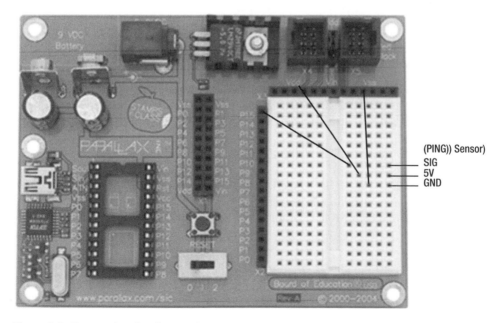

(PING)) Sensor)
SIG
5V
GND

Figure 6-6. *Connection for the PING sensor*

Figure 6-7 shows the completed connection.

Figure 6-7. *The connected BoE board and the two sensors*

Programming the PING Sensor

To program the PING sensor, you need to use the Parallax Basic (PBASIC) language. Parallax provides the free BASIC Stamp Windows Editor (`http://www.parallax.com/dl/sw/bs/win/Setup-Stamp-Editor-Lrg-v2.2.6.exe`), which makes programming the BS2 easy.

Once you have downloaded and installed the BASIC Stamp Windows Editor, you can launch it (see Figure 6-8).

Programming PBASIC is actually not a difficult task, and I will explain the syntax as I go along.

The first step is to add a PBASIC `BS2` directive to your program to tell the editor that your program is going to run on a BS2 module. You can insert the following directive by clicking the button labeled (1) shown in Figure 6-9:

```
' {$STAMP BS2}
```

Next, you need to insert the PBASIC `2.5` directive to specify the version of PBASIC you are using. Clicking the button labeled (2) in Figure 6-9 will insert the following directive:

```
' {$PBASIC 2.5}
```

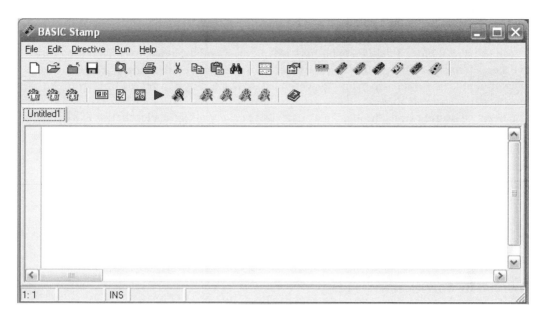

Figure 6-8. *The free BASIC Stamp Windows Editor*

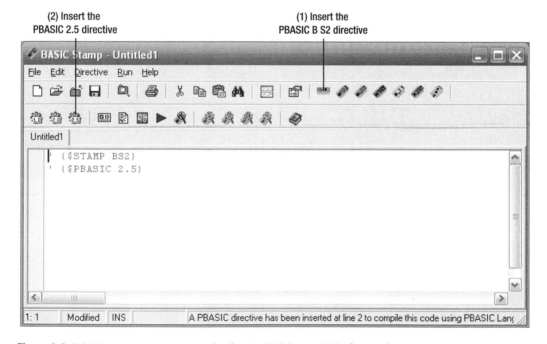

Figure 6-9. *Writing a program using the free BASIC Stamp Windows Editor*

To program the PING sensor, you need to understand how it works. To activate the PING sensor, you need to send a *low-high-low* pulse to trigger it. After it is triggered, it will wait for about 200 microseconds before it sends out an ultrasonic burst. In the meantime, you will wait for the burst to be bounced back; this entire pulse duration (which starts when the burst is sent) represents the round-trip distance from the sensor to the object you are detecting.

In the BS2, a *pulse* is defined to be 2μs (two microseconds). Hence, to convert the pulse to time, you multiply the number of pulses by 2. This will give you the time in μs. Because the measured pulse is for the trip to and fro, you need to divide it by 2 to get the time from the sensor to the detected object.

Because sound travels through air at 1,130 feet per second (at sea level), this works out to be 1 inch in 73.746 μs (or 1 cm in 29.034 μs). To convert the time in μs to a distance in centimeters, you need to multiply the time by 29.034 (or 30 for simplicity). This will give you the distance in centimeters. The following BS2 code summarizes what I have just described:

```
' {$STAMP BS2}
' {$PBASIC 2.5}

'---duration of the trigger; 1 represents 2 microseconds---
Trigger CON 1  '---CON represents constant---

'---variable to measure the pulse---
rawDist VAR Word  '---VAR represents variable---

'---the I/O Pin connected to the PING sensor---
Ping PIN 15  '---PIN represents pin on the BS2---

DO
    '---Set the pin to low first---
    Ping = 0

    '---trigger the sensor by sending a pulse ---
    PULSOUT Ping, Trigger

    '---measure the echo pulse by reading it---
    PULSIN Ping, 1, rawDist

    '---convert pulses to microseconds---
    rawDist = rawDist * 2

    '---get the single-trip timing---
    rawDist = rawDist / 2

    '---convert the distance to cm---
    rawDist = rawDist / 30

    '---print out the distance in cm---
    DEBUG DEC rawDist, CR

    '---delay for 100 milliseconds---
    PAUSE 100
LOOP
```

■**Note** I have modified the previous from the sample provided by Parallax (`http://www.parallax.com/dl/docs/prod/acc/28015-PING-v1.3.pdf`). Note that BASIC Stamp is able to deal only with integer division; for complex floating-point division, check out the language reference for PBASIC.

The `DEBUG` command will send a value (or string) to the BASIC Stamp Windows Editor (running on the PC). This command is useful for debugging your program running on the BS2. In this case, you are printing the calculated distance (`rawDist`) as a decimal value (`DEC`). The `CR` part indicates a carriage return.

Click the Run icon (or press Ctrl+R) to download the program onto the BS2. The Download Progress dialog box will appear (see Figure 6-10). You can observe from this dialog box that the BoE is connected to my computer via COM3.

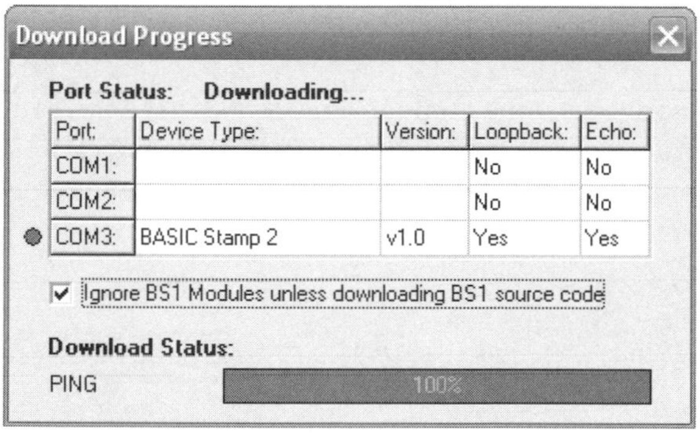

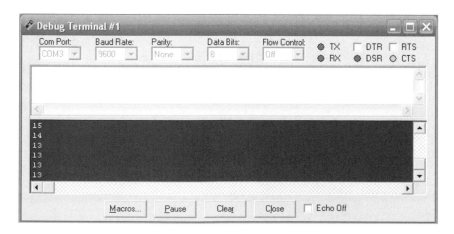

Figure 6-10. *The Download Progress dialog box*

The Debug Terminal dialog box will now appear; it shows the output from the BS2 (see Figure 6-11). Slowly move an object toward the PING sensor, and you will see that the distance gets smaller and smaller.

Figure 6-11. *Testing the PING sensor*

Integrating with the PC

So far, all the work has been done on the BoE. How do you integrate the PING sensor with your PC so you can do something useful? More specifically, how do you get the sensor values into your PC?

If you observe the top of the Debug Terminal dialog box, you will realize that it gets the debugging information from the BS2 through a serial connection (see Figure 6-12). In my case, it connects to COM3 with a baud rate of 9600bps. Hence, you can retrieve the sensor data through this serial connection.

Figure 6-12. *Serial connection information at the top of the Debug Terminal dialog box*

However, besides using the DEBUG function to send the output from the BS2 to the PC, you can also use the SEROUT command in PBASIC, which allows you to send asynchronous serial data out of the BS2. To use the SEROUT command, remove the DEBUG command in the program, and insert two SEROUT commands, as follows:

```
'---DEBUG DEC rawDist, CR    <--- comment out this line
SEROUT 16, 16468, [DEC RawDist]
SEROUT 16, 16468, [LF]
```

The SEROUT command takes the following arguments:

- 16 is the pin to use for the output. If 16 is specified, it indicates that it is using the dedicated serial output pin (S_{out}) of the BS2 (see Figure 6-13).

- 16468 is the baud mode. You can obtain this value from the Help documentation in the Basic Stamp Editor. This value specifies a baud rate of 9600bps, N81.

- [DEC RawDist] / [LF] is the data to send. DEC means decimal, and LF means linefeed.

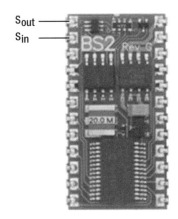

Figure 6-13. *The dedicated serial input/output pins of the BS2*

Note The BS2 has two dedicated serial input/output pins (S_{out} and S_{in}).

Using Visual Studio 2005, create a Windows application, and name it **SecuritySystem**. Populate the default Form1 with the following controls (see also Figure 6-14):

- Label

- ProgressBar

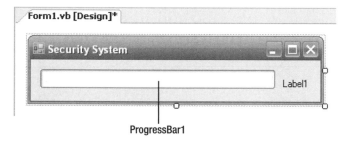

ProgressBar1

Figure 6-14. *Populating the default Form1*

For the ProgressBar control, set its Minimum property to 1 and its Maximum property to 160.

■**Note** For this project, I am interested only in measuring relatively short distances. Hence, I have set the maximum value of the ProgressBar control to 160 so you are able to detect small changes in the Progress-Bar control.

Switch to the code-behind of Form1, and declare the following member variables.

Visual Basic 2005

```
Public Class Form1
    Private WithEvents serialPort As New IO.Ports.SerialPort
    Private proximity As Integer
```

C# 2005

```
public partial class Form1 : Form
{
    System.IO.Ports.SerialPort serialPort =
        new System.IO.Ports.SerialPort();
    int proximity;
```

In the Load event of the form, open a serial connection to COM3 (assuming the COM port number used is COM3) using the SerialPort class.

> **■Note** Henceforth in this chapter, to make Visual Studio 2005 automatically create the event handler for a
> control (such as a form's `Load` event or a button's `Click` event), double-click the control to create the event
> handler.

Visual Basic 2005

```
Private Sub Form1_Load( _
   ByVal sender As System.Object, _
   ByVal e As System.EventArgs) _
   Handles MyBase.Load
    '---close the serial port if it is open---
    If serialPort.IsOpen Then
        serialPort.Close()
    End If
    Try
        '---configure the serial port with the various
        ' parameters---
        With serialPort
            .PortName = "COM3"
            .BaudRate = 9600
            .Parity = IO.Ports.Parity.None
            .DataBits = 8
            .StopBits = IO.Ports.StopBits.One
            .Handshake = IO.Ports.Handshake.None
        End With
        '---open the serial port---
        serialPort.Open()
    Catch ex As Exception
        MsgBox(ex.ToString)
    End Try
End Sub
```

C# 2005

```
private void Form1_Load(object sender, EventArgs e)
{
    //---close the serial port if it is open---
    if (serialPort.IsOpen)
    {
        serialPort.Close();
    }
    try
    {
        //---configure the serial port with the various
        // parameters---
```

```csharp
            serialPort.PortName = "COM3";
            serialPort.BaudRate = 9600;
            serialPort.Parity = System.IO.Ports.Parity.None;
            serialPort.DataBits = 8;
            serialPort.StopBits = System.IO.Ports.StopBits.One;
            serialPort.Handshake = System.IO.Ports.Handshake.None;

            //---wire up the event handler for the DataReceived
            // event---
            serialPort.DataReceived +=
               new
               System.IO.Ports.SerialDataReceivedEventHandler(
               DataReceived);

            '---open the serial port---
            serialPort.Open();
            serialPort.DiscardInBuffer();

    }
    catch (Exception ex)
    {
        MessageBox.Show(ex.ToString());
    }
}
```

In this project, you are interested only in getting data from the sensor (and not sending data to it); therefore, you just need to service the DataReceived event from the SerialPort class.

Visual Basic 2005

```vbnet
Private Sub DataReceived( __
   ByVal sender As Object, __
   ByVal e As System.IO.Ports.SerialDataReceivedEventArgs) __
   Handles serialPort.DataReceived
    '---read the data from the serial port---
    Dim str As String = serialPort.ReadLine
    If str <> String.Empty Then
        proximity = CInt(str)
        '---use the data received to update the ProgressBar
        ' control---
        ProgressBar1.BeginInvoke(New _
           myDelegate(AddressOf updateControl), _
           New Object() {})
    End If
End Sub
```

C# 2005

```csharp
private void DataReceived(object sender,
    System.IO.Ports.SerialDataReceivedEventArgs e)
{
    //---read the data from the serial port---
    string str = serialPort.ReadLine();
    if (str != string.Empty)
    {
        proximity = System.Convert.ToInt32(str);
        //---use the data received to update the ProgressBar
        // control---
        ProgressBar1.BeginInvoke(new
            myDelegate(updateControl));
    }
}
```

Once the value from the BoE is received, it is saved into the proximity variable. This value updates the ProgressBar control. However, because Windows Forms controls are not thread-safe, you need to use a delegate to update it.

A delegate is declared to write the received sensor data into the lblProximity control as well as update the ProgressBar control.

Visual Basic 2005

```vbnet
Public Delegate Sub myDelegate()
'---update the ProgressBar control---
Public Sub updateControl()
    Try
        If proximity <= 160 Then
            ProgressBar1.Value = proximity
            lblProximity.Text = proximity & " cm"
        End If
    Catch ex As Exception
        MsgBox(ex.ToString)
    End Try
End Sub
```

C# 2005

```csharp
public delegate void myDelegate();
//---update the ProgressBar control---
public void updateControl()
{
    try
    {
        if (proximity <= 160)
        {
```

```
            ProgressBar1.Value = proximity;
            lblProximity.Text = proximity + " cm";
        }
    }
    catch (Exception ex)
    {
        MessageBox.Show(ex.ToString());
    }
}
```

To test the application, press F5. Observe how the values change as you initiate some movements in front of the sensors (see Figure 6-15).

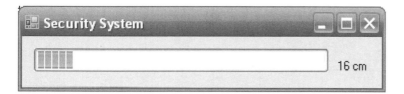

Figure 6-15. *Displaying the sensor information in a Windows application*

■Tip Remember to close the Debug Terminal dialog box of the BASIC Stamp Windows Editor. If you don't, you will have a problem opening the specified COM port (COM3 in my example) when you run the application because the debugging terminal is still using the port.

Programming the Webcam

The next step of the project is to program the webcam so you can use it to record footage as well as take snapshots of the surroundings. To program the webcam, you can use the AVICap class API available in the Windows operating system. Using this API, you can easily incorporate video capture capabilities into your Windows application.

The AVICap class (located in the avicap32.dll file) contains message-based interfaces to access video and waveform-audio acquisition hardware, and it provides the ability to capture streaming video to disk. The only downside to the AVICap class is that it is a Win32 API and is thus not exposed as a managed class to the .NET developer. Hence, as a .NET developer, you'll need to use Platform Invoke (P/Invoke) to use the API.

In the following sections, you will learn how to incorporate video capabilities into the Windows application that you built in the previous sections. In particular, you will learn how to do the following:

- Preview video input (within your Windows application) from your webcam

- Record streaming videos

- Capture images using your webcam

Using the AVICap Class

First, add the controls to the form (see Figure 6-16). You will need a PictureBox control so you can preview the video captures and three Button controls to start and stop the video recording as well as to stop a snapshot using the webcam.

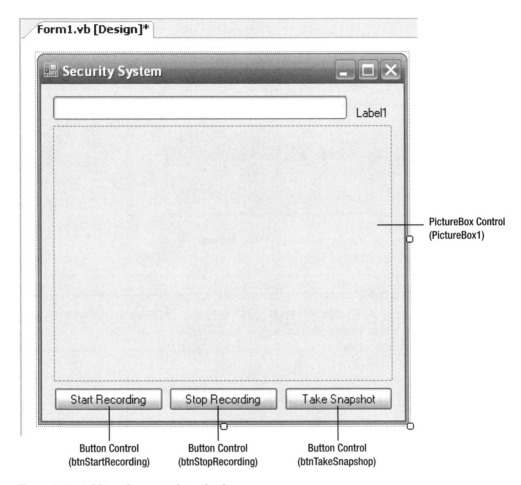

Figure 6-16. *Adding the controls to the form*

Switch to the code-behind of the form, and import the following namespace (required for P/Invoke).

Visual Basic 2005

```
Imports System.Runtime.InteropServices
```

C# 2005

```
using System.Runtime.InteropServices;
```

Within the Form1 class, declare the constants used by the AVICap class.

Visual Basic 2005

```
Const WM_CAP_START = &H400S
Const WS_CHILD = &H40000000
Const WS_VISIBLE = &H10000000

Const WM_CAP_DRIVER_CONNECT = WM_CAP_START + 10
Const WM_CAP_DRIVER_DISCONNECT = WM_CAP_START + 11
Const WM_CAP_EDIT_COPY = WM_CAP_START + 30
Const WM_CAP_SEQUENCE = WM_CAP_START + 62
Const WM_CAP_FILE_SAVEAS = WM_CAP_START + 23

Const WM_CAP_SET_SCALE = WM_CAP_START + 53
Const WM_CAP_SET_PREVIEWRATE = WM_CAP_START + 52
Const WM_CAP_SET_PREVIEW = WM_CAP_START + 50

Const SWP_NOMOVE = &H2S
Const SWP_NOSIZE = 1
Const SWP_NOZORDER = &H4S
Const HWND_BOTTOM = 1
```

C# 2005

```
const int WM_CAP_START = 1024;
const int WS_CHILD = 1073741824;
const int WS_VISIBLE = 268435456;
const int WM_CAP_DRIVER_CONNECT = (WM_CAP_START + 10);
const int WM_CAP_DRIVER_DISCONNECT = (WM_CAP_START + 11);
const int WM_CAP_EDIT_COPY = (WM_CAP_START + 30);
const int WM_CAP_SEQUENCE = (WM_CAP_START + 62);
const int WM_CAP_FILE_SAVEAS = (WM_CAP_START + 23);
const int WM_CAP_SET_SCALE = (WM_CAP_START + 53);
const int WM_CAP_SET_PREVIEWRATE = (WM_CAP_START + 52);
const int WM_CAP_SET_PREVIEW = (WM_CAP_START + 50);
const int SWP_NOMOVE = 2;
const int SWP_NOSIZE = 1;
const int SWP_NOZORDER = 4;
const int HWND_BOTTOM = 1;
```

Note You can learn how to use each of the constants listed previously by checking out the Windows Multimedia SDK Help Reference at ms-help://MS.VSCC.v80/MS.MSDN.v80/MS.WIN32COM.v10.en/multimed/htm/_win32_video_capture_reference.htm. You can view the Help files using the Help system that comes installed with Visual Studio 2005.

After declaring the constants, you need to declare the necessary functions in the AVICap class. You need the first two functions for video-capturing purposes, and you can find them in the avicap32.dll library; the next three functions (found in user32.dll) are for Windows management.

Visual Basic 2005

```
'---The capGetDriverDescription function retrieves the version
' description of the capture driver---
Declare Function capGetDriverDescriptionA Lib "avicap32.dll" _
    (ByVal wDriverIndex As Short, _
     ByVal lpszName As String, ByVal cbName As Integer, _
     ByVal lpszVer As String, _
     ByVal cbVer As Integer) As Boolean

'---The capCreateCaptureWindow function creates a capture
' window---
Declare Function capCreateCaptureWindowA Lib "avicap32.dll" _
    (ByVal lpszWindowName As String, ByVal dwStyle As Integer, _
     ByVal x As Integer, ByVal y As Integer, _
     ByVal nWidth As Integer, ByVal nHeight As Short, _
     ByVal hWnd As Integer, ByVal nID As Integer) As Integer

'---This function sends the specified message to a window or
' windows---
Declare Function SendMessage Lib "user32" Alias "SendMessageA" _
    (ByVal hwnd As Integer, ByVal Msg As Integer, _
     ByVal wParam As Integer, _
     <MarshalAs(UnmanagedType.AsAny)> ByVal lParam As Object) _
    As Integer

'---Sets the position of the window relative to the screen
' buffer---
Declare Function SetWindowPos Lib "user32" Alias "SetWindowPos" _
    (ByVal hwnd As Integer, _
     ByVal hWndInsertAfter As Integer, ByVal x As Integer, _
     ByVal y As Integer, _
     ByVal cx As Integer, ByVal cy As Integer, _
     ByVal wFlags As Integer) As Integer

'---This function destroys the specified window---
Declare Function DestroyWindow Lib "user32" _
    (ByVal hndw As Integer) As Boolean
```

C# 2005

```csharp
//---The capGetDriverDescription function retrieves the
// version description of the capture driver---
[System.Runtime.InteropServices.DllImport("avicap32.dll")]
static extern bool capGetDriverDescriptionA(
    short wDriverIndex, string lpszName,
    int cbName, string lpszVer, int cbVer);

//---The capCreateCaptureWindow function creates a capture
// window---
[System.Runtime.InteropServices.DllImport("avicap32.dll")]
static extern int capCreateCaptureWindowA(
    string lpszWindowName, int dwStyle, int x, int y,
    int nWidth, short nHeight, int hWnd, int nID);

//---This function sends the specified message to a window or
// windows---
[System.Runtime.InteropServices.DllImport(
    "user32", EntryPoint = "SendMessageA")]
static extern int SendMessage(
    int hwnd, int Msg, int wParam,
    [MarshalAs(UnmanagedType.AsAny)] object lParam);

//---Sets the position of the window relative to the screen
// buffer---
[System.Runtime.InteropServices.DllImport(
    "user32", EntryPoint = "SetWindowPos")]
static extern int SetWindowPos(
    int hwnd, int hWndInsertAfter, int x, int y,
    int cx, int cy, int wFlags);

//--This function destroys the specified window--
[System.Runtime.InteropServices.DllImport("user32")]
static extern bool DestroyWindow(int hndw);
```

Also, declare the following member variable.

Visual Basic 2005

```vbnet
'---used as a window handle---
Private hWnd As Integer
```

C# 2005

```csharp
//---used as a window handle---
private int hWnd;
```

When the form is loaded for the first time, preview the video after the serial port connection has been established.

Visual Basic 2005

```
Private Sub Form1_Load( __
   ByVal sender As System.Object, __
   ByVal e As System.EventArgs) __
   Handles MyBase.Load
   '---close the serial port if it is open---
   If serialPort.IsOpen Then
       serialPort.Close()
   End If
   Try
       '---configure the serial port with the various
       ' parameters---
       With serialPort
           .PortName = "COM3"
           .BaudRate = 9600
           .Parity = IO.Ports.Parity.None
           .DataBits = 8
           .StopBits = IO.Ports.StopBits.One
           .Handshake = IO.Ports.Handshake.None
       End With

       '---open the serial port---
       serialPort.Open()
       serialPort.DiscardInBuffer()
   Catch ex As Exception
       MsgBox(ex.ToString)
   End Try

   '---preview the selected video source---
   PreviewVideo(PictureBox1)
End Sub
```

C# 2005

```
private void Form1_Load(object sender, EventArgs e)
{
    //---close the serial port if it is open---
    if (serialPort.IsOpen)
    {
        serialPort.Close();
    }
    try
    {
        //---configure the serial port with the various
```

```csharp
            // parameters---
            serialPort.PortName = "COM3";
            serialPort.BaudRate = 9600;
            serialPort.Parity = System.IO.Ports.Parity.None;
            serialPort.DataBits = 8;
            serialPort.StopBits = System.IO.Ports.StopBits.One;
            serialPort.Handshake = System.IO.Ports.Handshake.None;
            serialPort.DataReceived +=
                new
                System.IO.Ports.SerialDataReceivedEventHandler(
                DataReceived);

            //---open the serial port---
            serialPort.Open();
            serialPort.DiscardInBuffer();
        }
        catch (Exception ex)
        {
            MessageBox.Show(ex.ToString());
        }
        //---preview the selected video source---
        PreviewVideo(PictureBox1);
    }
```

Define the PreviewVideo() subroutine as follows.

Visual Basic 2005

```vb
'---preview the selected video source---
Private Sub PreviewVideo(ByVal pbCtrl As PictureBox)
    hWnd = capCreateCaptureWindowA(0, _
        WS_VISIBLE Or WS_CHILD, 0, 0, 0, _
        0, pbCtrl.Handle.ToInt32, 0)
    If SendMessage( _
      hWnd, WM_CAP_DRIVER_CONNECT, _
      0, 0) Then

        '---set the preview scale---
        SendMessage(hWnd, WM_CAP_SET_SCALE, True, 0)

        '---set the preview rate (ms)---
        SendMessage(hWnd, WM_CAP_SET_PREVIEWRATE, 30, 0)

        '---start previewing the image---
        SendMessage(hWnd, WM_CAP_SET_PREVIEW, True, 0)

        '---resize window to fit in PictureBox control---
        SetWindowPos(hWnd, HWND_BOTTOM, 0, 0, _
```

```
            pbCtrl.Width, pbCtrl.Height, _
            SWP_NOMOVE Or SWP_NOZORDER)
    Else
        '---error connecting to video source---
        DestroyWindow(hWnd)
    End If

End Sub
```

C# 2005

```
//---preview the selected video source---
private void PreviewVideo(PictureBox pbCtrl)
{
    hWnd = capCreateCaptureWindowA(
        "0", WS_VISIBLE | WS_CHILD, 0, 0, 0, 0,
        pbCtrl.Handle.ToInt32(), 0);
    if (SendMessage(hWnd, WM_CAP_DRIVER_CONNECT, 0, 0) != 0)
    {
        //---set the preview scale---
        SendMessage(hWnd, WM_CAP_SET_SCALE, 1, 0);

        //---set the preview rate (ms)---
        SendMessage(hWnd, WM_CAP_SET_PREVIEWRATE, 30, 0);

        //---start previewing the image---
        SendMessage(hWnd, WM_CAP_SET_PREVIEW, 1, 0);

        //---resize window to fit in PictureBox control---
        SetWindowPos(hWnd, HWND_BOTTOM, 0, 0,
            pbCtrl.Width, pbCtrl.Height,
            SWP_NOMOVE | SWP_NOZORDER);
    }
    else
    {
        //---error connecting to video source---
        DestroyWindow(hWnd);
    }
}
```

The Start Recording button allows you to start capturing the selected video source.

Visual Basic 2005

```
Private Sub btnStartRecording_Click( _
   ByVal sender As System.Object, _
   ByVal e As System.EventArgs) _
   Handles btnStartRecording.Click
   btnStartRecording.Enabled = False
```

```
    btnStopRecording.Enabled = True
    Application.DoEvents()
    '---start recording---
    SendMessage(hWnd, WM_CAP_SEQUENCE, 0, 0)
End Sub
```

C# 2005

```csharp
private void btnStartRecording_Click(
    object sender,
    EventArgs e)
{
    btnStartRecording.Enabled = false;
    btnStopRecording.Enabled = true;
    Application.DoEvents();
    //---start recording---
    SendMessage(hWnd, WM_CAP_SEQUENCE, 0, 0);
}
```

When the Stop Recording button is clicked, the video stream is saved as an .avi file.

Visual Basic 2005

```vbnet
Private Sub btnStopRecording_Click( __
  ByVal sender As System.Object, __
  ByVal e As System.EventArgs) __
  Handles btnStopRecording.Click
    btnStartRecording.Enabled = True
    btnStopRecording.Enabled = False
    Application.DoEvents()
    '---save the recording to file---
    SendMessage(hWnd, WM_CAP_FILE_SAVEAS, 0, __
        "C:\" & Now.ToFileTime & ".avi")
End Sub
```

C# 2005

```csharp
private void btnStopRecording_Click(
    object sender,
    EventArgs e)
{
    btnStartRecording.Enabled = true;
    btnStopRecording.Enabled = false;
    Application.DoEvents();

    //---save the recording to file---
    SendMessage(hWnd, WM_CAP_FILE_SAVEAS, 0,
        "C:\\" + System.DateTime.Now.ToFileTime() + ".avi");
}
```

■**Tip** I have used the `ToFileTime()` method of the `Now` property as the unique filename of the video. A Windows *file time* is a 64-bit value that represents the number of 100-nanosecond intervals that have elapsed since 12 a.m., January 1, 1601 A.D. (C.E.) Coordinated Universal Time (UTC).

To take a snapshot, the user clicks the Take Snapshot button. The image captured by the webcam is then copied to the Clipboard and saved to a file.

Visual Basic 2005

```
Private Sub btnTakeSnapshot_Click( __
    ByVal sender As System.Object, __
    ByVal e As System.EventArgs) __
    Handles btnTakeSnapshot.Click

    Dim data As IDataObject
    Dim bmap As Image
    '---copy the image to the Clipboard---
    SendMessage(hWnd, WM_CAP_EDIT_COPY, 0, 0)

    '---retrieve the image from Clipboard and convert it
    ' to the bitmap format---
    data = Clipboard.GetDataObject()
    If data.GetDataPresent(GetType(System.Drawing.Bitmap)) Then
        bmap = __
            CType(data.GetData(GetType(System.Drawing.Bitmap)), __
            Image)
        bmap.Save("C:\" & Now.ToFileTime & ".bmp")
    End If
End Sub
```

C# 2005

```
private void btnTakeSnapshot_Click(
    object sender,
    EventArgs e)
{
    IDataObject data;
    Image bmap;

    //---copy the image to the Clipboard---
    SendMessage(hWnd, WM_CAP_EDIT_COPY, 0, 0);

    //---retrieve the image from Clipboard and convert it
    // to the bitmap format---
    data = Clipboard.GetDataObject();
```

```
if (data.GetDataPresent(typeof(System.Drawing.Bitmap)))
{
    bmap =
        ((Image)(data.GetData(typeof(
        System.Drawing.Bitmap)))));
    bmap.Save("C:\\" + System.DateTime.Now.ToFileTime() +
        ".bmp");
}
}
```

That's it! You can now test the application by pressing F5. Make sure you have the webcam connected to your computer. You can place the webcam on top of the PING sensor and use it to monitor the entrance of your company, for example. As someone approaches the door, you will be able to detect his distance and perhaps start a recording. To start recording, click the Start Recording button, and then click the Stop Recording button to save the video to a file. Click the Take Snapshot button to take a picture (see Figure 6-17).

Figure 6-17. *Testing the application*

Summary

In this chapter, you learned how to integrate external devices into your .NET application. In particular, you saw how to use a webcam in your Windows application, and you can combine this with an ultrasonic sensor to build a security system.

Index

You Need the Companion eBook

Your purchase of this book entitles you to buy the companion PDF-version eBook for only $10. Take the weightless companion with you anywhere.

We believe this Apress title will prove so indispensable that you'll want to carry it with you everywhere, which is why we are offering the companion eBook (in PDF format) for $10 to customers who purchase this book now. Convenient and fully searchable, the PDF version of any content-rich, page-heavy Apress book makes a valuable addition to your programming library. You can easily find and copy code—or perform examples by quickly toggling between instructions and the application. Even simultaneously tackling a donut, diet soda, and complex code becomes simplified with hands-free eBooks!

Once you purchase your book, getting the $10 companion eBook is simple:

❶ Visit **www.apress.com/promo/tendollars/**.

❷ Complete a basic registration form to receive a randomly generated question about this title.

❸ Answer the question correctly in 60 seconds, and you will receive a promotional code to redeem for the $10.00 eBook.

2560 Ninth Street • Suite 219 • Berkeley, CA 94710

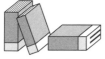

eBookshop

THE EXPERT'S VOICE™